DROPPING THE FIRE

The Decline and Fall of the Steam Locomotive

The first of the last. The form of the final generation of British steam locomotives, the BR Standards, introduced over thirty years later, was remarkably anticipated by R.E.L. Maunsells South Eastern and Chatham Railway mixed traffic 2-6-0s. The prototype pictured here, was completed at Ashford Works in mid-1917. The basic design had actually been completed on the eve of war in 1914, when already changing economics dictated maximum accessibility etc., for the 'golden years' of the Edwardian Era were already rapidly passing into history. NRM

By
Philip Atkins
(Librarian, National Railway Museum, York)

<u>Dedication</u>

*This book is dedicated to the memories of E.S. Cox, Brian Reed and Pat Ransome Wallis,
whose collective knowledge and experience of steam locomotives was profound.*

First Published in the
United Kingdom by
IRWELL PRESS 1999
59A, High Street, Clophill,
Bedfordshire MK45 4BE
Printed in Huddersfield by
The Amadeus Press

CONTENTS

ACKNOWLEDGEMENTS

This book has its origins in the early 1960s, when I made a first trip abroad and encountered Chapelon 4-6-2s and American-built 2-8-2s in Northern France, not to mention a Swiss compound 2-10-0 in steam at Lucerne. This aroused a keen interest in overseas locomotives, at a time when, though recently extinct in North America, the steam locomotive was still commonplace elsewhere, but not for very much longer. Compared to more recent times, relatively little information was readily available on the subject, although a major exception was the admirable *Concise Encyclopaedia of World Railway Locomotives* edited by Dr P. Ransome Wallis (Hutchinson, 1959). This illustrated the ultimate steam locomotive designs of several different countries, which inspired letters to many manufacturers and railway administrations for particulars, which sometimes resulted in generous and spectacular replies. Only a few years later, not least in regard to the British locomotive industry, the scene had changed so radically that such material was no longer available. Many of the illustrations in this book were obtained in this manner. Nearly twenty years later I was privileged to meet the good doctor, a number of whose photographs are reproduced in this book.

Contrary to the almost world-wide trend, it was curiously reassuring at the time to read in *The Railway Magazine* for May 1964, that in India steam locomotives were still being built in quantity. Over thirty years later, as this book was being completed, came the news that steam operation, even in India, had effectively come to an end.

I would like to pay tribute to my wife, Christine for word processing the manuscript for this book, with all its complexities. I am also indebted to Andrew Scott, Head of the National Railway Museum, York, for permission to reproduce a number of photographs from the Museum's collections, and to the following good friends for assistance in the provision of other illustrations; Joe Collias, John Edgington, Victor Hand, Laurie Marshall, Ted Talbot, Alan Wild and Bill Withuhn.

C.P.A. Harrogate, September 1998.

Author's Note. The references quoted at the end of each chapter have been carefully selected for their fullness in regard to the particular subject. They are not intended as a comprehensive list of the literature relating to each particular topic.

Shortly before this book went to press David Wardale published his long-awaited memoirs, The Red Devil and Other Tales from the Age of Steam, *which consists of a unique, highly detailed first-hand account of the final and ultimately forlorn attempts in South America, South Africa, the United States and China to produce a commercially viable coal-burning steam locomotive in the late Twentieth Century.*

Oblivious to the rapidly darkening international situation, streamlined LNER Class A4 4-6-2 No. 2510 QUICKSILVER (newly repainted in garter blue) powers the Silver Jubilee through Sessay North Yorkshire, on 28th July 1938. By the time the coming conflict had ended, in real terms the total cost of operating the nearly 20,000 strong British main line steam locomotive fleet would almost have doubled and the search would begin for viable alternative forms of motive power. A4s could still be seen at Sessay 25 years later, but by then the new order had all but taken over. M. W. Earley Collection NRM (MWE 3/2)

INTRODUCTION

In 1950, the mid-point of the Twentieth Century, the steam locomotive still numerically dominated the world's railways, including those in North America. It was also in regular production in no fewer than twenty countries, in four continents, not only for their own use but also for export to an almost equal number of others. Only ten years later the picture had changed considerably. By the end of 1960 the steam locomotive was effectively extinct in both the United States and Canada, and was in obvious retreat in Europe. Serial production was now confined to two Asian countries wherein it had been non-existent a decade earlier!

During the 1960s the main line steam locomotive was decimated in Western Europe, and indeed eliminated in the British Isles. At the beginning of the 1970s the two countries which possessed technologically the most advanced, and construction-wise the most modern

steam locomotives (the last in both cases dating only from 1958), Czechoslovakia and South Africa, began to plan their programmed demise. India terminated new construction, and only the following year, in late 1973, an escalation in the price of Middle East oil for political reasons, precipitated a world energy crisis.

This event undoubtedly deferred the final demise of steam in several countries, particularly in Eastern Europe, where the run-down was already well advanced. A further tripling in oil prices in 1979 actually aroused interest in the United States in returning to coal-fuelled locomotives in some form. At least one advanced steam locomotive project got seriously under way in the early 1980s in the USA. By this time only China was still actively building main line steam locomotives, but despite the availability of recently developed technology which could overcome two

of the age old problems, i.e. low thermal efficiency and smoke emission, even there interest rapidly faded. Even as the last new 2-8-2s and 2-10-2s were being built, their demise was being scheduled. The only fleet application of this technology was to be found on the most remote railway on earth, in Patagonia.

Why did the faithful steam locomotive fall from grace and become so universally reviled *by its operators*? Was the indecent haste of its replacement entirely justified? This book attempts to explore the underlying reasons beneath a world-wide phenomenon whose *rationale* has surprisingly rarely been publicly accounted for, something which the late E.S. Cox, writing at its height in 1966 aptly described as '**the world-wide contagion to be rid of steam at a rate beyond all common-sense**'.

An eight year old Louisville & Nashville RR 2-8-4 receives some attention at De Coursey Yard near Cincinati in 1956 shortly before its retirement. Photograph courtesy L&N.

And quiet flows the Don. A timeless Russian scene, with Class E 0-10-0 (No.709-84 of 1930) passing a peasant at work, at Apsheronsk in May 1993. Possibly as many as 13,000 locomotives of this basic design were built in at least 25 plants in 7 different countries between 1912 and 1957, making it by far the world's most numerous class of steam locomotive. N. Harris.

Chapter 1
HOW MANY, HOW LONG, HOW FAR AND HOW MUCH?

The highest life mileage ever officially ascribed to a British steam locomotive was 2,642,860 attained by the Gresley 4-6-2 FLYING FOX, pictured nameless and brand new at Doncaster as LNER No.1475 in April 1923. During its 41½ year life FLYING FOX carried 13 different boilers and was paired with ten different tenders. The main frames, and even the nameplates of all early Gresley 4-6-2s were renewed after only a few years and there was much routine interchange of parts during heavy repairs, making a given engine's identity purely nominal. NRM (DON 23/18).

It seems probable that the steam locomotive will have enjoyed an overall currency of about 200 years, from the construction of the first example by Richard Trevithick in Great Britain in 1803 until the demise of the last examples in everyday use in China sometime in the early 21st century. It is fascinating to speculate just *how many* steam locomotives have been built in total world-wide during the 19th and 20th centuries. Estimates have been few but there is little doubt that the number is well in excess of 600,000. *Significant* numbers were built in about 25 countries, for some of which exact totals, and for others accurate totals are known. Least precise are the estimated totals for the United States, Germany and Great Britain, which dominated the scene. Totalling up available figures from a variety of sources gives a figure of about 640,000.

When was the greatest number of steam locomotives built? There is little doubt that the most intensive period of construction was the first decade of the twentieth century. More specifically, given the dominant position of the two countries, this probably occurred during the year 1907, when American and British output peaked, at 7,400 and 1,800 respectively. German production was also very high at this time but has not been quantified. Whatever the German figure, it was almost certainly exceeded when a total of 5,370 engines was built there in 1921, a year not particularly notable for high production in the USA. Before the late 1950s, a probable all time low in world output came in 1932, a time of world

TABLE 1 <u>WORLD STEAM LOCOMOTIVE PRODUCTION BY COUNTRY</u>

COUNTRY	TOTAL	PERIOD
United States	177,000	1831 - 1955
Germany	155,000	1839 - 1966,1988F
United Kingdom	110,150	1803 - 1971
Russia	50,000	1833 -c1959
France	39,000	1839 - 1956
Belgium	15,895	1835 - 1956
Austria	15,000	1840 - 1959,1973F
Japan	11,000	1884 - 1967
China	10,000	1881 - 1995
Hungary	7,573	1873 - 1959
Canada	7,000	1860 - 1956
Czechoslovakia	7,000	1900 - 1959
Italy	5,741	1846 - 1955
Poland	4,797	1926 - 1963
India	4,256	1873 - 1972
Australia	3,460	1862 - 1958
Sweden	3,351	1853 - 1953
Switzerland	3,000	1873 - 1996
Spain	1,753	1883 - 1961
Romania	1,610	1896 - 1987
Finland	1,403	1900 - 1957
Holland	1,100	1900 - 1950
Ireland	750	1841 - 1942
New Zealand	550	1873 - 1956
Yugoslavia	550	1939 -c1960,1965F
Norway	322	1861 - 1941
Denmark	190	1900 - 1950
Chile	123	c1870- 1920
Argentina	82	1883 - 1942
South Africa	21	1935 - 1968
Latvia	11	1933 - 1934
Rhodesia (Zimbabwe)	10	1954 - 1955
Indonesia	6	c1900- 1923
Bulgaria	3	1948 - 1950
Majorca	2	1902 - 1903
Turkey	2	1961
Vietnam	2	1961 - 1962
Mexico	2	?
Portugal	1	1944
Brazil	?	1937 -
GRAND TOTAL	**c640,000**	

F   fireless steam locomotives were built in Germany, Austria and Yugoslavia several years after conventional steam locomotives.

TABLE 2

PEAK MAIN LINE STEAM LOCOMOTIVE STOCKS OF VARIOUS COUNTRIES
1914 - 1980

COUNTRY	MAXIMUM STEAM STOCK	YEAR	EXTINCTION
SWITZERLAND	1,590	1914	1963
GERMANY	c.33,000	1917	(West) 1977
			(East) 1988
FRANCE	c.20,000	1923	1975
UNITED STATES			
(Class 1 railroads)	65,000	1924	1960
(all railroads)	70,000	1921-24	1968
GREAT BRITAIN	24,000	1924	1968
CANADA	c.5,600	1924	1960
AUSTRALIA	3,950	1931	1973
JAPAN	5,958	1946	1976
FINLAND	817	1951	c.1974
NEW ZEALAND	650	1953	1971
SPAIN	3544	1954	1975
EGYPT	744	1954	1963
RUSSIA	c.36,000	1956	-
SOUTH AFRICA	2,755	1959	-
INDIA	10,810	1964	1998
CHINA	7,800	1975-1980	-

main line locomotive units; a great unknown for any country was the number of locomotives in *industrial* service. In 1995 the only steam locomotives still in regular production were the Chinese Class SY 2-8-2s built for industry - it is probable, in fact, that the 2-8-2 has been the most prolific steam locomotive wheel arrangement. The most numerous locomotive classes in such diverse countries as France (141R), Spain (141F), India (WG) and Japan (D51) were all 2-8-2s. It was also one of the most numerous wheel arrangements in North America in the Twentieth Century. By 1924 the steam locomotives of the world numbered something like 250,000, and their decline is charted as follows:

1928	227,000	1960	120,000
c.1952	163,000	1964	100,000
1958	150,000	1978	25,000

What was a reasonable working life for a steam locomotive? A legal rating wrangle known as the Hitchin Case which involved the Great Northern Railway in England in 1906, put this at 30.4 years. In practice a working life (through premature retirement) ranged from as little as five years (or even less) in the United States and Great Britain to over a century in Spain and Indonesia.

For depreciation purposes the former London Midland & Scottish Railway ascribed the following

economic slump. When was the greatest number of steam locomotives in service? Peaks for individual countries varied from as early as 1914 in Switzerland to as late as 1980 in China. All time peaks, it turns out, were attained simultaneously in North America and Great Britain, during 1924. By this time electrification and road competition were beginning to make themselves felt. Although several countries, including Spain, South Africa, India and China, did not reach their steam locomotive peak until after World War Two, individually their magnitude was insufficient to reverse the unmistakable downward trend, driven by developments in the USA.

Contemporary estimated global totals have been rare and are tabulated below. The early and late 1950s totals are almost certainly inconsistent with each other. Strictly speaking, moreover, these totals relate only to

Madrid, Zaragosa & Alicante Railway 0-6-0 No.250, built by E.B. Wilson & Co. of Leeds in 1857, still at work as Spanish National Railways (RENFE) No.030-2016 in 1961. In fact it enjoyed an active life of at least 106 years and probably retained many of its original components. P. Ransome Wallis Collection, NRM (PRW 5419).

'standard lives' to different categories of locomotive:-

Express passenger	30 years
Mixed traffic	40 years
Superheated goods	45 years
Non-superheated goods and shunting tank engines	50 years

In practice these were frequently exceeded, and several non-superheated 0-6-0s, however, built in the 1870s, were still at work in the 1950s and early 1960s. It is questionable how much (if any) of the original locomotives lasted throughout. The London & North Eastern Railway took the following view regarding the renewal of the major components of an average locomotive:-

Tyres	once every 6 years
Boiler	once every 12 years
Cylinders	once every 15 years
Frames	once every 20 years
Crank axle	once every 30 years
Wheel centres	once every 60 years

In effect *total renewal* fell due after 60 years. However, locomotive life was not so much a matter of time as of mileage. Obviously an express passenger locomotive would accrue a given mileage in a much shorter period than a goods locomotive. A particularly dramatic instance of this could be found on the London & North Western Railway whose 2-4-0 No.955 CHARLES DICKENS entered service in February 1882. It had covered 500,000 miles by September 1886, 1,000,000 miles by September 1891,

and 2,000,000 miles by August 1902. When condemned in October 1912 it had covered an estimated 2,345,107 miles during 30½ years compared to 'only' 1,240,900 miles by LNWR 0-6-0 No.944 between February 1873 and August 1953, over a period of 80½ years.

The consistent average annual mileage of 100,000 miles achieved by the 2-4-0 during its first 20 years was truly remarkable by contemporary standards and was scarcely equalled in Britain even in the twentieth century. One LMS 4-6-2 achieved 108,000 miles in 1936, whilst one or two BR Class 7 4-6-2s also hit six figures when new in 1953.

Life mileages of around two million appear to have been the general limit for passenger locomotives, with a few reaching 2½ million. Seemingly, the highest credited to a British engine was 2,642,860, for the LNER Class A1/A3 4-6-2 No.4475 *Flying Fox* between 1923 and 1964, during which time it was completely renewed. Not so the one-off Timken 'Four Aces' roller bearing 4-8-4 in the United States which covered 2,125,000 miles between 1930 and 1957. Likewise, something similar was probably achieved by the first two Norfolk & Western Railway 4-8-4s between late 1941 and early 1959, for both had already accumulated two million miles during their first thirteen years. But for abrupt dieselisation in 1958, their mileages would probably have risen to

three million each by the end of 1960, something never seen in a steam locomotive, yet achieved by several British Railways 3,300HP diesel-electric 'Deltic' Co-Cos during just twenty years. This average of 150,000 miles per annum, which would have been rather higher in earlier years, nevertheless fell somewhat short of the 220,000 miles called for in the original 1958 contract. Even this has since almost certainly been exceeded by the High Speed Train power cars on British Railways, which have frequently covered 800 miles per day on the East Coast Main Line.

The steam locomotive possessed one unassailable virtue, its remarkably low capital cost. Comparisons can be odious, however, as within a given country these could vary considerably with time or between builders. These variations did not derive entirely from inflation, but could also be due to raw material prices. One of the most enduring British locomotive designs was the North Eastern Railway Class E1 (LNER Class J72) 0-6-0T, built between 1898 and 1951. Actual building costs, it can be seen, varied considerably; in the figures for the E1/J72 given below, 1995 equivalent sterling prices, calculated according to official Bank of England conversion factors, are quoted in brackets.

1898	£1,456 (£73,000)
1920	£4,075 (£68,175)
1922	£6,950 (£158,600)
1951	£5,314 (£88,000)

Timken 'Four Aces' 4-8-4 No.1111, sponsored by the roller bearing manufacturer to promote the application of its products to steam locomotives, and built by the American Locomotive Company in 1930. It is pictured when fairly new, prior to eventual purchase by the Northern Pacific Railway. When the NPR condemned it in 1957 it was credited with 2,125,000 miles. As a 'one-off' the 4-8-4 probably retained most of its original major components, boiler, cylinders, and especially running gear. Timken.

Very rarely was it possible to ascertain quoted prices for the *same design* of locomotive in different countries, but such figures were published for 37 broad gauge 0-6-0s for India by 26 builders in nine countries in 1923.

The prices of several latter-day major steam locomotives are also worth quoting; the costs of an American compound 2-8-8-2 and much smaller French compound 2-8-2 in 1952 were seemingly very close, even though the American engine would have contained at least twice as much steel—see below table 4.

The costs of contemporary British Railways Class 9F 2-10-0s and English Electric 2,000HP diesel-electrics also make an interesting

TABLE 3

PRICES QUOTED IN 1923 BY PRIVATE LOCOMOTIVE BUILDERS IN DIFFERENT COUNTRIES FOR 37 5FT 6IN GAUGE 0-6-0s FOR INDIA

COUNTRY	NO. OF BUILDERS	PRICE RANGE
United Kingdom	8	£4041 - £5852
France	2	£4566 - £4606
Germany	7	£4760 - £5290
Czechoslovakia	1	£4729
Belgium	3	£4900 - £7520
Italy	2	£5230 - £5336
Switzerland	1	£5491
Sweden	1	£5855
United States	1	£7143

The ultimate British 0-6-0 design was the hugely distinctive Bulleid Southern Railway Class Q1 of 1942. Remarkably its 8ft + 8ft 6in coupled wheel spacing could be directly traced back to the mid-19th century Kirtley 0-6-0s of the Midland Railway. Seen here at Feltham in June 1963 is No.33011. Peter Groom

comparison. Despite the disparity owing to the premature demise of the steam locomotive (average life for the batch was about 7 years) and long life of the diesels (average life about 26 years) the average rate of depreciation

for both was remarkably close at something over £4,000 per annum.

General Bibliography

Concise Encyclopaedia of World Railway Locomotives, Ed. P. Ransome

Wallis, Hutchinson, 1959, 512p
World Steam in the Twentieth Century, E.S. Cox, Ian Allan, 1969, 191p
Locomotive Panorama Vol.2, (Chapters 2 and 3) E.S. Cox, Ian Allan, 1966, 158p

TABLE 4	BUILDING COSTS OF SELECTED POST-WORLD WAR 2 STEAM LOCOMOTIVES				
COUNTRY	TYPE	DATE	ACTUAL PRICE	£ EQUIVALENT	1995 PRICE EQ'VAL'NT
USA	NYC 4-8-4	1946	$239,000	£59,750	£1,225,000
USA	L&N 2-8-4	1949	$255,000	£63,750	£1,185,000
USA	N&W 2-8-8-2	1952	$260,000	£93,000	£1,400,000
France	SNCF 2-8-2	1952	87,000,000F	£89,300	£1,345,000
Germany	DB 2-6-2	1955	441,500 DM	£37,600	£520,000
GB	BR 2-10-0	1958	£30,200	£30,200	£373,000
GB	BR EE Co 1Co-Co1 DE	1958	£106,800	£106,800	£1,318,000
South Africa	SAR 4-8-4	1953	£67,500	£67,500	£987,000
	SAR 4-8-4 condensing	1953	£112,000	£112,000	£1,637,000
India	IGR 2-8-2	1964	(£33,600)	£33,600	£359,000
China	CR 2-10-2	1981	Y270,000	£90,000	£180,000

A Chinese SY 2-8-2 was reported to cost the equivalent of £38,000 in 1995.

A Glasgow-built Class WG 2-8-2 in triumphal mode on display in London, at South Bank, during the Festival of Britain in 1951. By this time construction had recently begun in India (actually utilising imported parts) and would continue there for almost 20 years. A sister engine was similarly displayed, somewhat closer to its birthplace, in George Square, Glasgow, prior to dispatch. The last active WG was one sold into industrial service, which was still at work during 1997. P. Ransome Wallis Collection, NRM (PRW 3626).

Generally considered the world's largest steam locomotive, the Union Pacific Railroad 4000 series 4-8-4 of which twenty-five were built by Alco between 1941 and 1944. No.4002 is pictured with crew in pristine condition following delivery.

Chapter 2
THE AMERICAN STEAM LOCOMOTIVE

Around 1900, owing to extremely urgent requirements, a number of railways in England, Belgium, France and Germany imported locomotives from the United States to the builders' own designs. To European eyes many of these American engines must have appeared somewhat crude, but the Americans were to have the last laugh. Only a few years later, in June 1907, the Pittsburgh plant of the American Locomotive Company delivered an experimental 4-6-2 to the Pennsylvania Railroad (No. 7067) which can be perceived as having been the world's first 'modern' steam locomotive. It combined a large wide-firebox boiler with bar frames, two outside cylinders and external Walschaerts valve gear. These basic features not only sufficed for the remaining forty or so years of domestic US steam locomotive construction, but were also to be found in the world's last new steam locomotives still being built in China *eighty* years later.

PRR No.7067 lacked only one major refinement, a superheater, which was then still under development. This feature was incorporated in a further 4-6-2 completed by the same manufacturer at its Schenectady plant in July 1910. Numbered 50000 this was a 'demonstrator' and resulted from a careful study of locomotive and particularly boiler proportions under the leadership of Francis J. Cole. By employing weight-saving vanadium steel in the main frames, and cast steel cylinders, the boiler was made as large as possible. No.50000 was given trial by several railroads before being purchased by the Erie, and developed a maximum cylinder horsepower of

2,216, or 18.45 hp per ton (2,240lb). No.50000 was closely studied by the Pennsylvania Railroad in developing its own celebrated K4 4-6-2 in 1914, whose boiler was in turn later credited with influencing the design of the Gresley 4-6-2s and their successors in England (1922-1949). In *overall* concept, it almost certainly inspired the British Railways Standard 4-6-2s of the early 1950s. By the 1950s, steam locomotives of fundamentally American concept, particularly 4-6-2s and 2-8-2s, were to be found in such diverse countries as Australia, South Africa, India, the Soviet Union, and even France.

Long before this, the characteristics of two outside cylinders, external valve gear and large boilers were enshrined in the range of United States Railroad Administration standard designs produced during 1918-20, several of which proved to be remarkably enduring, the 0-8-0 in particular remaining in production until 1953. Although nearly two thousand locomotives were built to direct USRA order, ranging from 0-6-0 to 2-8-2, but notably including many 4-6-2, 2-8-2, 4-8-2, and 2-10-2s, a huge demand for new locomotives by US railroads was predicted in the aftermath of World War One. In the event, nowhere did matters even approach the heady days of the pre-1914 era, but there was also a need for improvements in locomotive design.

Having entered the market building geared and small industrial locomotives the Lima Locomotive Works adopted an aggressive stance by evolving a new locomotive concept more suited to the perceived new requirements of the early 1920s, in response to the first stirrings of road

transport competition. These included reduced maintenance costs, increased running speed, and improved efficiency, and were contained in a large 2-8-2 No.8000, completed in June 1922 for the Michigan Central, a subsidiary of the New York Central Railroad. This was masterminded by William E. Woodard (1873-1942) who had been recruited in 1916 from the American Locomotive Company as Vice President (Engineering). Woodard had played a part in the design of 4-6-2 No.50000, and for good measure he had also spent some time with the Baldwin Locomotive Works in Philadelphia, early in his career.

When the design of 2-8-2 No.8000 was initiated the paramount consideration was fuel economy. In 1920 the average price of coal to the US railroads was $4 per US ton. This was more than double the 1916 figure, and about 50 per cent up on that for 1919 during which there had been a long and bitter miners' strike. This had been abruptly terminated through the intercession of the Vice President of the miners' union, one John Llewelyn Lewis (1880-1969) who secured a major pay award. The high price of coal was reflected in the proliferation of proprietary feedwater heating equipment prominently fitted to US steam locomotives in the early 1920s in an attempt to reduce fuel consumption. The price of coal afterwards subsided over the next twenty years.

Lewis was confirmed as President of the United Mineworkers Union in 1920 and dominated the American domestic scene for the next forty years. He thus unwittingly played a significant part in the evolution of what became known as the super

Northern Pacific Railway Class Z5 2-8-8-4 No.5000, built by the American Locomotive Company in 1928. This was designed to burn the on-line low grade Montana 'Rosebud' lignite, and so had an unsurpassed firegrate area of 182ft², intended to consume an (unrealised) fuel rate of 20 US tons per hour. Alco.

TABLE 5

**IMPROVING MAXIMUM INDICATED HORSEPOWER
IN RELATION TO ENGINE WEIGHT AND GRATE AREA,
AMERICAN EXPRESS PASSENGER LOCOMOTIVES 1911 - 1945**

YEAR	RAIL ROAD	CLASS	WHEEL ARR	WEIGHT TONS	GRATE AREA FT^2	MAX IHP	IHP/ TON	IHP/ FT^2
1911	Alco	50000	4-6-2	120.0	59.8	2126	17.7	35.6
1914	PRR	K4	4-6-2	135.9	69.3	3200	23.5	46.2
1927	NYC	J1A	4-6-4	153.1	82.0	3900	25.5	47.6
1937	NYC	J3A	4-6-4	160.7	82.0	4700	29.2	57.3
1939	PRR	K4	4-6-2	152.0	69.9	4267	28.1	61.0
1942	PRR	T1	4-4-4-4	222.0	92.0	6550	29.5	71.2
1945	NYC	S1A	4-8-4	210.3	101.0	6900	32.8	68.3

power steam locomotive. A quarter of a century later, Lewis would be personally credited with promoting the rise of the diesel locomotive.

No. 8000, it turned out, was only the beginning, for Woodard and his team soon embarked on a locomotive design which would have an entirely new wheel arrangement, the 2-8-4. Built as a speculative venture for evaluation by any interested railroads, the legendary Lima A1, progenitor of the final generation of American steam locomotives, was completed in 1925. It has been calculated that over the next 25 years, a total of approximately 400 4-6-4, 600 2-8-4, 900 4-8-4 and nearly 400 2-10-4 engines were built for United States railroads. These never existed simultaneously, for even as Lima was constructing its last 2-8-4s and 4-8-4s during 1948-49, some early examples had already been broken up. The celebrated Lima A1 had been purchased by the Illinois Central Railroad, which operated it in modified form until 1954. It was not preserved.

Even during the relative short period of the 'Super Power' era, considerable improvements were made. Though the prototype 2-8-4 produced a maximum cylinder

horsepower of 3,675, and a corresponding drawbar horsepower of 3,240, the penultimate US 2-8-4 design, the Louisville & Nashville M1 of 1942, produced a maximum DBHP of no less than 4,500. Similarly, the original New York Central J1A 4-6-4 of 1927 produced only 3,950 indicated horsepower as against no less than 4,700IHP by the ultimate development, the J3A of 1937. In both instances a major modification had been the provision of a combustion chamber in the firebox in the later designs. Power to weight ratios steadily improved and on the New York Central alone had doubled between about 1905 and 1945 using entirely conventional technology, particularly as regards boilers and valve gear, and in the 4-8-4s aluminium for cabs and smoke deflectors.

Proposals for rigid-frame locomotives with *six*-wheel trailing trucks were made as early as 1929, e.g. a 4-10-6 for the Texas & Pacific, just at the time the collapse of the US economy effectively scotched any such developments for the time being. In the event only one such locomotive was ever built, the enormous Pennsylvania four-cylinder 6-4-4-6 express passenger engine built at Altoona in

1939 with the collaboration of the three leading US locomotive builders. It was capable of hauling 1,200 US tons at 100 mph but despite recent research in the railroad archives the precise *raison d'être* for this monster (especially as its sphere of operation was greatly circumscribed) has never been made clear.

In theoretical capacity, with a grate area of 132ft^2, this engine was the high speed equivalent of the various Mallet articulated heavy freight engines. These were invariably compounds at first, as per Anatole Mallet's original concept, with low pressure cylinders as large as 48in diameter in the exceptional Virginian Railway 2-10-10-2s of 1918. From about 1924 the compounds were rapidly superseded by four-cylinder simple expansion engines. Again these had been extremely slow machines, but by 1929 larger wheeled 'high speed' Mallets began to be envisaged and a pair of experimental 2-6-6-2s on this principle appeared on the Baltimore & Ohio Railroad in 1930. Almost simultaneously, in 1936, fast 2-6-6-4s and 4-6-6-4s appeared on the Norfolk & Western and Union Pacific respectively which were both capable of 70 mph. The home-built 2-6-6-4 was

TABLE 6

**IMPROVING MAXIMUM DRAWBAR HORSEPOWER
IN RELATION TO ENGINE WEIGHT AND GRATE AREA
AMERICAN FREIGHT LOCOMOTIVES 1925 - 1952**

YEAR	RAIL ROAD	CLASS	WHEEL ARR	WEIGHT TONS	GRATE AREA FT^2	MAX DBHP	DBHP TONS	DBHP FT^2
1925	Lima	A1	2-8-4	171.9	100.0	3240	18.8	32.4
1942	L & N	M1	2-8-4	200.0	90.3	4500	22.5	49.9
1938	ATSF	5001	2-10-4	240.3	121.5	5310	22.1	43.7
1936	N & W	A	2-6-6-4	255.8	122.0	5300	20.7	43.4
1941	C & O	H8	2-6-6-6	347.3	135.2	7050	20.3	52.1
1941	UP	4000	4-8-8-4	344.8	150.0	6290	18.2	41.9
1952	N & W	Y6b	2-8-8-2	273.0	106.2	5600	20.5	52.7

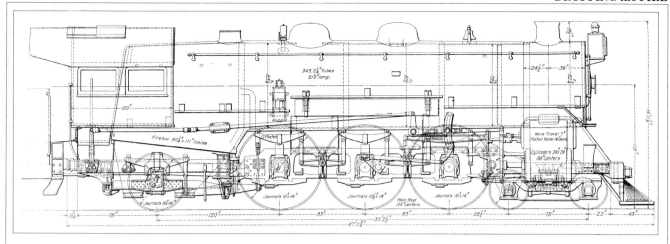

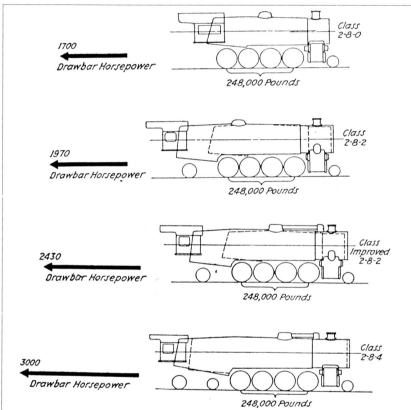

Above. Scale drawing of the world's first 'modern' steam locomotive, Pennsylvania Railroad 4-6-2 No.7067 built in 1907. Although non-standard on a highly standardised railroad, this engine was superheated in 1916, and lasted until 1933.

Left. A diagrammatic representation of the evolution of Super Power. The 2-8-0 would have been typical of the 1913 period, the smaller 2-8-2 of about 1918, whilst the larger 2-8-2 is the Michigan Central No.8000 of 1922. The 2-8-4 appeared in 1925.

remarkable for its high power output, whilst the 4-6-6-4, developed by Alco, would five years later be extrapolated into the 'Big Boy' 4-8-8-4s for the Union Pacific.

The year 1941 was notable for the almost simultaneous production of the Union Pacific 4-8-8-4 (by Alco) for heavy mountain freight, the Chesapeake & Ohio 2-6-6-6 (by Lima) for trans-Allegheny heavy coal trains, and the Duluth, Missabe & Iron Range 2-8-8-4 by Baldwin, to work heavy iron ore trains in Minnesota. Dimensionally speaking there was no single design which exceeded the others in every respect, although the six-wheeled trailing truck of the Lima engine was unique in a locomotive in series production. The 'Big Boy' has generally been regarded as the largest, although with six-coupled engine units the Chesapeake & Ohio, in its 'H8', had an enormously high *specified* axleload. At 80,000lb this was exceptional even by US standards, and it was actually exceeded, through poor estimation, by 11 per cent.

TABLE 7

LEADING DIMENSIONS OF LARGEST AMERICAN MALLET ARTICULATED STEAM LOCOMOTIVES BUILT 1918 - 1948

RAILROAD	C & O	DRGW	NP	DM & I	UP	VGN
Class	H8	3800	Z5	M4	4000	800
Wheel Arr.	2-6-6-6	2-8-8-2	2-8-8-4	2-8-8-4	4-8-8-4	2-10-10-2
Built	1941-8	1930	1928-30	1941-3	1941-4	1918
Driving W. dia.	5'7"	5'3"	5'3"	5'3"	5'8"	4'8"
Cylinders	(4)	(4)	(4)	(4)	(4)	(2) 30"X32"
	22.5"x33"	26"x32"	26"x32"	26"x32"	23¾"x32"	(2) 48"x32"
Boiler prs. lb	260	240	250	240	300	215
Evaporative HS ft2	7240	8111	7673	6758	5755	**8605**
Superheater	3186	**3476**	3219	2770	2043	2120
Grate area	135.2	136.5	**182.0**	125.0	150.3	108.7
Adhesive wt tons	226.3	255.4	246.9	252.2	243.3	**275.4**
Engine weight	**347.3**	296.9	320.0	312.4	344.6	305.4
Tractive effort lb	110,200	131,800	140,000	140,000	135,375	**176,000**
Booster			13,400			
Boiler dia (max)	9'1"	9'2"	9'2"	9'0"	8'11"	**9'11"**

It will be noted that the remarkable Virginian Railway 2-10-10-2s of 1918 boasted five major dimensions which were never subsequently exceeded in locomotive practice.

NB The UP 4-8-8-4s of 1941-1944, although often cited as the largest steam locomotives ever built, did not actually exceed any other design in any single respect. **Maximum dimensions are shown in bold.**

The largest two-cylinder simple rigid frame steam locomotives ever built were thirty-five AT&SF '5001' Class 2-10-4s built by the Baldwin Locomotive Works between 1937 and 1944. Oil-burner No.5004 is pictured new at Eddystone in 1937. AT&SF.

This necessitated weight reductions in subsequent repeat orders, but such repeats of the other two designs showed a slight increase in weight due to the high grade steels being unobtainable in wartime. No sooner had the pilot batches of each of these designs appeared than the United States entered World War Two in December 1941, and locomotive development was virtually frozen by the immediately instituted War Production Board. Even so it is difficult to conceive of, in strictly practical terms, any larger locomotives than these, none of which would enjoy an operational span of as much as twenty years. Happily several examples of each have been preserved.

The rigid-frame two-cylinder steam locomotive also attained a prodigious size in the United States, most notably on the Atcheson, Topeka & Santa Fé. Between 1938 and 1944 the Santa Fé received from the Baldwin Locomotive Works two series

of 4-8-4 and 2-10-4 locomotives. At 228 tons without 16-wheel tender, the final batch of 4-8-4s was the heaviest ever built. All oil-burners, these undertook the 1,787 mile through workings between Kansas City and Los Angeles, and ran up to 800,000 miles between heavy repairs. In a different respect the 2-10-4s were also quite remarkable, although all were oil burners after 1948, of the first ten built in 1938, half were originally coal-fired. In conjunction with a boiler pressure of 310lb (the highest figure ever employed with a conventional locomotive boiler, other than in short term experiments) were two cylinders of 30in diameter by 34in stroke. The 5001 class neatly encapsulated the problems encountered by contemporary designers in embracing such dimensions. Piston loads were nearly *three times* those of the most powerful British two-cylinder locomotives. To transmit such power required very heavy machinery, and it

was to balance this adequately that coupled wheels of no less than 6ft 2in diameter, larger than those of several 4-8-4 designs, were adopted. Such large cylinders were served by piston valves of 15in diameter, but having a maximum travel in full fore gear of little more than 7½ inches. Piston valves were normally made approximately half the diameter of the cylinders they served, but as the latter became larger simple mathematics indicated that, in relation to cylinder *volume,* the valves became progressively smaller.

It was to overcome these problems which compromised cylinder efficiency that experiments began with poppet valves in the late 1930s. There had been a few experiments in the USA around 1929 with Caprotti valve gear but this proved unsuited to robust American operating conditions. Subsequently the Franklin Railway Supply Company evolved a home-grown oscillating cam system. When

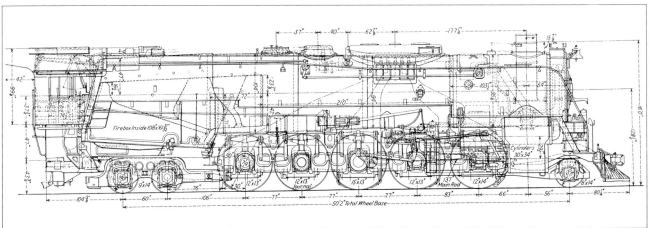

A scale elevation drawing of this remarkable AT&SF '5001' Class 2-10-4.

The highly complex cast-steel engine bed, incorporating all four cylinders and their poppet valve steam chests, produced by the General Steel Castings Corporation for the Pennsylvania Railroad Class T1 4-4-4-4 described in Chapter 3

applied to a Pennsylvania Class K4 4-6-2 in 1939, it dramatically increased maximum indicated cylinder horsepower, from 3,500 to 4,267, an increase of 22 per cent. A major disadvantage was the highly inaccessible driving mechanism encased between the frames and the outbreak of World War Two inevitably curtailed further development. After the war a rotary cam version (Type B) only just managed an appearance, before the final curtain fell.

One of the most notable features of many American steam locomotives built from about 1930 onwards was the cast steel engine bed with integral cylinders. Those incorporated in the Santa Fé 2-10-4s described above, about 64 ft long and weighing 39 tons, are seen as amongst the largest such units ever produced. One can only marvel now at the technology involved, which derived from heavy gun carriage manufacture during World War 1.

Such engine beds featured in many 4-8-4s, a wheel arrangement which combined high boiler capacity and high adhesion in conjunction with a high speed capability. A total of thirty US railroads operated some 900 4-8-4s of no fewer than 70 officially recognised varieties, which could probably have been reduced to some four or five 'standard' designs. Though such a concept would have been anathema in the steam era, it was accepted readily enough when diesels took over. The 4-8-4 epitomised the high point of American steam locomotive design, and was a casualty probably more than any other of the diesel in view of its essentially recent construction and confinement by virtue of its weight to major routes.

A particularly outstanding 4-8-4 was the speculative 'Four Aces', commissioned by Timken and built by Alco in 1930. The idea of the project was to promote the use of roller bearings in steam locomotives. In this it proved highly successful, and led to many locomotives, 4-8-4s especially, being so equipped, on journals and (later) on crankpins. Legislation delayed the final major development until it was all but too late. Development work on all-welded boiler shells commenced around 1937 at Alco, which immediately after the war in 1945 installed a stress relieving furnace at Schenectady capable of accommodating the largest Mallet boilers.

TABLE 8	LEADING DIMENSIONS OF ULTIMATE AMERICAN RIGID FRAME TWO-CYLINDER STEAM LOCOMOTIVES 1938-1948				
Railroad	C & O	L & N	Western Maryland	Lima	ATSF
Class	L2a	M1	J1	Proposed	5001
Wheel Arr.	4-6-4	2-8-4	4-8-4	4-8-6	2-10-4
Built	1948	1942-9	1947	-	1938-44
Driving wheel dia.	6'6"	5'9"	5'9"	5'10"	6'2"
Cylinders	(2)	(2)	(2)	(2)	(2)
	25"x30"	2"x32"	26½"x32"	28"x32"	30"x34"
Boiler pressure lb	255	265	255	280	310
Evaporative HS ft²	4178	5114	4974	5263	6075
Superheater	1785	1908	2170	2028	2675
Grate area	90.0	90.3	106.7	132.9	121.5
Adhesive weight, tons	98.0	119.4	129.5	125.0	165.9
Engine weight	197.8	200.0	226.1	234.4	243.4
Tractive effort lb	52,100	61,500	70,600	74,600	93,000
Booster lb	14,200	14,000	-	12,400	-

A typical final generation (post-1933) American steam locomotive, showing the clean functional lines and neat pipework associated with the period. A 2-8-4 fast freight engine for the Virginian Railway poses at the Lima plant in 1946. A total of 299 of this basic design were produced by all three builders for six different railroads between 1934 and 1949 (the first and last for the Nickel Plate Road). This was the nearest approach to a modern US standard steam locomotive design, although individual batches varied considerably in detail. N&W.

Only a limited number of welded boilers, including one for a new 4-6-6-4, were actually constructed before Alco quit the steam locomotive business only three years later. Oddly, a non-locomotive builder, the Combustion Engineering Co. of Chattanooga, Tennessee, subsequently produced a number of welded boiler shells, around 1950. These included several for Santa Fé 4-6-4s, 4-8-4s and 2-10-4s, which in the event saw very little service. Curiously, as late as 1951 the by-then rapidly dieselising New York Central announced its intention to equip forty 4-6-4s with welded boilers.

Only one locomotive combined all four features, i.e. cast steel engine bed, roller bearings, poppet valves, and all-welded boiler. This was the final New York Central 4-8-4, No.5500, delivered by Alco in June 1946. An indication of what might have been, No.5500 nevertheless proved something of a disappointment. Equipped with the original form of Franklin poppet valve gear, just as it appeared the improved rotary cam operated Type B variety became available. The latter was specified for a mixed-traffic 4-8-6, a pet project of Will Woodard's successor at Lima, A. J. Townsend, in early 1949, after some five year's gestation. This was also to incorporate a novel feature, Townsend's Double Belpaire firebox.

The Belpaire firebox was relatively rarely employed in modern American practice, outside the Pennsylvania Railroad. In the so-called double version, the underside of the combustion chamber was also squared off in order to increase total free gas area by about 10 per cent compared to a conventional round-topped boiler. This increased evaporative capacity and enhanced the free gas area/grate

area ratio which was inherently very low in modern American boilers. Dimensionally the Lima 4-8-6 was clearly derived from the NYC 4-8-4s. The coupled wheel diameter of 5ft 10in had not prevented a Norfolk & Western 4-8-4, even with half worn tyres from achieving 110 mph on the Pennsylvania Railroad. It is interesting to note that the *adhesive* weight of the NYC 4-8-4 and the projected Lima 4-8-6 slightly exceeded the *total engine* weight of Pennsylvania 4-6-2 No.7067, such had been the level of progress over a period of forty years.

But hopes to build a demonstrator 4-8-6, 25 years on from the prototype 2-8-4, were dashed when Lima underwent major re-organisation in mid-1949. The firm determined not to continue steam locomotive development and A.J. Townsend resigned in protest; a bitter and disillusioned man, he died the following year. There was clearly a

feeling of regret amongst the older hands, for the veteran Alco designer A.W. Bruce concluded his classic study of American steam locomotive design, published in 1952, with the words **'they concede the streamlined cleanliness of the diesel electric locomotive, but they miss the throb and visual signs of life found in steam. For them there is no creative inspiration in a piece of wire!'** In 1948 even a senior executive of General Motors, who had been raised close to the railway, conceded that he found it hard to conceive of a time when the steam locomotive whistle would not be heard.

References
The Locomotive Cyclopaedia, Simmons Boardman Publishing Corporation, various editions (1922, 1930, 1938, 1941, 1947 and 1950/1952).
The Steam Locomotive in North America - its development in the

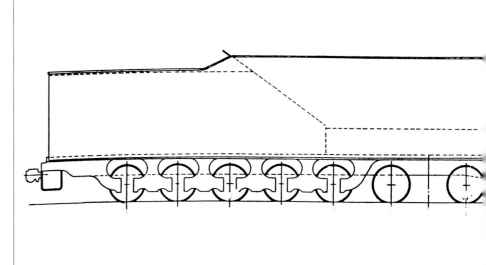

Chesapeake & Ohio Railway Class L2a 4-6-4 express passenger locomotive built by the Baldwin Locomotive Works in 1948. The five engines of this class were the heaviest six-coupled locomotives ever built, having an axleload of 33 tons, and represented the only fleet application of the Franklin Type B (rotary cam) poppet valve gear. BLW.

Radial-Stayed Type   Double Belpaire Type

	Radial stayed	Double Belpaire	Per cent increase
Heating surface, sq. ft.:			
Tubes and flues	5,327	5,670	6.44
Firebox and comb. chamber	865	890	2.89
Superheating	2,440	2,892	18.52
Firebox volume, cu. ft.	1,341	1,392	3.80
Grate area, sq. ft.	162	162	...
Steam space, cu. ft.	288	363	16.67
Water space area, around combustion chamber below center line, sq. in.	948	1,061	11.92
Steam area, sq. in.	97.21	115	18.30
Gas area, sq. in.	1,805	1,995	10.53

Twentieth Century, A.W. Bruce, Bonanza Books, 1952, 443p.

The Case for the American Steam Locomotive, V.L. Smith, *Trains,* August 1967, 22-28.

The Big Engines, R.A. Le Massena, *Trains,* June 1968, 38-45.

Loco Profile 31, Lima Super Power, C.P. Atkins and B. Reed, Profile Publications, 1973, 24p.

Was There Ever a Super 4-8-4? R.A. Le Massena, *Trains,* February 1975, 48-53.

The Ultimate Development (AT & SF 2-10-4s), L. Stagner, *Trains,* August 1975, 18-55.

Lima, The History, E. Hirsimaki, Hundman Publishing Inc., 1986, 351p.

Left. Comparative dimensions of similar boilers having round-topped and Double Belpaire fireboxes, showing the improvement wrought by the latter.

Below. Diagram of A.J. Townsend's proposed 4-8-6 mixed traffic locomotive, as outlined at Lima in early 1949 and regrettably, not proceeded with.

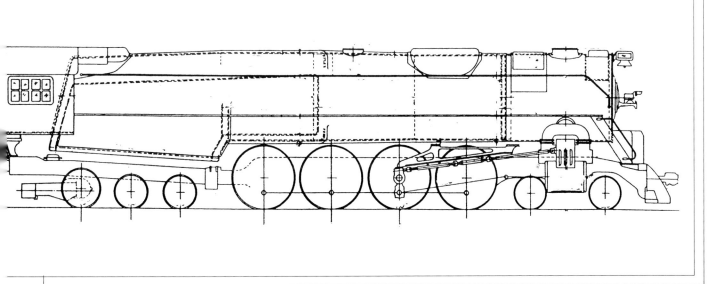

American perfection. The first production New York Central 4-8-4 No.6001 poses on its builder's test track at Schenectady, NY in October 1945. Running qualities were reported to be superb for a 2-cylinder locomotive. Alco.

Baldwin-built Pennsylvania Railroad Class T1 4-4-4-4 No.5533 as delivered in May 1946. The streamlined casing is similar to that applied to the two 1942 prototypes, but provided better access to the rear cylinders. It was soon further modified. BLW.

Chapter 3

THE LAST WORD : NEW YORK CENTRAL 'NIAGARA' VERSUS PENNSYLVANIA 'DUPLEX'

The rival Pennsylvania and New York Central railroads were the largest operators of coal burning steam locomotives in the United States. For many years their combined locomotive fleets accounted for more than one quarter of the national total. The Pennsylvania Railroad steam locomotive stock peaked at 7,486 units in 1924, and that of the New York Central at 4,919 in 1931. Whereas the New York Central collaborated closely with the American Locomotive Company, which built almost all of its engines, the Pennsylvania designed and built the majority of its locomotives itself, at Altoona, PA passing contracts to Baldwin (and occasionally Lima) at times of high demand.

Both railroads operated between New York and Chicago by very different routes. The NYC ran north of New York up the Hudson River Valley to Albany, where it swung west along the southern shores of the Great Lakes to Chicago. From 1906 the first 33 miles out of New York were electrically worked as far as Harmon, where steam took over for the

remaining 928 miles to Chicago, over what was popularly known as the 'Water Level Route.' In contrast the Pennsylvania route was more direct but entailed passage through the Allegheny mountains via Pittsburgh. Between 1930 and 1942 no new steam locomotives whatever were built for the PRR (with the exception of the mammoth 6-4-4-6), but despite the severe economic conditions, by 1938 electrification extended west as far as Harrisburg, and possible electrification through to Pittsburgh was still under debate 20 years later.

Steam locomotive development on both lines followed a steady pattern. The 4-6-2 appeared on the NYC as early as 1903, and on the PRR in 1907. On the Pennsylvania the outstanding K4 4-6-2 was introduced in 1914 and remained in production until 1928, whereas on the NYC a stoker-fired 4-6-4 had been produced in 1927. This was progressively developed until 1937, whereas the only response from the PRR was a 'super 4-6-2', the K5 in 1929, which was originally hand-fired. Both the NYC and PRR also operated large fleets of fast mixed traffic 4-8-2s.

During the 1930s passenger trains between New York and Chicago became progressively heavier. The NYC 4-6-4s initially kept pace, but the PRR frequently resorted to 4-6-2s in pairs, although by this time many were being equipped with mechanical stokers. Around 1940 Lima presented to the PRR a scheme to rebuild a 4-8-2 as a 4-8-4 with the added benefit of poppet valves. But for World War Two the New York Central would probably have moved on from the 4-6-4 to the 4-8-4 rather sooner, but by mid-1943 it was drawing up a basic specification for a 4-8-4 under the direction of Paul W. Kiefer, Chief of Motive Power. This was to exploit to the maximum New York Central loading gauge, which at a maximum height of 15ft 3in, and width 10ft 9in, was somewhat restricted by US standards. Existing 100ft diameter turntables also circumscribed overall loco length, but by adopting a 4-10-0 'centipede' tender with considerable 9ft rear overhang, it still proved possible to accommodate an exceptionally high coal capacity of 43 short (2000lb) tons, which would require only one replenishment en

Altoona-built 4-4-4-4 No.5511, completed in February 1946, with streamlining as modified after only six months to a standard to which all fifty engines soon conformed. PRR.

TABLE 9

NYC STEAM V. DIESEL-ELECTRIC TRIALS, 1946

	STEAM 4-8-4 6000HP[1]	DIESEL ELECTRIC TWIN UNIT 4000HP	STEAM:DIESEL STEAM = 1.00
UNIT COST (DEC 1946)	$238,854	$351,115	1.47
COST PER HP	$39.8	$88.0	2.21
DRAWBAR THERMAL EFFICIENCY %	6	22	3.7
ANNUAL MILEAGE (Passenger working)	288,000	324,000	1.13
UTILISATION[2]	63.0	70.4	1.12
AVAILABILITY[2]	69.0	74.2	1.08
TOTAL FUEL COST	$118,080	$90,720	0.77
TOTAL REPAIR COST	$102,528	$114,048	1.11
TOTAL CREW COST	$55,987	$64,055	1.14
TOTAL OPERATING COST 3	$325,642	$320,630	0.99
TOTAL ANNUAL COST 3	$350,095	$359,471	1.03
FUEL COST/MILE	$0.410	$0.280	0.68
REPAIR COST/MILE	$0.356	$0.352	0.99
OPERAT.COST/MILE	$1.131	$0.990	0.88
ANNUAL COST/MILE	$1.22	$1.11	0.91

1   The 4-8-4 had a nominal rating of 6000HP but was assumed to work at   of this, ie 4000HP
2   % total annual hours
3   In the interests of simplification, lesser costs, eg water and fixed charges, have been omitted.

route. A solitary prototype, to be numbered 6000 on account of its nominal horsepower, was ordered from Alco in April 1944. This was to be supplied with both 6ft 3in and 6ft 7in coupled wheelsets and was described as 'dual purpose', i.e. mixed traffic, possibly to keep the War Production Board happy, although the prestigious *Twentieth Century Limited* between New York and Chicago was to be its prime duty.

No.6000 was delivered in March 1945, by which time 25 more had already been ordered two months earlier. Delivery of these commenced in October 1945 whilst No.6000 was only just beginning exhaustive road tests with 275lb against 290lb boiler pressure and 6ft 3in *versus* 6ft 7in coupled wheels. On the plus side these incorporated larger ashpans, but a seemingly retrograde move was the increase in tube length from 19ft to 20ft. This somewhat reduced the firebox volume and hence the maximum evaporative capacity of the boiler, from 110,000lb to 105,000lb per hour. This was established during exhaustive tests with No.6023 in late 1946, which also involved trials with the experimental 6ft 3in wheelsets originally supplied with No.6000.

The trials with No.6023 were also for comparative purposes with No.5500, an additional 4-8-4 with Franklin Type A poppet valve gear which had been ordered in June 1945, following earlier consideration of a

4-4-4-4 'Duplex' version of the standard 4-8-4s, which the NYC referred to as 'Niagaras' for publicity purposes. The delivery of No.5500 in June 1946, like the last three piston valve 4-8-4s, had been delayed by a strike at Schenectady. Classified S2a, compared to the S1a (No.6000) and S1b (Nos.6001-25) No.5500 also had a welded boiler shell and unique twin stoker screw. The tender was also redesigned to accommodate 47 in place of 43 short tons of coal, and only 16,000 as against 18,000 US gallons of water. (Consideration had even originally been given to providing a phenomenal 75 short ton coal capacity on the 4-8-4 tenders).

The poppet valves on No.5500 brought no dramatic improvement in performance, piston valves actually delivered marginally higher drawbar and indicated horsepowers over the speed range 30-75mph, and notably superior acceleration characteristics. In terms of specific fuel and water consumption, No.5500 demonstrated a slightly enhanced efficiency, which was markedly outweighed by the greater maintenance involved. Indeed the engine proved notably troublesome, sometimes shedding its coupling rods at speed. In 1951 it was retired after a life of only five years and cannibalised to provide spare parts for Nos.6000-25.

Meanwhile No.5500 also participated with Nos.6007, 6009, 6012, 6024 and 6025 in the exhaustive NYC steam versus diesel tests which

took place between October 1946 and March 1947. The opposition consisted of six 4,000HP twin unit diesels (normal operation called for the 4-8-4 to operate at two thirds full power). Engine house procedures were highly organised in order to reduce servicing and turning to only 2½ hours per day, and the 4-8-4s were covering 24,000 miles per month. No.6024 was given special treatment and monitored from new in May 1946 until March 1947, during which it ran 228,849 miles, or effectively 250,000 miles per year.

The results were written up in detail by Paul Kiefer in *An Evaluation of Railroad Motive Power*, which was published by the then almost defunct Steam Locomotive Research Institute of New York in 1947. In view of the long established association between the NYC and the American Locomotive Company the latter had a strong vested interest in the outcome of the tests in order to shape its future policy, and was probably their true instigator. It was a very closely fought contest as will be seen from the data tabulated below.

Although finely balanced, the disruption to coal supplies during the currency of the trials, caused by John L. Lewis calling the miners out on strike, 'tipped the scales'. The New York Central top management was moved to hand down a directive to Kiefer, that steam locomotive development should cease forthwith. Nevertheless, the effective elimination of steam traction on the New York Central within a decade was probably not envisaged in 1947. During that year, however, the pride of its steam fleet, the 4-8-4s, were partially immobilised. Crystalline fatigue cracks were discovered around the circumferential riveted joints of the high tensile carbon silicon steel boiler plates.

Twenty four welded barrels of carbon steel were ordered from Alco, and fitted in association with the existing fireboxes from late 1947 through 1948. In addition three riveted shells were obtained from the Combustion Engineering Co. of Chattanooga, Tennessee in 1950.

In early 1948 the 'Niagaras' handled the newly accelerated 'Twentieth Century Limited' between Harmon and Chicago, but it was not long before diesels took over this prime task. The 4-8-4s continued on lesser named passenger services until well into the 1950s - No.6000 itself was the last to receive a major overhaul at the NYC Beech Grove Shops in Indianapolis, in December 1953. A few months earlier, on 7 August, No.6020 powered the last steam working out of Harmon, (rather anticipating the last steam operations out of London King's Cross almost exactly ten years later). The 'Niagaras' appear to have been retained in traffic in accordance with

In a highly atmospheric study an unidentified NYC 4-8-4, early in its all-too short career, battles against adverse weather conditions.

the trust (hire purchase) agreements under which they had been funded. They were rapidly retired during 1955-56, and despite at least two attempts to preserve an example, one by the Smithsonian Institution in Washington, DC, none survived. By this time the steam locomotive conflicted with the by then impoverished New York Central's modern image and it had no desire to see a steam locomotive bearing its insignia, however modern, in a national museum.

This attitude contrasted sharply with that of the rival Pennsylvania, which in 1956 was also in dire financial straits, yet which nevertheless conscientiously set aside for posterity representatives of each of its major steam locomotive classes, with one notable exception.

The New York Central 4-8-4 may be regarded as the ultimate development of the basic conventional simple expansion reciprocating steam locomotive. It was by no means the world's largest two-cylinder design, but even here such factors as high piston loads, heavy reciprocating masses, and less than ideal valve/cylinder volume factors were becoming acute. It was to circumvent these problems that in 1939 the newly re-constituted Baldwin Locomotive Works decided to revive a 1932 scheme for four-cylinder rigid-frame so-called 'Duplex' locomotives, for which it enumerated the following virtues:-

1. **Short piston stroke, resulting in lower piston speeds at a given locomotive speed and thereby providing a higher mean effective pressure (and hence greater cylinder horsepower).**
2. **Small cylinders and hence low piston loads and resultant lighter machinery, thus easier to balance and inflicting lower 'hammer blow' on the track. Reduced maintenance.**
3. **(Alleged) reduction in internal machine friction thus increasing drawbar horsepower.**
4. **Small cylinders permitted relatively larger valves, steam ports, and enhanced steam passages.**

Baldwin proposed to build a demonstrator operating on this principle. However before this could be designed, let alone built, the Pennsylvania Railroad entered into discussions in early 1940 with the builders regarding the construction of two 4-4-4-4s.

Elegant Loewy-styled GG1 electrics worked into Harrisburg from the east, and what was required was a steam equivalent capable of working the remaining 713 miles through the mountains to Pittsburgh and on to Chicago. Employing K4 4-6-2s in pairs was an expensive operation and the company was anxious to avoid any increase in this sort of working - hence the projected 4-4-4-4. The resultant T1 has been the subject of myth and legend and only long after its premature demise has much light been thrown on its evolution and alleged defects. This has been made possible through the labours of Charles Meyer, the stepson of a leading Pennsylvania Railroad executive who had much direct involvement with these locomotives when they entered fleet operation.

For forty years the Pennsylvania Railroad 4-4-4-4s were traditionally dismissed as exotic failures, expensive on maintenance and prone to violent bouts of uncontrollable slipping. Mr Meyer's diligence in researching the extensive railroad archives has uncovered a very different story as revealed in *Milepost*, the Journal of the Friends of the Railroad Museum of Pennsylvania, between 1989 and 1993.

The PRR outline requirement was the ability to haul 11-car trains of 880 short tons at 100mph on straight and level track. The only technical details specified were the traditional Belpaire firebox, clasp brakes, and a 65,000lb axleload. Eddystone got to work, quickly suggesting that the design incorporated Franklin poppet valve gear, on the strength of the dramatic 22 per cent increase in

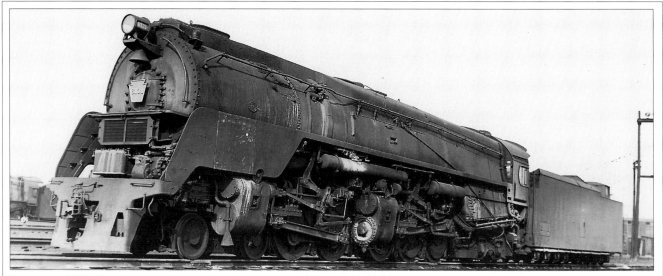

Prototype PRR Class Q2 4-4-6-4 heavy freight locomotive No.6131, built in 1944. The twenty-six engines of this class were the most powerful rigid-framed steam locomotives ever built, and on test proved capable of almost 8,000IHP. However the axleload of almost 80,000lb and the long rigid wheelbase of 26ft. 4½in. limited route availability. Like their 4-4-4-4 passenger counterparts, the Q2s saw little if any active service after 1952, though ten were not sold for breaking up until early in 1956. In 1948 a Q2 was tested against a Norfolk & Western Railway 2-6-6-4.

cylinder horsepower (from 3,500 to 4,267) achieved by its provision on K4 4-6-2 No.5399 in 1939. This, however, considerably increased the estimated weight, producing an axleload of 72,000lb which the PRR refused to accept. It was then pointed out by the PRR that the greater economy in steam consumption made possible by the poppet valves could permit a smaller and therefore lighter boiler. By January 1941 a revised scheme had been produced with axleload down to 67,500lb (which was still a little above the original specified limit). Theoretical boiler maximum evaporation was reduced from 90,000lb/hr to 85,000lb/hr, as the grate area was to be reduced from 100 to 92ft². Strangely, Vernon L. Smith, then a designer with the Franklin Railway Supply Co., and actively involved in the detailed design of the poppet valve gear, has ventured the opinion that the grate area should have been 100ft², rather than 92ft², apparently unaware of preceding events. He also had profound misgivings concerning the highly inaccessible oscillating drive mechanism (actuating the Franklin poppet valves) which lay between the frames. His strong recommendations

for the adoption of a rotary cam arrangement incorporating external propeller shafts went disregarded by Baldwin.

Nearly two years elapsed between the initial placing of the order for two engines, one of which was to be provided with an auxiliary booster, in July 1940, and delivery of the first engine in April 1942, - a long while by normal Baldwin standards. Extensive stationary plant and road tests ensued, with both engines notching up around 150,000 miles during their first two years. Design expectations were certainly exceeded in that on one occasion one of them hauled 16 passenger cars (rather than 11) at an average of 102mph for 69 miles. It was, however, during this period that the design also acquired notoriety for violent and uncontrollable slipping of the separate power units, the non-booster fitted engine especially.

In November 1944 the War Production Board restrictions were greatly relaxed and the placing of locomotive orders actively encouraged. The Pennsylvania Railroad wasted no time in authorising fifty more 4-4-4-4s, with construction to be divided equally between Altoona and Baldwin, with

the former building all the tenders. These incorporated relatively few modifications when compared to the 1942 pair, apart from revised compensated suspension which allegedly reduced the propensity to slipping. The omission of boosters, which would also have greatly assisted in getting away with a heavy train, was later criticised in some quarters. Once again, rotary cam poppet valve gear was recommended but rejected on the grounds of the extra time and cost that this would incur.

Delivery of the new engines from both sources commenced in November 1945 and continued into the summer of 1946. It is now known that a few weeks before the emergence of the first production 4-4-4-4s, in response to developments on the rival New York Central, the Pennsylvania Railroad placed its first order for fleet passenger diesels and cutting back the T1 order was considered but not implemented.

Almost within days of entering service the new 4-4-4-4s suffered derailments on the tight curves in the vicinity of Pittsburgh, and had to be diverted elsewhere pending design modifications to their lateral play.

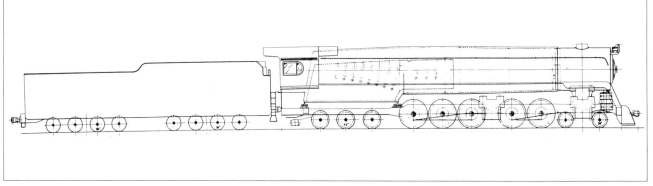

A powerful 4-4-6-6 engine proposed for the PRR by Alco in November 1946, for reasons which are now unclear. Boiler pressure would have been 325lb and grate area 144ft², both exceptionally high figures. The diagram appears to imply poppet valves despite recent PRR adverse experience of these.

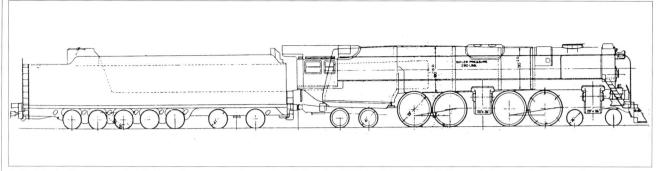

A foot in both camps. 4-4-4-4 Duplex strangely outlined by the NYC in March 1945, by which time the 25 production 4-8-4s were already on order and a new enlarged turntable would have been required at Harmon. Quotations were sought, it seems, but the solitary poppet valve 4-8-4 No.5500 was ordered instead.

Curiously this had seemingly not occurred with the pilot pair, which in the event had only briefly run through the 713 miles between Harrisburg and Chicago on account of en route re-coaling problems, despite a *Railway Gazette* (19 April 1946) claim that overhead coal chutes could dispense 43 (short) tons of coal in 75 seconds. In the event the post-war T1s never operated in this fashion, although the derailment problem was solved in early 1946. Despite this, double-heading with K4 4-6-2s persisted over the Crestline-Chicago stretch. In other words the 1940 Harrisburg-Chicago dream was never realised.

The last four T1s were delivered from Baldwin in August 1946, around which time another problem began to become apparent - fractures (although the incidence varied greatly from one engine to another) of the mild steel poppet valves. A top speed of 100mph had been indicated to Franklins, whose representatives covertly rode in T1-hauled passenger trains and timed them. Little if anything can be authenticated almost fifty years later, but very high speeds indeed were allegedly recorded, 130mph and even 140mph was claimed. (As an intriguing

aside the driving wheel diameter of 6ft 8in, and piston stroke of 26in were the same as those of an LNER Class A4 4-6-2, and so at a given locomotive speed *rotational* and *piston* speeds would have been identical). The problem of fracturing in the poppet valves was eventually solved by using new materials. In addition the roller bearing big ends performed badly as some required complete replacement after only 100,000 miles rather than 500,000 miles. These had been a rather unnecessary luxury as like most American locomotives the T1s rarely if ever ran more than 200 miles between stops.

As early as the spring of 1947, diesels began to take over some of the most prestigious passenger duties on the PRR. An early analysis showed that they returned an average repair cost of only 32 cents per mile, compared to 54 cents for a 4-4-4-4. This represented an annual total saving of no less than $1.3 million, to which could be added a further saving of $900,000 in fuel costs! Scrapping of the revered K4 4-6-2s commenced with a vengeance as early as 1947, including one of the last to be built, as recently as 1928.

Against this background, in 1948 (following accident damage) T1 No.5500 was rebuilt with rotary cam poppet valve gear (Franklin Type B) to produce what was claimed to be the best T1 of all. It was credited with attaining 135mph in 1950 *and* was sure footed. A little later, for reasons which are now inexplicable, No.5547 was rebuilt with piston valves and Walschaerts valve gear, possibly also after accident damage.

By 1949 there were numerous reports of T1s engaged upon menial tasks, even working coal trains and on banking duties out of Altoona. By late that year, some were already standing out of use and at least three were cut up as early as 1951. The 4-4-4-4s appear to have been finally in active operation, sometimes working in pairs on mail trains, and others working local passenger trains, during 1952. To satisfy the accountants the last eight Baldwin engines rusted at Altoona for several years before finally being cut up in March 1956. The PRR 4-4-4-4s therefore had an operational span of only ten years, slightly less than that of the NYC 4-8-4s.

The violent slipping sometimes encountered with the T1s has

Two 'Niagaras' on the eve of their demise, including the prototype No. 6000, stand at Collinwood Depot, Cleveland, Ohio, in 1956. The NYC systematically dieselised from east to west, and the last reported sighting of an NYC 4-8-4 in steam was of No.6015 at Indianapolis in late June 1956. The prototype NYC 'Hudson' 4-6-4 No. 5200 of 1927 had been scrapped only three years earlier, so rapid was the rundown of the New York Central's elite with no survivors.

New Altoona-built T1 4-4-4-4 No.5507 pauses at Englewood, just east of Chicago, in 1946. At this location for a few brief years it was possible to watch Pennsylvania 4-4-4-4s and New York Central 4-8-4s powering prestigious passenger trains on adjacent tracks, approaching and departing from Chicago.

blackened their name, but evidently this was *not* a major problem with the production series on account of their revised compensated suspension. A few engines also had their cylinder bore reduced from 19¾in to 18¾in in order to increase the adhesive factor. One major criticism of the T1s by crewmen was that their cabs could become intensely hot and dusty.

In early 1945 the New York Central had considered a 4-4-4-4 'Duplex' version of its 4-8-4 and for which a diagram at least was produced. Other railroads, notably the Texas & Pacific, also showed interest

in the type, as did the Canadian Pacific briefly in 1947. Alternative CPR plans for a conventional 4-8-4 also failed to materialise at this period. In 1946 a T1 ran experimentally on the Chesapeake & Ohio, which possibly hoped it would combine mountain climbing with fast work on the plains. However, the 4-4-4-4 slipped extremely violently and was quickly sent back, with the C & O subsequently ordering 4-6-4s and 4-8-4s instead. A brief exchange between a PRR 4-4-4-4 and a Norfolk & Western 4-8-4 also took place in 1948 for reasons which are now obscure. An even larger and more

powerful freight version of the T1, the Q2 4-4-6-4 was also built, a prototype in 1944, followed by 25 production engines in 1945. Capable of almost 8,000IHP, these were the most powerful rigid frame locomotives ever built. Although they incorporated sophisticated electrically actuated devices in order to arrest slipping, in reality this equipment was apparently not even connected up!

After only a few months in service, the entire 4-4-6-4 fleet succumbed to serious cracks in their boilers. There is a possibility that the American Locomotive Company, which

Put out to grass. Not yet seven years old, the second Altoona production series T1, No. 5501, stands out of use, never to be steamed again, at Crestline, Ohio, in 1952, the final year(?) of Pennsylvania 'Duplex' operation.

TABLE 11

MAXIMUM CYLINDER (IHP), DRAWBAR (DBHP) HORSEPOWERS, AND MAXIMUM EVAPORATION ATTAINED BY NYC CLASS S1\S2 4-8-4s AND PRR CLASS T1 4-4-4-4

	NYC S1a	NYC S1b	NYC S1b	NYC S2a*	PRR T1*
Boiler Pressure lb	290	275	275	275	300
Driving Wheel diam.	6'7"	6'3"	6'7"	6'7"	6'8"
Max IHP @ mph	6900 @ 85	6600 @78	6550 @ 84	6620 @ 90	6552 @86
Max DBHP @ mph	5375 @ 62	5100 @58	5050 @ 62	5000 @65	-+ - +
Max Evaporation lb/hour	110,000	105,000	-	-	101,200
Coal Rate lb/hour	17,000	17,000	-	-	18,500
Steam consumption lb/IHP hr	15.7	15.9	16.0	15.9	15.4
Coal consumption lb/IHP hr	2.46	2.58	2.60	2.57	2.82

*   Equipped with Franklin (Type A) poppet valve gear

+   Not determined on a comparable basis

did not normally contract to the PRR, designed an all-welded boiler for them. This work would have been done on a speculative basis, though in the event the originals were (evidently) satisfactorily repaired. In November 1946 Alco also submitted an even larger rigid frame 4-4-6-6 proposal, possibly because a little earlier the PRR had considered ordering a further 75 Q2 4-4-6-4s. At this time the Pennsylvania Railroad's financial position was dire, and James Symes, its rapidly rising star, had begun to wean the road away from steam and towards the diesel in order to cut back on rising financial losses. Significantly, the 4-4-6-4s were outlived by the slightly older and less powerful C&O type two-cylinder 2-10-4s built by the

PRR as a wartime emergency measure during 1942-44. All 125 were still in stock, if not all active, at the beginning of 1957.

Despite the relative diversity of their respective designs, the one ultra-conservative, and the other distinctly unorthodox, there were remarkable parallels between the NYC 4-8-4s and PRR 4-4-4-4s. Built to fairly tight constraints by American standards, both were of almost identical power capacity, around 6,500IHP. Outstanding by whatever yardstick, the seeds of their premature destruction were already germinating in late 1945 before either design was in fleet operation. Such defects as cracked boiler plates, poppet valve and roller bearing big end failures, were

only incidental and did not change the course of history. These short term problems, all of which were overcome, merely facilitated the progress of the inevitable. No 'Niagara' or 'Duplex' can be admired in Washington DC or Strasburg, PA today but, happily, numerous photographs and moving film exists (now transcribed onto commercial video) depicting them in operation during their (albeit brief) eleven year operational spans.

Summary
NYC Sla   4-8-4 No. 6000 Alco March 1946, rtd March 1956
NYC Slb   4-8-4 Nos 6001-25   Alco Oct 1945 - May 1946, rtd Aug 1955-Aug 1956
NYC S2a   4-8-4 No. 5500 Alco June 1946, rtd May 1951 scr 1956
PRR T1   4-4-4-4 Nos 6110-1 BLW April-May 1942, scr Dec 1953
PRR T1   4-4-4-4 Nos 5500-24 PRR Nov 1945-June 1946, scr 1951-56
PRR T1   4-4-4-4 Nos 5525-49 BLW Nov 1945-Aug 1946 scr 1951-56
rtd = retired
scr = scrapped

References
Modern Steam Passenger Locomotives - Research and Design, P.W. Kiefer. *Transactions of the American Society of Mechanical Engineers*, January 1942, 1-18.
A Practical Evaluation of Railroad Motive Power, P.W. Kiefer, Steam Locomotive Research Institute, Inc., 1947, 65p.
Road Testing of the Niagaras, R.W. Dawson, *Central Headlight* (Journal of the New York Central System Historical Society), August 1975, 5-25.
The Strange Story of Mr. Kiefer's Superlative S Class 4-8-4s, R.A. Le Massena, *Trains,* March 1984, 46-51.
Classic Power 5, Pennsy Q Class, E.T. Harley, N.J. International Inc., 1982, 88p
One Man's Locomotives, 50 Years Experience with Railway Motive Power, V.L. Smith, Trans-Anglo Books, 1987, 181p.
Articles by C. Meyer, in *Milepost* (Journal of the Friends of the Railroad Museum of Pennsylvania) from 1988.
Pennsy Power III, A.F. Stauffer, W.D. Edson & E.T. Harley, A.F. Stauffer, 1993, 496p.
The Great (Motive) Power Struggle, The Pennsylvania Railroad v. General Motors, 1935-1949, M. Reutter, *Railroad History*, 170, Spring 1994, 15-33.

TABLE 10

LEADING DIMENSIONS OF NEW YORK CENTRAL 4-8-4 AND PENNSYLVANIA 4-4-4-4 LOCOMOTIVES

	NYC S1a 4-8-4	NYC S1b 4-8-4	NYC S2a 4-8-4	PRR T1 4-4-4-4
Driving Wheel diameter	6'7"/6'3"	6'7"	6'7"	6'8"
Cylinders	(2) 25"x32"	(2) 25½"x32"	(2) 25"x32"	(4) 19¾"x26"
Boiler Pressure lb	275/290	275	275	300
Evaporative HS ft²	4632	4819	4819	4218
Superheater	1977	2073	2073	1680
Grate Area	101.0	101.0	101.0	92.0
Adhesive Wt tons	122.8	122.8	122.8	119.7
Engine Wt	210.3	210.3	216.5	222.0
Tractive Effort lb	62,400	61,570	61,570	65,000

Spirit of the Norfolk & Western personified. A compound 2-8-8-2 of the ultimate Y6b variety, with clear exhaust and only a 'feather' at the safety valves, heads a train of loaded coal hoppers over well ballasted track alongside the New River, west of Roanoke. This timeless view dates from the zenith of Norfolk & Western Railway steam operation, the late 1940s/early 1950s, and would vanish within a decade. N&W.

The ultimate in Mallet elegance. The last five of the forty-three N&W Class A 2-6-6-4s incorporated roller bearing big-ends and crank pins. No.1238 was recorded brand-new at Roanoke in 1949. N&W.

Chapter 4
NORFOLK & WESTERN · THE MAVERICK

Even as the diesel tide continued to sweep remorselessly across the United States in 1951, one railroad could not only lay claim to be entirely steam operated, but it still continued to build new steam locomotives in its own workshops. It is probably fair to say that prior to the 1950s, the Norfolk & Western Railway had attracted little attention as it had pursued its prime business of hauling Pocahontas coal from the deep valleys of West Virginia, eastward across the Allegheny mountains to Norfolk for export, and north to Columbus, Ohio for consumption in the American Mid-West.

From the mid-1930s the N&W developed three highly refined types of steam locomotive which increasingly dominated its operations, 2-8-8-2 compound for working coal trains over the mountains, 2-6-6-4 simple for fast freight over the western portion of the system, and 4-8-4 passenger. All were provided with cast steel engine beds, roller bearings on all axles, and pressure lubrication. As these were all built as well as designed on the N&W's own workshops at Roanoke, in this respect the Company was not dependent upon developments at Alco, Baldwin and Lima, even when this meant adopting an increasingly isolated stance. Just why was succinctly expressed by H.C. Wyatt, Assistant General Superintendent of Motive Power, at the Norfolk & Western Railway's annual staff conference in April 1951.

"You probably are interested to know why our railroad - almost alone among the country's roads - not only continues to operate steam locomotives, but continues to build new ones. Our situation differs from that of most other roads in two respects. First, we have available along our railroad, in almost unlimited quantities, the cheapest known fuel - coal. It is coal of the finest quality for power generation. Second, when other railroads began to turn to other types of power, we already had in service a substantial number of modern coal-burning steam locomotives. The railroads on which the greatest number of steam locomotives were replaced by other types did not have fleets of steam power as reliable, efficient or as modern as our own J's, A's, or Y-6's.

Regardless of what you may have read or heard about the steam locomotive, you should not overlook its virtues. First of all, it is an extremely rugged and simple machine. It will better withstand abuse than any other type of locomotive in existence. It has the ability to develop its maximum power quickly when needed. The best illustration of this quality is the locomotive boiler's ability to evaporate in a given time ten times as much water as the most efficient stationary steam plant boiler. Yet its size and weight is only one-tenth that of a stationary boiler. In spite of the steam locomotive's virtues, however, we are not complacent over what we now have. The relatively low overall efficiency of the conventional steam locomotive is recognised."

Wyatt had personally been much involved in the design and development of the outstanding N&W motive power servicing facilities at Williamson, West Virginia, which probably had no parallel on a steam worked railway anywhere in the world. Earlier in his address he had made interesting comparisons between operations during the previous year, 1950, with the situation 25 years earlier. In 1925 twice as many locomotives had worked considerably less traffic than was handled in 1950, when locomotive miles per engine failure were five times better. The 'trademark' of the Norfolk & Western Railway was the compound 2-8-8-2, first introduced in 1918, and of which there were 111 in service by 1925. Who could have guessed then that an almost exactly equal number were yet to be built, and that construction and development would still be proceeding in 1950? These were ideally suited to the arduous main line extending 470 miles east of Williamson, with the triple summits of Bluefield, Christiansburg, and Blue Ridge on the long haul to the Atlantic port of Norfolk. Remarkably, cylinder dimensions remained unchanged throughout, but in 1930 (in the new Y5) boiler pressure was increased from 240lb to 300lb, and grate area enlarged from 96 to 106ft² to match. Low pressure piston valve diameter was also increased from 14in to 18in to produce the Class Y5, of which thirty were built.

During 1933-35 the effects of the Depression meant that no new N&W locomotives appeared. Many of the earlier 2-6-6-2s were scrapped, but from 1936 to 1940 35 additional 2-8-8-2s were built. Designated Class Y6, these were based on the Y5 but incorporated cast steel engine beds and roller bearings to all engine axles. A further 16 generally similar Class Y6a

engines were produced during 1942-43. During the 1940s a number of the older 2-8-8-2s were sold to a variety of other railroads, but in 1948 new construction resumed at Roanoke with the Y6b.

In the Y6b, firebox volume was increased and the draughting improved. The final six engines were turned out new with a so-called booster arrangement whereby live steam at reduced pressure could be admitted to the low pressure cylinders, boosting tractive effort. This meant incorporating 12½ tons of lead ballast in the leading engine unit to increase the adhesive weight. Peak drawbar horsepower was boosted from 4,600 to 5,600, at a speed of 25 mph.

Y6bs built in 1950 had a unique distinction, for they were built to replace electric locomotives. The latter dated back to 1914 and worked between Bluefield and Iager where the ruling grade was 2 per cent. After World War Two, a new deviation line was built incorporating a tunnel and in which the ruling gradient was reduced to 1.4 per cent, which came into full use in 1952. Despite their distinctly ponderous appearance, the later 2-8-8-2s had a remarkable turn of speed, indeed the last of all, No.2200, when on its trial trip when brand new in April 1952 reputedly hit 70 mph.

Such speeds, in fact, were already commonplace with the Class A 2-6-6-4; high speed simple expansion engines, the initial pair had been completed at Roanoke in 1936. These were almost exactly contemporaneous with the first Alco 'Challenger' 4-6-6-4s, but their symmetrical engine units rendered them aesthetically superior. On test a maximum of 6,300DBHP was claimed, but this was disputed by other authorities at the time. Indeed no more than 5,300DBHP was recorded in 1952. By that time, boiler pressure had been increased from 275lb to 300lb for the class as a whole, and all contributory factors had been significantly increased on the engine in question.

The As were principally used west of Roanoke on fast freight and even passenger trains. However, a speciality with which they came to be particularly associated was working heavy coal trains over the almost dead level 111 mile route between Williamson, West Virginia and Portsmouth, Ohio. A development in 1952 was the provision of additional 16,000 US gallon water tenders or 'canteens', which not only enabled the run to be made in four hours, but also the loading to be increased from 11,600 to 13,000 long (224lb) tons due to the complete elimination of intermediate

The acme of the N&W 2-8-8-2 saga was the highly efficient Class Y6b, of which the prototype No.2171 is illustrated here. Although introduced in 1948, development continued up to the final batch delivered in 1952. However, the final thirty 2-8-8-2s enjoyed nothing like the life of the Y5s of 1930—eight were still on the books at the beginning of 1960, by which time half of the Y6bs had already been retired. N&W.

stops for water. (Unlike in Britain, with its twin tracks *and* the additional benefit of water troughs, the need for water stops on single tracks greatly circumscribed line capacity as far as steam working was concerned in the USA, Russia and, eventually, China).

The same coupled wheel diameter of 5ft 10in was employed in the Class J semi-streamlined express passenger 4-8-4, introduced in late 1941. This was a remarkable design and ranked amongst the largest and most powerful of all 4-8-4s. The tractive effort of 80,000lb was unequalled. While experimentally running on the Pennsylvania Railroad in 1944, one had attained 110 mph with half worn (5ft 8½in) tyres. As with the A class after World War Two, boiler pressure was increased, from 275lb to 300lb and a final trio was built at Roanoke in 1950. With careful rostering, each engine regularly achieved 15,000 miles per month. The first two 4-8-4s. Nos.600-601, completed in late 1941, almost simultaneously notched up 2 million miles each in February 1954. Although the engines operated to Norfolk in the east and to Cincinnati in the west, a total distance of 677 miles, the longest single run actually undertaken was the 424 miles between Roanoke and Cincinnati, which was modest when compared to the 928 mile through runs undertaken by the NYC 4-8-4s. One can only guess what might have been achieved on runs of much greater length, of the sort found on larger railroad systems.

In early 1950 the Norfolk & Western Railway purchased the 30 Baldwin 1948-built 0-8-0 shunters from the Chesapeake & Ohio Railway, at about half their new cost and then proceeded to build 45 more to the same drawings, (except for enlarging the tenders) at Roanoke. This design, in essence, dated back to 1918, being one of the USRA standards, and constituted the American steam locomotive design to which the greatest number of units, 1,340, was ultimately built. They were all hand-fired and the only major innovations were increased boiler pressure and cast steel engine beds. N&W 0-8-0 No.244, outshopped on 10 December 1953, was the last conventional steam locomotive to be built for service in North America.

Roanoke Shops probably retained the capacity for building new steam locomotives for another two or three years. In December 1955 a 2-8-8-2 suffered very extensive firebox damage only a fortnight after completing a major overhaul and was subsequently completely rebuilt. The General Steel Castings Corporation at Eddystone continued to supply steam locomotive engine beds to European locomotive builders until 1957, but the difficulties of procuring other specialist components undoubtedly lay behind the sudden and dramatic demise of the steam locomotive on the Norfolk & Western Railway in the late 1950s.

Steam operation on the Norfolk & Western Railway reached its zenith in early 1955, when 100 Y5/Y6 2-8-8-2s, by then all upgraded to Y6b standards, 43 2-6-6-4s and 14 4-8-4s (the 'Magnificent Three') accounted for 94 per cent of the gross ton miles, and 84 per cent of the passenger train miles. Furthermore, in that year with steam the N&W achieved the highest productivity in gross ton miles per hour in freight train operation of any railroad in the United States, what Roanoke liked to call 'Precision Transportation'. Why then did 'The Great Black Fleet' vanish within just five years?

The fundamental answer is that the Norfolk & Western Railway was *not* devoted to the steam locomotive as such, but *was* devoted to working its heavy coal traffic as efficiently as possible. By the mid-1950s this amounted to 50 to 60 million tons per year. After the bleak years of the late 1940s, the US coal industry was enjoying something of a resurgence, enjoying (through much lower costs) particular success with exports to Europe. This was reflected in changing traffic patterns on the N&W which was experiencing an increasing proportion of its tonnage moving *east* to Norfolk. The saw-tooth gradient profile was particularly demanding, even with the excellent 2-8-8-2s both pulling and pushing, and operating costs began to rise. The N&W decided to dieselise, cautiously at first.

Back in 1952 a comparative trial had taken place between a General Motors F7 unit and a hand-picked 2-6-6-4 (No 1239) and 2-8-8-2 (No 2197). How this came about is not clear. Obviously GM would have liked to have cracked the final nut in the pursuit of its goal of total national dieselisation, yet it has been suggested that it was Roanoke which threw down the gauntlet. Over thirty years later, many details were still shrouded in secrecy, but it is known that both parties performed sleight of hand. The diesel men secretly up-rated their champion from 6,000 to 6,800HP, whilst the N&W temporarily increased the boiler pressure of the 2-6-6-4 and 2-8-8-2 from 300lb to 315lb, and ballasted the frames to increase the adhesive weight to match. For good measure the 24in cylinders of the 'A' were bored out by an extra ¼in, and the coupled wheel tyres reduced by ½in, which collectively increased the tractive effort from 114,000lb to 126,000lb, or 10 per cent. Surviving data show that it was a very close run thing, not least in specific fuel costs. The diesel showed a slight but distinct advantage in tackling the steeper gradients, but against this had to be set the advanced infra-structure already in place for the servicing of steam locomotives, and the high calibre of the steam locomotives themselves. Moreover, given the N&W's continued allegiance to the coal industry there was no good reason to abandon steam. Indeed the low average age of the N&W locomotive stock, its high degree of standardisation, and advanced servicing facilities prompted the observation that it had already effectively 'dieselised without diesels'.

The dieselisation programme began, innocuously enough, in the spring of 1955 - a few months after David P Morgan published his article 'Faith in Steam', in *Trains* for November 1954. Then the N&W ordered eight general purpose diesels, four each from Alco (1,600HP) and General Motors (1,750HP), specifically for service on the 115 mile Durham - Lynchburg branch. President R.H. Smith explained the move in the following terms:

"This does not mean that we have changed our view that our modern roller-bearing coal-burning steam locomotives can handle the major part of our traffic economically. Nor does it mean that our interest in new and better types of coal burning locomotives has diminished in any way. The major reason for switching to diesels on the Durham line is based on our need at the present time for additional motive power elsewhere, and particularly for the large type power we are at present using on the Durham line, where, because of comparatively thin traffic, we are not able to get out of this large power the full service of which it is capable. We have therefore concluded that the smaller diesel units will be sufficient for that territory."

The first diesels arrived on the N&W from General Motors in September 1955. Singly they could be employed on shunting operations, and in multiple on passenger or freight workings. Operating economies of 37 per cent were quickly demonstrated. By the end of the year the order had been increased to 25 units for freight service between Cincinnati and Portsmouth, Ohio. It was perhaps no

coincidence that the N&W's long awaited coal burning steam electric locomotive (see Chapter 14) had apparently proved to be unsuccessful.

During 1956 a further 148 diesel locomotives were ordered by the N&W but the official line was that the railroad 'planned to use these on its lighter traffic and variable traffic side lines ..... and release the heavy steam power at present being used on those lines for handling its heavy and increasing main line freight traffic.'

At this point, President Smith and his team clearly had no *immediate* intention of eliminating steam power on the Norfolk & Western Railway, which he had joined in 1911 as a humble inspector of masonry, working his way up to become President in 1946. Yet when he retired at the end of March 1958 at his last official public appearance that month it was revealed that dieselisation of the 238 mile Hagerstown branch had achieved operating economies of around 30 per cent. Furthermore, heavy repairs to steam locomotives had *already* ceased at Roanoke in September 1957. The 'count down' had begun.

Smith's departure coincided with a deep economic recession, which doubly facilitated the swift moves made by his successor, Stuart T Saunders, who had originally joined the N&W in a legal capacity in 1939. Only a few weeks later Saunders' deputy, H. C. Wyatt announced:- **'Without doubt, the one single development having the greatest impact on our operation today and in the near future is the diesel locomotive.'**

This was a very different opinion indeed from that which he had expressed only seven years earlier. The final bastion had fallen. On 2 June

1958 the Norfolk & Western Railway announced that it was ordering 268 diesel units in order to permit the *complete* elimination of steam working by the end of 1960. It was proposed, however, to retain a total of sixty steam locomotives (hand-picked 4-8-4s, 2-6-6-4s, and 2-8-8-2s) for standby duties, but in the event this did not happen.

The wind-down process began immediately with neither fear nor favour. On 17 July 4-8-4s powered the prestige passenger trains for the last time, to be superseded by borrowed diesels the following day. During August the final Sla 0-8-0, No.244, barely 4½ years old, was withdrawn from service. Inroads were rapidly made into the ranks of the As, Js, and Y6s as they fell due for their annual overhauls. The last 4-8-4s and 2-6-6-4s finally operated in ordinary service during mid-1959, just after which, scarcely five years after his 'Faith in Steam' article, David P Morgan published 'The Morning After Steam' in *Trains* for September 1959—once again a little prematurely, as it turned out. A subsequent upturn in traffic deferred the end of steam working from the close of that year, into the early months of 1960. The end finally came on 6 May 1960, at Williamson, when nine year old Y6b 2-8-8-2 No.2190 dropped its fire for the last time, although a few 2-8-8-2s and 0-8-0s remained officially on the books until September.

Ironically no other major US railroad had made the steam/diesel transition as rapidly as had the N&W. It had been assisted by the 1958 recession, however, in that it hired surplus diesels from other railroads. These included fifty brand new units from the Pennsylvania Railroad, which

TABLE 12

COMPARATIVE TEST RESULTS BETWEEN GENERAL MOTORS F7 DIESEL ELECTRIC LOCOMOTIVE AND NORFOLK & WESTERN RAILWAY CLASS A 2-6-6-4 AND Y6b 2-8-8-2 STEAM LOCOMOTIVES, 1952

Section	Williamson - Portsmouth		Portsmouth - Williamson		Williamson - Farm		Farm - Bluefield	
Distance	111 miles		111 miles		62 miles		36 miles	
Ruling gradient	0.32%		0.66%		0.6%		1.4%	
	A 2-6-6-4	F7	A 2-6-6-4	F7	Y6b 2-8-8-2	F7	Y6b 2-8-8-2	F7
Load (tons)	16,028	15,763	4,130	4,126	7,422	7,481	3,818	3,512
Time	3hr 31min	3hr 33min	3hr 8min	3hr11min	2hr 29min	2hr 31min	1hr40min	1hr26min
Speed (mph)	31.6	31.4	36.3	35.8	25.36	24.9	19.3	22.7
Fuel cost per 1000 gross ton miles	$0.0638	$0.0617	$0.1987	$0.1861	$0.1800	$0.1778	$0.4362	$0.3709

Note: It seems possible that these trials were initiated by the N&W in order to establish yardsticks of efficiency in anticipation of its long awaited steam-electric locomotive. See Chapter 14.

Roanoke built three additional Class J 4-8-4s in 1950 and this is the first, No.611, brand new. Last operated under 'normal' circumstances in October 1959, it evaded the scrapper's torch, and saw extensive employment on railfans' excursions between 1982 and 1994, before its second enforced retirement and preservation. N&W.

amounted to one third of a batch of 150 which that enterprise had ordered the previous autumn. This was in order to eliminate steam working once and for all; there would not even be any locos left stored, in the event of any unlooked-for traffic upsurge.

The Pennsylvania Railroad had enjoyed a secretive controlling interest in the N&W for several years, and Stuart Saunders sat upon the PRR Board. No evidence, however, has ever been uncovered to suggest that Philadelphia handed down a directive to Roanoke to eliminate steam working. Nevertheless, a posthumous pen portrait of Saunders pulled no punches:

"His first move as president was to push ahead, quickly and decisively, with dieselisation. No railroad in the United States had stuck with steam as long as the N&W, which had done so out of loyalty to the coal industry that was its main customer; it had built new steam locomotives as late as 1952. There was a strong professional and emotional attachment to steam on the N&W, and this intellectual non railroader who eliminated it with such ruthlessness caused great dismay among many of the railroad's employees. The episode set the tone for style of management; profits mattered, sentiments did not."

Not entirely unrelated to all this was the take-over of the Virginian Railway by the N&W in late 1959, which

Saunders also engineered. This provided a much less demanding route for export coal to the port of Norfolk, with the N&W's own severely graded line thereafter utilised for return empties. Other mergers followed and by late 1964 the Norfolk & Western Railway was a very different concern from that of 1954. A 2,134 route mile enterprise operated by 441 steam locomotives had expanded into a 7,577 mile network operated by 1,396 diesel units. Also under discussion at this point was a possible merger with the Chesapeake & Ohio Railway (which failed to materialise), even though the

once unimaginable amalgamation of the New York Central and Pennsylvania railroads *did* go through shortly thereafter, in the early post-steam era.

An evocative and highly acclaimed record of the twilight of Norfolk & Western Railway steam operation during the late 1950s was made by the New York-based photographer, O. Winston Link, in black and white still photographs, moving colour film and sound recordings. After 1960 it seemed virtually impossible that any of the sights and sounds thus recorded would ever be experienced again, but by sheer

N&W 0-8-0 No.244, a humble hand-fired shunting engine, completed at Roanoke in December 1953 was the last conventional steam locomotive to be built for service in North America. Its basic design dated back no less than 35 years, but No.244 was retired in August 1958 after a working life of less than five years. N&W.

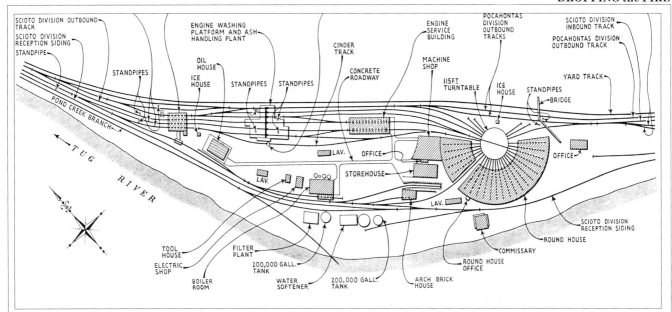

accidents of history both a 4-8-4 and a 2-6-6-4 each eluded the scrappers. Many years later, in 1982 and against all the odds, both No.611 and No.1218 reappeared in main line operation and enjoyed a further twelve years of active life. Ironically no Y6b 2-8-8-2 survives. Inexplicably, a Y6a was presented to the National Museum of Transportation in St. Louis in 1959, rather than the rarely photographed Y6b No.2200, the last US main line steam locomotive to be built, which was retired early the following year when not yet eight years old.

In many ways the Norfolk & Western Railway during the 1950s can be perceived as a *world* high point in steam locomotive operation, but despite considerable finesse in design and unparalleled servicing facilities, even there the steam locomotive succumbed to seemingly irresistible factors during a remarkably short period of time.

References

Faith in Steam: the Story of Norfolk & Western Locomotives, D.P. Morgan, *Trains,* November 1954, 18-30.
The Morning After Steam, D.P. Morgan, *Trains,* September 1959, 27-33.
Norfolk & Western Railway: Pocahontas Coal Carrier, R.E. Prince, 1980. 352p.
N. & W. Giant of Steam, L.I. Jeffries, Pruett Publishing Co., 1980, 333p
4-8-0s to Mallets to Jawn Henry, C.E. Pond, *Trains,* October 1984, 34-45.
Effect and Cause in Dieselization, R.A. Le Massena, *Trains,* November 1990, 80.
Norfolk & Western: Diesel's Last Conquest, W.E. Warden, Walsworth Publishing Co., 1991, 62p.
N&W's Secret Weapons, R.A. Le Massena, *Trains,* November 1991, 64-69.

Above. The highly developed steam locomotive servicing facilities established by the Norfolk & Western Railway at Williamson, West Virginia, during the 1940s. It was here that N&W steam operations finally ended, in early May 1960.

TABLE 13

CHARACTERISTICS OF MAJOR NORFOLK & WESTERN RAILWAY STEAM LOCOMOTIVE CLASSES

Class	Y3	Y6b	A	J
Wheel Arrangement	2-8-8-2	2-6-6-4	2-6-6-4	4-8-4
Built	1919-1923	1948-1952	1936-1950	1941-1950
Driving Wheel dia	4'10"	4'10"	5'10"	5'10"
Cylinders	(2) 25"x32"	(2) 25"x32"	(4) 24"x32"	(2) 27"x32"
	(2) 39"x32"	(2) 39"x32"		
Boiler Pressure lb	270	300	300	300
Evaporative HS ft²	5753	4915	6639	5271
Superheater	1582	1478	2703	2177
Grate Area	96.3	106.2	122.0	107.7
Adhesive Weight tons	216.6	244.9	193.0	128.6
Engine Weight	240.6	273.0	255.8	220.5
Tractive Effort lb	114,154	126,838	114,000	80,000
Maximum DBHP	3400	5600	5300	5150
	@ 15 mph	@ 25 mph	@ 40 mph	@ 40 mph
Cost in 1950	($98,000*)	$236,307	$289,772	$251,524

* cost in 1919

TABLE 14

THE RUN-DOWN OF MAJOR N & W RAILWAY STEAM LOCOMOTIVE CLASSES DURING 1958 - 1960

CLASS	YEARS BUILT	TOTAL	STOCK AT:			
			1.1.57	1.1.58	1.1.59	1.1.60
S1 0-8-0	1948	30[1]	30	30	23	0
Sla 0-8-0	1951-53	45	45	45	34	6
J 4-8-4	1941-50	14	14	14	13	0
A 2-6-6-4	1936-50	43	43	43	26	0
Y5 2-8-8-2	1930-31	20[2]	19	19	17	8
Y6 2-8-8-2	1936-40	35	35	35	29	16
Y6a 2-8-8-2	1942	16	16	16	14	3
Y6b 2-8-8-2	1948-52	30	30	30	30	16
TOTAL		**233**	**232**	**232**	**186**	**49[3]**

[1] Built BLW for C & 0, sold to N & W in 1950

[2] Rebuilt to Y6 standard in 1940-41, except for one engine destroyed in an accident in 1937

[3] Engines remaining in stock on 1.1.1960 were all retired between January and September 1960

The last entirely new Mallet locomotive design for a US railroad was the stylish EM1 2-8-8-4 for the Baltimore & Ohio Railroad, which had received the first US Mallets (compound 0-6-6-0s from Alco) in 1903. Thirty EM-1s were supplied by Baldwin during 1944-45, of which an early example poses in the huge Eddystone complex, some of which was only demolished as recently as 1994. B&O.

The B&O EM1 was a relative lightweight when compared to the not-dissimilar Duluth Missabe & Iron Range 2-8-8-4s Baldwin had supplied during 1941-43. The latter, in its dimensions, challenged the Alco 4-8-8-4 and Lima 2-6-6-6 designs as the world's largest steam locomotives. The DM&IR 2-8-8-4s worked the heaviest loadings of the steam era, 17,000 ton iron ore trains single-handed over easy gradients. No.231 was at work in June 1959, just one year before steam working finally ceased.

Chapter 5
USA 1920 - 1960, THE LEWIS YEARS

The total steam locomotive stock of the United States Class 1 railroads attained a peak of 65,000 in 1924 and thereafter declined steadily until 1940, after which World War Two brought a temporary levelling out. What is interesting is that the trend prior to 1941 (before which the diesel had made no *significant* impact), if statistically projected, indicated an extinction date for steam of 1964. The rate of decline after 1924 had been remarkably uniform and was not accelerated, it would seem, by the very severe economic depression of the early 1930s. The total 'book stock', however, did not give an entirely realistic picture of the position in that large numbers of engines were laid up in storage in both serviceable and unserviceable condition. At the nadir of the Depression in mid-1932, no less than *fifty per cent* of the stock, including half that of the New York Central Railroad (for example) was inactive. This would inevitably have included quite new locomotives put aside when due for heavy repairs. On the Pennsylvania Railroad, for instance, there were 1920s built 4-6-2s, 4-8-2s and 2-10-0s still languishing in sidings in 1939, some of them not having turned a wheel in years.

With so little work for the existing stock to perform, it is hardly surprising that new construction fell to a negligible level. During 1933 only a single new steam locomotive (and that an experimental one) entered service on US railroads, compared to 972 in 1930. Statistical projection of the widely fluctuating new construction over the period 1926-1940, indicates that the cessation of domestic steam locomotive construction in the United States could have been reached in 1938!

In fact, new construction continued for a further fifteen years, although from that date new steam units per annum would never outnumber diesel. It is also interesting to note that the American commentator, Robert Le Massena, discerned a distinct decline in the quality of American steam locomotive design after 1937. For example, the Alco 2-8-4s for the Pittsburgh & Lake Erie in 1948 carried only 230lb boiler pressure and were distinctly heavy in relation to their modest tractive effort. In his opinion even the NYC 4-8-4s could have been better still with the benefit of a more sophisticated draughting arrangement. Some revival in economic fortune became apparent

during 1934-37 when several railroads ordered new power for the first time for some years. Early off the mark was the Nickel Plate in 1934 with fifteen fast mixed traffic 2-8-4s from Alco, which soon after developed the 4-6-6-4 high speed simple expansion Mallet. This was the 'Challenger' and the foe to be challenged was the fast developing trucking industry. The first Challengers were delivered in 1936, to the Union Pacific, and the following year it also received twenty sophisticated 4-8-4s from the Schenectady plant. During 1938 these each averaged 180,000 miles and an availability of 93.4 per cent on passenger duties which frequently called for speeds above 80 mph. Replacing 1922-built 4-8-2s, they demonstrated dramatic savings in costs, in just twelve months the 4-8-4s recovered just over fifty per cent of their original cost, even though fuel costs per mile were 15 per cent greater due to increased train weights and speeds. The second (1939) series of these undertook the longest scheduled through runs by coal burning locomotives anywhere, of 1394 miles. Several smaller railroads also invested in fast 4-8-4s (though for freight) at this time and in some instances these

Louisville & Nashville Railroad Class M1 2-8-4 No.1970, completed by the Lima Locomotive Works in early 1949. Despite incorporating every modern conventional refinement, operating costs for such 'state of the art' power such as this continued to escalate during the 1940s; all were out of service by late 1956.

also proved to be their last new steam locomotives.

The economic strictures of the Depression enabled the main line diesel to gain the toe hold it needed. A straight cost comparison between steam and diesel on the Chicago - Los Angeles passenger service was made by the Atcheson, Topeka & Santa Fé Railroad as early as 1935. These showed that total operating costs with diesel traction amounted to almost exactly *half* those for steam.

In early 1935 the Baldwin Locomotive Works had gone into receivership. It had a vested interest in the survival of the steam locomotive which it still considered invincible and not under serious threat from the diesel, of which some experimental units had indeed been built at Eddystone. In April 1935 the company's philosophy was forcefully expressed by its Sales Manager in New York in a speech he had entitled 'Muzzle Not the Ox that Treadeth Out the Corn', Subsequently encouraged by a perceptible upturn in the economic situation, Baldwin produced a detailed 76 page report in September 1937 entitled *The Motive Power Situation of American Railroads*. This contained a mass of statistical data and concluded that over ninety per cent of the current motive power could be considered obsolete. This situation was exacerbated by the fact that the period which immediately preceded the advent of 'Super Power' in 1925 had witnessed something of a boom in locomotive building, so many engines had been rendered obsolescent soon after their construction. Obviously, with its huge new Eddystone plant and parlous financial position, Baldwin had no wish to see the steam locomotive overthrown. Whilst giving some credit to diesel traction it averred that **'the steam locomotive must continue to be the mainstay of railroad operation for the indefinite future'**.

A similar attitude existed at Baldwins' chief rival Alco, whose President proclaimed in April 1938 **'the possibilities of the Diesel-electric locomotive are already**

fixed and known. Not so with the steam locomotive. Although it is over one hundred years old it is still in the process of evolution.'

The year 1938 showed a return to a depressed economy with low demand for new locomotives and the following year, as war commenced in Europe, Baldwin was re-constituted. Its new board resolved on adopting a more positive policy towards diesel development. It also proposed to espouse 'Duplex' rigid frame four-cylinder locomotives and investigate steam turbine propulsion. On both fronts it would find a willing collaborator in the Pennsylvania Railroad. Such schemes were still on the drawing board when the situation in Europe prompted a massive upsurge in traffic on the US railroads and a growing realisation that the country would also become engulfed in war. It was no coincidence that during the latter half of 1940 all three builders received orders for simple expansion Mallet articulateds; each of these were contenders for the accolade of the largest steam locomotives ever built.

In January 1942 the War Production Board came into being and immediately froze steam (and diesel) locomotive development. Even minor design changes in repeat orders had to be specifically authorised, but several 'new' hybrid designs appeared, particularly 4-8-4s, by mating existing boiler with existing chassis designs. One might have expected greater standardisation to have been enforced than was the case, as in World War One, yet there were strange exceptions. The 220 ton turbine 4-8-4 ordered by the Pennsylvania Railroad from Baldwin in May 1941 still progressed, using available lower grade steels and eventually emerged over three years later as a 260 ton 6-8-6, in September 1944. As regards diesels, the traditional locomotive builders were restricted to producing 1,000 HP switchers, yet General Motors was permitted to build 2,000 HP main line diesels, giving them something of a head start once the war had ended. Even so, some railroads which would have preferred diesels were obliged to accept new steam in lieu in the strategic interest of conserving copper. This consideration underlaid the supply of thirty relatively 'light' 2-8-8-4s of new design by Baldwin to the Baltimore & Ohio during 1944-45. Similarly against its own inclinations, the Santa Fé received its final oil-burning 4-8-4s and 2-10-4s in 1944. That railroad experienced particular water supply problems in arid desert regions, and daily shipped 250,000 gallons for locomotive purposes. By 1944 more than half the locomotives on the

Class 1 railroads were estimated to be over 25 years old, and seventy per cent to be 20 years or over. After the titanic rigours of World War Two a massive re-equipment programme was overdue and it was estimated that there would be an initial annual requirement for 1,300-1,700 new locomotives of all kinds. Indeed eight thousand new units *were* put into service between 1945 and 1949, but only a mere five per cent would be steam. After 1944 all new American steam locomotives were exclusively coal burners, ordered by railroads centred east of Chicago and adjacent to the vast Appalachian coalfield. Several felt a strong allegiance to the coal industry, a loyalty which would be sorely tested over the next five years. As of August 1945 the American Locomotive Company, no less, confidently declared that there would be major advances in coal burning steam locomotive design over the next decade. This opinion would very soon radically change.

In 1941 it was estimated that 83 per cent of US railroad operations were fuelled by bituminous or 'soft' coal, while much of the remaining 17 per cent was accounted for by oil burning steam locomotives. The railroads annually consumed between 20 and 30 per cent of the national bituminous output, a much higher proportion than in Great Britain, and some derived up to 70 per cent of their gross revenue from its movement. There was thus a necessarily close relationship between the American railroad and coal industries. Towards the end of World War Two there was a growing awareness, however, that the supremacy of the steam locomotive was seriously threatened, with far reaching repercussions for both industries. For many years efficient locomotive operation had not necessarily been perceived by the coal industry as in its best interests, now it came to be regarded as vital, in order to avert the prospect of the decline of a major consumer.

In January 1945 a special committee was set up under the auspices of Bituminous Coal Research Incorporated, to promote the development of new types of coal-fired locomotives (not necessarily steam) and thereby counter the diesel threat. The committee consisted of senior representatives of six leading coal hauling railroads (the Pennsylvania, New York Central, Baltimore & Ohio, Chesapeake & Ohio, Louisville & Nashville, Norfolk & Western and Virginian) and three leading coal producers. There were high hopes of quickly developing a coal-fired gas turbine locomotive and there was confident talk of a prototype entering service in 1948. It was still being developed well into the 1950s but had not appeared by 1956, due to major technical problems. It was finally

TABLE 15

COMPARATIVE COSTS OF OPERATION, STEAM & DIESEL-ELECTRIC ON THE ATCHESON, TOPEKA & SANTA FÉ, CHICAGO - LOS ANGELES - CHICAGO, 4458 MILES, 1935

	STEAM	DIESEL
Operating Costs:		
Fuel	$1143	$519
Water	82	6
Lubrication	40	103
Supplies	16	16
Depot expenses	171	72
Repairs	1172	560
Total	2624	1276
Cost per mile	0.59	0.29

abandoned soon afterwards. However, anxious to utilise its local Montana coal the Union Pacific Railroad, which had wide experience of oil-fired gas turbines, in 1961 completed an experimental coal-fired gas turbine. This did not progress beyond road tests which were concluded in 1964.

A fundamental problem lay within the coal industry itself, which experienced particularly turbulent times during the 1940s. Twenty five years on John L. Lewis was still President of the National Union of Miners. Lewis had provoked public outrage by calling four strikes during the war, the most serious in early 1943, but worse was yet to come. The first year of peacetime in the United States witnessed considerable industrial unrest in the pursuit of wage claims, particularly in the steel industry. The miners were not far behind, and on 1 April 1946 Lewis called them out. Railway passenger services were quickly curtailed, and after five weeks an estimated 551,000 railroad employees were laid off, with the early prospect of another 100,000 plus 400,000 similarly affected in other industries. The city of Chicago was afflicted with repeated electric power cuts. As on previous occasions, Lewis secured a substantial pay rise for the miners and ordered them back to work, after six weeks of stoppage, on 13 May.

At the beginning of November 1946 when officially accepting the railroad's first passenger diesel locomotive from the builder at Eddystone, the Chief Executive of the Central Railroad of New Jersey (which only 21 years earlier had put into service the nation's first diesel locomotive) did not mince his words:

"We are sympathetic with the difficulties of our friends in the bituminous coal industry, but the Jersey Central Lines and its patrons cannot and will not be placed at the mercy of the whims of any man who decides to call a strike in the soft coal mines when it suits his fancy. This condition has prevailed too frequently in the past, but it is going to end as far as the Jersey Central and its operations are concerned. The aim of the Jersey Central Lines management is to give the railroad complete independence from the use of bituminous coal, and we will continue to replace bituminous-burning with oil-burning Diesel-electric locomotives as rapidly as possible."

Barely three weeks later Lewis called another coal strike, in breach of a prior agreement, and while negotiations with the government were still in progress. This ended after nearly three weeks, but Lewis was referred to in the railway press as the man who had done more for the cause of the diesel locomotive than any man alive. Such was Lewis's massive national status that one ponderous biography of him hardly even mentioned his impact on the US railroad industry. He was also venerated in Venezuela, the source of

much American oil. Even on the eve of the US entry into World War Two five years earlier, several railroads with strong coal interests, for example the Louisville & Nashville, which served the Kentucky coalfield, had purchased diesel-electric locomotives to power their most prestigious passenger services. In December 1941 the Pennsylvania Railroad aroused considerable interest by placing an order with General Motors for a Standard E7 unit to work a Chicago - Florida through service, in concert with several other railroads. The Japanese attacked Pearl Harbour and the order was cancelled. The possibility of reviving it was raised by the Pennsylvania President in March 1944, and later the order was indeed implemented. A vast enterprise, the self-styled 'Standard Railroad of the World', the Pennsylvania Railroad was closely associated with the powerful coal and steel empires, and derived a substantial proportion of its revenue from the movement of coal. There was an understandable reluctance to endanger the goose which laid the golden eggs. There was another factor, however; the PRR was traditionally sensitive (maybe over much) to any developments from the arch rival, the New York Central, and the NYC was not so closely allied to the coal interest. In 1945 the New York Central began to show interest in dieselising its major passenger services. Notwithstanding the fact that the PRR had fifty sophisticated T1 4-4-4-4s on order, in October 1945 James M Symes, (1897-

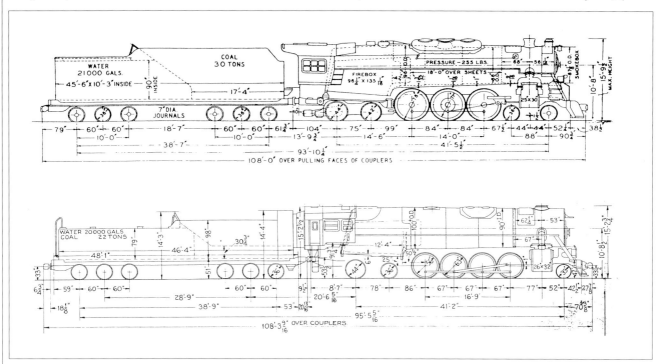

Steam locomotive development by American private industry effectively ceased in mid-1948. Alco supplied seven (out of ten originally ordered) 2-8-4s to the Pittsburgh & Lake Erie Railroad during May-June, and Baldwin five heavy 4-6-4s to the Chesapeake & Ohio Railway during July-August. The P&LE was a subsidiary of the New York Central and dimensionally (especially in their boilers) its 2-8-4s were closely related to the NYC 4-8-4s though, curiously, they carried only 230lb boiler pressure. The 4-6-4s had the latest Franklin Type B rotary cam poppet valve gear. Both designs were doomed; reputedly, all the 2-8-4s were nearly cancelled, whereas the passenger services for which the 4-6-4s were envisaged had dwindled by the time they appeared. Both classes had active lives of barely five years and after storage they were sold for scrap in 1956/57.

An unusual nocturnal study of the last new Canadian steam locomotive, CPR 2-10-4 No.5935, near the end of its brief working life at Medicine Hat, Alberta, in September 1956. It was only seven years old, but had been displaced by diesels in the Rockies for five years past. J.G. Collias.

1976) Vice President, Western Region PRR) advocated the purchase of fifteen twin diesel units to work designated named trains and the cancellation of up to twenty T1s. The PRR demurred; all fifty T1s *were* built and even after the last of these was delivered in August 1946 (the PRR's centennial year) the railroad was still steam-minded. Financially, the year proved disastrous, ruined by the coal strikes which put the company into the red for the first time in its history. In December 1946 the implications of national dieselisation, in order to reduce operating costs, were reviewed in some detail. The following points were made:-

1. *The railroads in 1945 accounted for roughly one quarter of the coal market, and if this market disappeared, many mines would close.*
2. *Railroad orders provided the coal industry with a steady and dependable high volume backlog of production which kept costs down. It its absence, costs would assuredly rise.*
3. *The coal industry would be faced with over-capacity and provoke strong competition for a reduced market in which necessary price rises could not be sustained, thereby resulting in acute financial difficulties. The*

inroads already made by alternative energy sources, i.e. oil, natural gas, and hydro-electricity would inevitably increase and so force up the price of coal.

As far as the Pennsylvania Railroad itself was concerned, not only was it a major consumer, purchasing almost 18 million US tons of coal in 1944, and almost 16 million tons in 1945 (rather more that that of the main line British railways *combined*), but around 10 per cent of its revenue was derived from moving locomotive coal to other railroads. Even modest dieselisation meant reductions in coal consumption of some two million tons, threatening serious implications for the coal industry. The PRR was very anxious to avoid offending its coal customers and diplomacy was a feature of the time - some diesel units purchased in 1946 by the Louisville & Nashville (for banking duties) were painted plain black.....

This conventional wisdom was called into question again by James Symes, who maintained that steam locomotives made for high operating costs and that *large scale* dieselisation was the only option. Soon after, in early 1947, Symes assumed the position of Vice President - Operations, diesel-electric locomotives took over some of the PRR's most prestigious passenger services from steam 4-4-4-4s delivered only the previous year. No fewer than 235 new diesels were ordered in 1947 compared to only 20 in 1946, and

before the year was out substantial numbers of the Class K4 4-6-2s had gone for scrap. Nearly 600 steam locomotives were withdrawn by the PRR during 1948, including about one hundred K4s, and 371 diesels were ordered. By 1949 recently built 4-4-4-4s and 4-4-6-4s were standing idle and the first inroads were made into the 4-8-2 and 2-10-0 workhorses which for so long had earned the railroad's bread and butter.

In 1947, a year which witnessed an all-time high in US coal production with no strikes, John L. Lewis sought by legal action (unsuccessfully) to dissuade the PRR from adopting a pro-diesel policy. About 100 million tons of this would have been hauled by the Chesapeake & Ohio, which publicly affirmed its allegiance to the steam locomotive, backing this up by placing orders for eighty more. These were express passenger 4-6-4s and 4-8-4s from Baldwin and Lima (five of each), fifteen 2-6-6-6 heavy Mallets from Lima, and twenty-five branch line compound 2-6-6-2s and thirty 0-8-0 heavy shunters from Baldwin. All except the 2-6-6-2s were delivered during 1948, when monetary inflation forced up energy costs. On the Santa Fé, for example, fuel costs rose by forty per cent on 1947, even though a minority of its locomotives were coal burners. Although *effectively* already resolved, the steam *versus* diesel debate in the United States in 1948 centred primarily on the respective fuel costs. Mindful of the still recent World War, some factions criticised the railroads for forsaking coal and thereby depleting precious finite national oil reserves. Legislation was seriously considered in order to ensure the annual construction of a limited number of coal burning steam locomotives. Other more parochial interests had fought campaigns *against* the steam locomotive for decades, on the grounds of smoke pollution in urban areas. Steam locomotives had been prohibited by statute from entering New York City since mid-1926. Because of the sensitive smoke issue in many districts many US steam locomotives in the 1940s were provided with prominent 'over fire' steam jets along the (out)sides of their fireboxes in order to reduce smoke emission. The Norfolk & Western Railway provided overhead suction pipes at some of its depots to 'take away' smoke from stationary locomotives. The Pennsylvania Railroad actively co-operated with the authorities in America's grimiest city with the happy result, largely through dieselisation, that Pittsburgh by 1956 was a very much cleaner place than it had been in 1946.

Diesel fuel was more than four times the cost of coal in terms of the price per 'British Thermal Unit', or BThU, but set against this was the several-fold superiority in the overall thermal efficiency of diesel-electric locomotives. The initially high capital cost of the diesel was now falling, due to quantity production. Moreover, it was realised that, whereas a diesel might cost twice as much as an equivalent steam locomotive, it was also capable of twice as much work in terms of annual mileage, enhanced as it was by less servicing, quicker turnround and so on. Fewer locomotives were also therefore required

During 1949 the cost of oil declined, but not that of coal, which at $5 per US ton now stood at twice its 1941 price. This was due to further industrial action in the coalfields ordered by Lewis, for two weeks during March 1949, and a very sustained stoppage later in the year which extended from 19 September until 6 March 1950. As on previous such occasions, railway passenger services were considerably curtailed by government decree, and even the Norfolk & Western Railway borrowed diesels from the Southern. The Union Pacific had already permanently converted all 45 of its 4-8-4s to oil burning in 1946. Although experiments with a 4-8-8-4 had proved unsatisfactory, many UP 4-6-6-4s also became oil burners.

One consequence of the inevitable loss of revenue was the curtailment by the C&O of its order for 25 2-6-6-2s to only ten, which were delivered in the autumn of 1949. These were the last steam locomotives to be built commercially for an American railroad, and strange to relate the design was identical with one produced for the rival Norfolk & Western Railway in 1911, many of which had been scrapped during the Depression in 1934. In early 1950 the C&O sold to the N&W at a knockdown price the 30 0-8-0s it had only recently obtained from Baldwin, for just as the 2-6-6-2s began to appear, so too did the first diesels (initially shunters) on the Chesapeake & Ohio. Later, in 1951, the C&O's limited passenger services quietly transferred to diesel traction, with practically non-existent publicity. In March 1952 the C&O President declared: **'The greatest single advance in railroad efficiency in recent years has been the introduction of the diesel-electric locomotive, and the Chesapeake & Ohio is making use of this new tool.'**

The 1949 strikes had several profound effects. Industrial demand for coal waned as users resorted to natural gas and other energy sources and railway traffic patterns changed accordingly. Less coal from the Pocahontas region was routed towards Chicago following the strikes; instead it began to move east for export to Europe. The Louisville & Nashville Railroad employed the diesels it had hitherto religiously used as bankers as train engines instead and was greatly impressed by the operating economies which resulted. In early 1949 it had obtained 22 new 2-8-4s from Lima, and had then considered ordering more, but in view of the above and the decline in the coal market, soon abandoned this plan.

The L&N M1s, of which the first had been built by Baldwin in 1942, represented the ultimate in American 2-8-4 design. In *Railway Mechanical Engineer* for October 1949 the L&N had published an analysis of the operating costs of the class since its introduction, which showed considerable savings when compared to older 2-8-2s. Unwittingly these figures also showed the escalating costs of operating even modern steam power in 1940s America and by the end of 1956 even the Louisville & Nashville was fully dieselised.

The final Louisville & Nashville 2-8-4 had been despatched by Lima only two days before the Ohio plant outshopped what proved to be its last steam locomotive. This was 2-8-4 No.779, on Friday 13 May 1949, one of ten engines ordered by the New York, Chicago & St Louis Railroad (known as the 'Nickel Plate Road') following comparative operating cost evaluations of a 4,500 HP diesel and a steam 2-8-4 in early 1948. Fuel costs had been almost identical but the speed/drawbar horsepower curve of the 2-8-4 was better suited to the exacting NKP express freight services on routes which were not cursed by severe gradients. The Nickel Plate also enjoyed highly advanced engine house equipment and procedures. It continued to develop these in 1950 and was anxious to order further 2-8-4s. At this very time, November 1950, Lima Hamilton had amalgamated with Baldwin and although 'Baldwin Lima Hamilton' was still in the steam business, this was to be concentrated in Philadelphia - NKP afterwards looked to the Canadian Locomotive Co. in Kingston, Ontario. Although this plant built 4-6-2s for India as late as 1956 the Nickel Plate enquiries came to nothing, for reasons which are unclear.

General Motors had had a head start over the traditional US locomotive builders as regards the main line diesel market, which it increasingly dominated. By the mid-1950s Baldwin was in severe difficulties, though despite quoting a price twice as high as those of European builders it secured an order for fifty 2-8-2s for India, delivered in 1955. In happier times Baldwins had built thousands of steam locomotives, and more recently not a few diesels for its largest single customer, the Pennsylvania Railroad. The final humiliation came in 1956 when the PRR wished to complete its dieselisation programme and placed the order with General Motors, despite a personal plea from the head of Baldwin to James Symes, who by now was the Pennsylvania President. Baldwin quit the locomotive industry forever a few weeks later.

The American Locomotive Company fared rather better at first, doubtless because it had recognised the rise of the diesel early on, and it remained in the locomotive business until 1969. Alco had become fully committed to diesel-electric production from 16 June 1948 when it despatched its last steam engine, a green 2-8-4, to the Pittsburgh & Lake Erie Railroad.

TABLE 16

OPERATING COSTS PER MILE* OF LOUISVILLE & NASHVILLE RAILROAD CLASS M1 2-8-4 LOCOMOTIVES

PERIOD	COST PER LOCOMOTIVE
1943 (Feb - Dec)	$0.38
1944	0.44
1945	0.60
1946	0.60
1947	0.68
1948	0.97
1949 (Jan - May)	1.10

* based on four locos Nos 1960 - 1963, including fuel, water, lubricants, depot expenses and repairs.

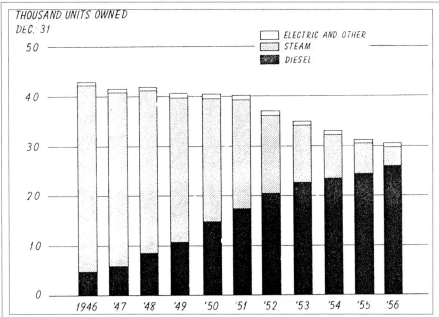

A dramatic representation of US railroad motive power trends between 1946 and 1956. The relatively small contribution by electric traction throughout is apparent.

Originally the so-called 'Little Giant' line had ordered ten of these 2-8-4s; the order at one stage came close to being cancelled altogether and eventually, to counter rising costs, was cut back to seven engines. The final three are said to have been cut up when already in an advanced state of construction... The last of the curtailed batch was, it has always been said, Pittsburgh & Lake Erie No.9401 rather than No.9406, but the class in any event enjoyed but a short life. The engines were displaced by diesels after barely five years, and scrapped in 1957. June 1948 had effectively marked the beginning of the end of steam locomotive manufacturing.

Alco initially retained the necessary facilities in the event of receiving a substantial steam order, which appeared increasingly unlikely. Its Canadian subsidiary, the Montreal Locomotive Works, continued to build steam locomotives through 1948, for export and for the Canadian Pacific Railway. Its 'swan song' in this regard was the delivery of six powerful oil-fired 2-10-4s for passenger service between Calgary and Revelstoke, the last of the CPR 'Selkirks', during February and March 1949. The following month Alco sold its steam spares business to Lima, which since 1946 had assembled locomotive tenders under sub-contract for Alco, whose tank shop had been turned over to diesel production. (The construction of the tenders for Baldwins' last steam locomotives in 1955 was sub-contracted to the Vulcan Ironworks).

In 1947 even Lima had acquired diesel interests, becoming the 'Lima Hamilton Corporation'. Two years later, in mid-1949, it underwent a major reorganisation, with a decision to discontinue steam locomotive development. One outcome of this was the immediate cessation of its

customary advertisements extolling the virtues of the modern steam locomotive (*Don't sell this giant short!* and so on) in the American railway trade journal *Railway Age*. Diesel orders in 1949 were well down on those for 1948, but with improved financial prospects, redoubled in 1950. Nevertheless, during 1949 the diesel got the upper hand in terms of passenger operation, as measured in train miles, and in shunting, as measured in yard hours. In 1951 freight operation, in terms of a majority of gross ton miles, also succumbed to the diesel.

Nevertheless, *Railway Age* in January 1952 remarked that '**if the rate of replacement of steam by diesel were to continue at the rate of installations and retirements for the year 1951, it is obvious that many years would elapse before all of the steam power disappears**. *Whether or not this ever will actually take place is, at the moment, a matter of conjecture.*' [author's italics].

Only four months later, in May 1952, the Rubicon was crossed with the record monthly condemnation of 689 steam locomotives, thereby rendering the diesel-electric locomotive *numerically* superior in the United States. Though certain railroads, particularly the Nickel Plate and Illinois Central, had no immediate plans to dieselise their highly efficient steam operated freight services, even at this time, dieselisation of the US railroads was *effectively* achieved between 1947 and 1952.

It had early been pointed out that the spectacular operating economies achieved by pilot diesel trials on prestige high mileage duties could not be expected to be extended right across the whole range of tasks, some quite mundane and adequately performed by steam locomotives.

However, as dieselisation advanced, far more rapidly than originally envisaged, it was realised how impractical and costly it was to maintain dual servicing and repair facilities. The Gulf, Mobile & Ohio Railroad claimed to be the first Class 1 railroad to achieve 100 per cent dieselisation, in October 1949.

Within four years, many railroads had also (effectively) achieved this; they maintained steam locomotives in reserve only, to meet peak traffic surges, for it was sound economy to utilise expensive new diesels to the maximum extent possible. One statistic made much of was the relative amount of work achieved from one dollar spent on fuel. In 1947 this was put at 2.2 times as much tonnage moved by a diesel as by a coal fired steam locomotive. Tactics of this kind were much employed by General Motors, which preferred to make comparisons between diesels and *oil*-burning steam locomotives. By late 1952, at the height of the Korean War GM played on patriotic susceptibilities with '*America Wins This Scrap! - the average steam locomotive displaced by a General Motors Diesel provides enough scrap metal to meet steel production requirements for one Diesel locomotive plus TEN 40-TON TANKS!*' Two months later, in February 1953, the message was: '*If all steam locomotives in the United States were replaced with General Motors Diesels the scrap metal thus recovered would meet steel production requirements for building the Diesels plus 100 Aircraft Carriers as large as the Midway!*'

Recession hit the railroads in 1954 when General Motors calculated that the remaining seven thousand steam locomotives could be replaced within five years. The cost of re-stocking with diesels was not as formidable as might be thought. These were obtained under hire purchase agreements, and the operational savings greatly exceeded the monthly repayments. The high degree of standardisation of the diesel units themselves facilitated their repossession and re-assignment if they could not be paid for. During 1955-56 a traffic upsurge resulted in many steam locomotives returning to service, not only on their parent lines, but sometimes leased to others. A particularly interesting development concerned the huge 2-10-4s of the Santa Fé, where steam working had been eliminated at the beginning of 1954. Quite unexpectedly, several saw further service on hire to the Pennsylvania Railroad in Ohio, in 1956. The same traffic upturn had also resulted in several of the C&O 2-6-6-6s, which had laid out of use since 1953, being pressed back into service. At least one of the final series received a full overhaul. Even so, steam working on the Chesapeake & Ohio ended forever in September 1956, when the seven year old 2-6-6-2s ceased operation from Peach Creek, in West Virginia.

From then on it was downhill all the way, for by this time even the Norfolk & Western Railway had begun to dieselise. Although the last remaining New York Central 4-6-4s, 4-8-2s, and 4-8-4s continued to operate well into 1956, it would be a 1920-built 2-8-2 which would drop its fire at Cincinnati on 2 May 1957 and end an era on the NYC. This was one of the few such events to be recorded at the time because for two or three years steam locomotives would be held in reserve by several railroads against another possible traffic upturn. A 2-10-0 would make the final steam working on the Pennsylvania on 28 February 1957, and a 2-8-2 on the Baltimore & Ohio three months later in February 1958. It was often the humble pre-Super Power workhorses of the 1920s which performed the last rites, the 'glamour' 4-6-4s and 4-8-4s of the 1930s and 1940s being the first casualties of dieselisation because their weight and general characteristics rendered them unsuited to secondary duties.

By this period obtaining spare parts for steam locomotives following the demise of a host of specialist component manufacturers, with such evocative names as Flannery, Hannah, and American Arch was becoming a major problem for the remaining operators. This certainly afflicted the Nickel Plate, which obtained some from other dieselised railroads, and was reflected in the fact that steam locomotive repair costs doubled between early 1954 and late 1956. Nickel Plate 2-8-4s continued to receive heavy repairs until early 1958 (when they were still being equipped with cab radio telephones) yet they abruptly ceased operation in early July, almost four years ahead of schedule. Probably the final instance of

comparative operation costs for steam *versus* diesel in the United States related to Union Pacific freight operations in March 1957. Steam cost $7.33 per mile as against $2.97 for diesel power. The Union Pacific was also the world's only fleet operator of gas turbine locomotives, for which the figure was $3.74, itself an indication as to why this alternative did not achieve wider adoption, for oil now reigned supreme. The UP 4-8-8-4s 'Big Boys' last operated during the early summer of 1959, when a national steel strike in July finally ended their activities.

At the end of 1959, John L Lewis finally stepped down after almost forty years in supreme office. Several hundred steam locomotives still remained on the books by this date, but there was only a handful active on main lines in North America. During the early months of 1960 scattered steam operation could be found on the Norfolk & Western, Grand Trunk Western, Illinois Central, and Duluth, Missabe & Iron Range railways in the United States, and on both the Canadian Pacific and Canadian National railways. Ironically, for 18 months the last regular steam hauled passenger working in the USA (on the GTW) passed within sight of the General Motors headquarters in Detroit. An era can truly be said to have ended when DM & IR 2-8-8-4 No.222 made a final ore movement on 5 July 1960, just two months after the Norfolk & Western *finale*.

Total dieselisation of the US Class 1 railroads had thus effectively been achieved in only 15 years. At this point their diesel fleet attained an all time peak of 28,200 units, which was credited with saving the American railroad industry from bankruptcy by holding down operating costs and thereby the Operating Ratio (total operating costs/gross receipts) below 100 per cent. As President Smith of the Norfolk & Western Railway, the last

US railroad to capitulate to the diesel, put it in 1957, since 1940 freight rates had increased by only 50 per cent, but wages and materials costs had tripled. This was a problem which was afflicting railways to a greater or a lesser degree the world over, not least in Britain. However, the 1950s and 1960s was a time of cheap oil, priced at only a few cents per US gallon. In 1960 no US railroad could have envisaged that during the still-distant 1970s, Middle East politics would see the cost of fuel increase *seven*-fold, from an average of 10.7 cents per gallon in 1970 to 83 cents by 1980. Some roads, for example the Union Pacific, were actually paying an undreamed of *one dollar* per gallon. Ironically, almost a quarter of a century after its effective demise, a serious reappraisal of the coal-fired steam locomotive was made, even though the fuel efficiency of modern US diesels was also considerably greater than in 1960. The efficiency mountain was even higher to climb, but any thoughts of a return to steam were discarded when the oil price fell to 49 cents in 1986.

THE RISE OF THE DIESEL-ELECTRIC LOCOMOTIVE IN THE UNITED STATES

1924 June
Alco builds 300HP Bo-Bo diesel-electric demonstrator locomotive, first given trial by New York Central Railroad, followed by fourteen others. Finally sold to the Central Railroad of New Jersey to become the first US railroad-*owned* diesel locomotive. Retired 1957 and now preserved.
1925 June Baldwin Locomotive Works completes demonstrator 1000HP Bo-Bo diesel-electric freight locomotive. Later returned to builder and scrapped.
1928 June Alco delivers first successful diesel-electric main line freight locomotive to the New York Central Railroad, 750HP 2Bo-Bo2 No.1550.
1928 July
Alco delivers first US main line diesel-electric passenger locomotive to New York Central Railroad, 900HP 2Bo-Bo2 No.1500.
1934 February
First streamlined diesel-electric passenger train delivered to Union Pacific Railroad.
1936 June
Electro-Motive Division of General Motors commences diesel-electric

TABLE 17

DIESEL POWERED OPERATIONS ON SELECTED MAJOR US RAILROADS IN 1946, 1951, AND 1952 EXPRESSED AS A PERCENTAGE

Railroad	PASSENGER			FREIGHT			SHUNTING		
	1946	1951	1952	1946	1951	1952	1946	1951	1952
Pennsylvania	0.5	41.3	51.0	0.1	44.7	59.6	2.7	67.2	73.0
New York Central	6.7	38.7	50.8	1.4	36.5	66.2	28.0	50.5	61.1
Baltimore & Ohio	41.9	62.7	64.5	6.0	44.5	58.7	18.0	61.2	64.5
Chesapeake & Ohio	2.2	28.1	90.5	0.0	15.8	52.8	5.3	60.9	80.6
Norfolk & Western	0.0	0.0	0.0	0.0	0.0	0.8	0.0	0.0	0.0
Nickel Plate	0.0	93.8	97.1	0.0	2.1	2.4	12.0	62.6	77.9
Reading	10.5	35.4	74.3	21.3	59.3	69.8	39.7	71.3	80.7
Illinois Central	13.1	58.2	73.O	0.0	0.2	2.6	21.4	49.6	67.4
Louisville & Nashville	42.4	78.0	93.7	0.0	45.2	61.0	23.9	68.3	84.5
Santa Fe	19.2	83.6	89.4	34.4	64.1	72.7	48.2	77.7	88.6
Southern Pacific	1.5	27.2	32.1	0.0	58.9	66.1	36.8	54.7	60.2
Union Pacific	11.1	50.4	56.8	0.1	32.0	32.9	44.0	74.5	77.3

NB By implication the balance percentages would have been steam operated, except the Pennsylvania Railroad which operated a significant electrified mileage.

Twilight of a giant. Due to a major recession, steam locomotive operations in the USA were at a low level as early as 1954. A sudden upturn in the economy and a sharp increase in demand for export coal wrought a dramatic, albeit short-lived, change in fortunes during 1955-56. After long periods of storage many steam locomotives were fired up once again. This brought new life in particular to the Chesapeake & Ohio 2-6-6-6s; one of these is No.1644, recorded near Handley, West Virginia in the early summer of 1956 on one of its final duties. Many of these engines were not cut up until 1961. J.G. Collias.

Turbine Locomotive, *Railway Age*, 31 January 1948, 254-256, 262.

Fuel and Future Motive Power Selection, G.J. Weihofen, *Railway Age*, 8 January 1949, 180-182.

The Shift from Steam, D.P. Morgan, *Trains*, April 1949, 26-30.

How Many Diesels, How Soon? D.P. Morgan, *Trains*, April 1952, 52-57.

Abandonment of Steam Power in the USA, A.G. Hoppe, *The Railway Gazette*, (1) 3 May 1957, 507-509, (2) 14 June 1957, 682-684, (3) 28 June 1957, 738-741.

Diesel Traction in North America, D.P. Morgan, Chapter 2 of *The Concise Encyclopaedia of World Railway Locomotives*, Ed. P. Ransome Wallis, Hutchinson, 1959, 512p.

Dieselisation of American Railroads, a Case Study, J.B. McCall, *The Journal of Transport History*, Third Series, Vol 6 No.2, September 1985, 1-17.

locomotive production at purpose-built plant, at La Grange, ILL.

1949 October
First US Class 1 railroad (Gulf, Mobile & Ohio) becomes fully dieselised.

1952 May
Diesel-electric locomotives outnumber steam locomotives on US railroads for the first time.

1960 July
Diesel locomotives completely supersede steam on US Class 1 railroads and attain all time peak total.

References:
What About the Steam Locomotive? R.A. Binkerd, *Railway Age*, 25 May 1935, 800-804.

The Motive Power Situation of American Railroads. The Baldwin Locomotive Works, September 1937, 86p.

The Possibilities of the Modern Steam Locomotive, W.C. Dickerman, *Railway Age*, 7 May 1938,. 796-801.

Operating Characteristics of Steam and Diesel Electric Locomotives, *The Railway Gazette*, 7 August 1942, 128-131.

Coal Burning Gas

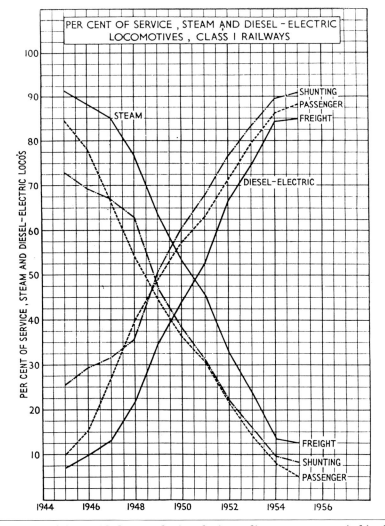

A further indication of the rapid changes during the immediate post-war period in the USA, as regards passenger, freight, and shunting ('switching') operations. Steam operations in all three categories ended in early 1960.

Chapter 6
GREAT BRITAIN - STAGNATION

For about seventy years steam was the only viable form of main line railway traction, but as the 19th century drew to a close, electricity began to pose a possible alternative. Thus in January 1896, Francis Webb, Chief Mechanical Engineer of the London & North Western Railway, predicted **'In 10 to 15 years from now trains moved by electricity will run from all the large centres of the country at a rate of speed which can hardly be realised, probably 100 mph.'**

Fifteen years later *The Railway Gazette* (for 15 September 1911) at a time when it had been computed that British coal stocks could become depleted in less than 200 years commented **'it is quite possible that before the time limit put upon the continuation of the coal supply has expired, the steam-actuated railway engine may have been relegated to the limbo of forgotten inventions and another more potent type of motor will have taken its place.'** Only six months later Dr Rudolph Diesel addressed the Institution of Mechanical Engineers and remarked **'whether a Diesel locomotive can be made a practical commercial success remains to be seen, but there can be no doubt that no effort will be spared to make it work.'**

Meanwhile railway electrification had made some

headway, initially of a suburban nature in such centres as Liverpool, Newcastle and London during 1903-05. In 1913 the South Eastern & Chatham Railway seriously investigated the implications of *total* electrification, and in 1919 the North Eastern Railway commissioned detailed proposals to electrify its main line between York and Newcastle. Equally abortive was a 1927 Great Western Railway proposal to electrify Taunton - Penzance and branches, a scheme which was re-examined in 1938. In 1931 the London & North Eastern Railway looked at electrifying London-Grantham and some branches, and almost simultaneously the London Midland & Scottish considered 'wiring up' Crewe-Carlisle. In each instance the necessary capital expenditure was not forthcoming and the calculated rate of return sometimes marginal. Also in 1931 the Weir Committee had costed electrification of the *entire* British network. The editorial of the May 1934 issue of the *Locomotive Magazine* was entitled 'Steam Still Predominant', and that very month witnessed the advent of the most advanced British steam locomotive to date, Nigel Gresley's magnificent three-cylinder 2-8-2 No 2001 COCK O' THE NORTH, to work the Edinburgh - Aberdeen passenger services. The prototype of Britain's only eight-coupled express passenger locomotive class, it incorporated Lentz rotary cam poppet valve gear and double Kylchap

exhaust. Six months later it was despatched to France for evaluation at the new Vitry Locomotive Testing Station near Paris. Despite its sophisticated French-style features, not least the ACFI feedwater heater, its coal consumption proved to be prodigious.

Similar features were shown in the first draft for the proposed Class A4 4-6-2 but were subsequently discarded in favour of piston valves, a single plain exhaust and a Bugatti-style front end which made its *début* in September 1935. Four later engines turned out in early 1938 were equipped with double-Kylchap exhaust, one of which, No 4468 *MALLARD*, attained 125 mph downhill between Grantham and Peterborough on 3 July 1938, which the LNER claimed as a world speed record for steam traction on rail (126 mph was later specified on commemorative plaques affixed to the engine in 1948).

For its part the LMS in 1937 produced the streamlined 'Coronation' four-cylinder 4-6-2s which were likewise capable of working Anglo-Scottish expresses through over the 400 miles with only one crew change. One of a small batch of non-streamlined engines, No 6234 DUCHESS OF ABERCORN, was subjected to full power trials in early 1939. When experimentally equipped with double exhaust it achieved an instantaneous 2,511 equivalent

The last major advance in British steam locomotive design, the short-lived Gresley LNER Class P2 3-cylinder 2-8-2 express passenger engine No.2001 COCK O' THE NORTH, brand new at Doncaster in 1934. The Lentz RC poppet valve gear was replaced by piston valves and Walschaerts gear in 1938, and the engine rebuilt as a 4-6-2 in 1944. Interestingly, No.2001 was a close contemporary of the outstanding Chapelon PO 4-8-0s in France, and was tested at the new Vitry locomotive testing station when new. In firegrate area (50 ft²), adhesive weight (80½ tons), and nominal tractive effort (43,500lb), it would remain unsurpassed in British practice. NRM (DON 34/151).

The High Noon of the British steam era epitomised by LMS streamlined 4-6-2 No.6223 PRINCESS ALICE with matching silver striped blue rolling stock approaching Shap Summit with a London-Glasgow express in 1938. M.W. Earley Collection, NRM (MWE 3702).

drawbar horsepower on Shap Bank, a record which remained unchallenged for the remainder of the steam era in Britain.

By this time the LMS was already drafting a proposed streamlined four-cylinder 4-6-4 with 24 ton axleload, 300lb pressure boiler and 70ft² of mechanically fired grate. The LNER had considered a super A4, but like a proposed 4-8-2, this would have been hand fired, thereby imposing a severe limitation on sustained maximum power output.

The late 1930s undoubtedly represented the high noon of the steam locomotive, which had attained a high degree of mechanical and technical perfection, especially metallurgically speaking. In Britain, attendant labour and good quality coal was still available at low cost, despite a sharp but short-lived price rise in 1938.

After August 1939 things would never be quite the same again. Only three years later in a December 1942 appraisal entitled *LMS Post War Steam Traction Policy and Development* E.S. Cox recorded:

"In the various plans for post-war development which are being worked out it is desirable that the part to be played by steam traction should not be overlooked .... There are at present some 7,500 steam locomotives on the LMS and whatever decisions are taken for large scale electrification they will not all disappear overnight, but will continue to burn coal, and require repairs and in some cases even renewal for a number of years to come. Indeed it is difficult to see complete elimination of the steam locomotive in this country in the next 20 years even under the most drastic decisions."

Cox recommended the proposed 1938 4-6-4 be built, together with a smaller-wheeled 4-8-4 fast freight development of it. Existing standard designs were to be improved to increase mileage between repairs and to facilitate servicing. Similar recommendations, such as the provision of roller bearings and poppet valve gear on Class 5 4-6-0s followed Cox's visit to North America in late 1945 as a member of a joint LMS/LNER delegation to investigate at first hand current developments there, his personal remit being Steam Traction Policy. The already rapid transition to diesel traction was very evident, and in his extensive January 1946 report Cox observed:

"It is an undoubted fact that with many American railways the immediate future lies entirely with the diesel, and it is very doubtful if some of them will ever purchase another new steam locomotive. This is particularly true of those Western and Southern roads remote from coal supplies and accessible to oil......

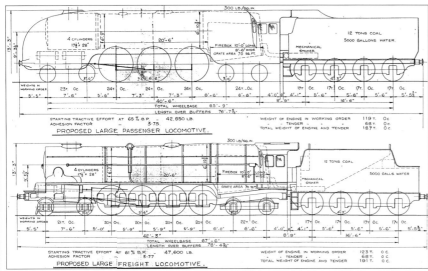

LMS 'Super Power' might-have-been, streamlined stoker-fired 4-cylinder 4-6-4 express passenger engine and 4-8-4 fast freight equivalent, proposed in 1942 for post-World War Two construction. The 4-6-4, with 24 ton axleload and 300lb boiler pressure, had originally been outlined as a major advance on the preceding streamlined 4-6-2s in 1938, when its firebox would have been round-topped in order to be accommodated within the loading gauge. As shown 'naked' on the 4-8-4 it has become Belpaire, which would have presented clearance problems. It is regrettable that neither design was built as they would have represented a major advance in tractive capacity. The 4-6-4 would assuredly have been built without streamlining, as this was soon removed from the 4-6-2s after the end of World War Two.

The Way Ahead? Immediately after the Second World War there was considerable interest in the possibilities of gas turbine propulsion on railways. Compared to contemporary diesel engines, the gas turbine offered greater simplicity and a far higher power to weight ratio. During 1946 the Great Western Railway ordered two prototype locomotives, a 119 ton A1A+A1A rated at 2,500HP from Brown Boveri in Switzerland and a 130 ton 3,500HP Co-Co from Metropolitan Vickers of Manchester. The Swiss engine, No.18000, was delivered first, at the beginning of 1950 and remained in intermittent service on BR until 1959 and is still in existence. However, the Metrovick, No.18100 saw less than two years service, during 1952-53. Here No.18000, popularly dubbed 'Kerosene Castle', is near Didcot on an up express, on 22 September 1951. J.F. Russell Smith Collection, NRM (JFRS 459).

The relation between oil and coal costs is much the same (in the USA and UK), but fuel costs are on a lower level generally in the USA. ...... There are, however, certain conditions profoundly different from those obtaining in this country."

In Britain in early 1946 the diesel-electric was by no means assumed to be the way ahead. By virtue of its rapid development during the recently ended war, high hopes were held as regards the potential of the gas turbine for a variety of peacetime uses. At the Annual General Meeting of the Great Western Railway held on 6 March

1946, the Chairman, Lord Portal, announced that the Company 'had **under consideration plans for the construction of a gas-turbine locomotive.'** The *rationale* behind this could later be found in an internal appreciation of GWR motive power policy dated 7 April 1947:

The rather brutal yet strangely imposing experimental Fell 2,000HP diesel-mechanical 2D2 No.10100 heads a down London-Manchester express near Elstree on 22nd March 1952. Later altered to 2BB2 by removal of the centre section of the coupling rods, it proved to be a dead end in British locomotive development and was condemned in 1958. E.D. Bruton Collection, NRM (EDB 5748).

A stirring view of the penultimate LMS 4-6-2, No.(4)6256 SIR WILLIAM A STANIER FRS hauling the down 'Mid-Day Scot' at Scout Green in 1949. This engine was one of a pair built at Crewe in 1947 incorporating all 'mod cons', such as roller bearings and hopper ashpans for NYC-style comparison with the pioneer diesel-electrics, Nos 10000 and 10001, then also under construction. The intention that these 4-6-2s should achieve 100,000 miles per annum and between heavy repairs was never realised. P. Ransome Wallis Collection, NRM (PRW 8497).

"In the gas turbine, while the overall thermal efficiency does not, as yet, attain that achievable by the diesel engine, its prime cost, even for initial experimental projects, appears to be likely to become stabilised at lower price levels than the diesel, while no elaborate maintenance organisation, such as is required by the diesel, is necessary ... These considerations have led the Company to place orders for two gas-turbine-electric locomotives, one with the Brown-Boveri firm of Switzerland and the other with Metropolitan-Vickers."

These locomotives eventually entered service after the demise of the GWR, in February 1950 and December 1951 respectively. However, as a prime mover the gas turbine proved unsuited to the ever fluctuating power demands of railway service. Overall thermal efficiency proved to be no higher than that of a steam locomotive, and fuel costs were appreciably higher.

Only six days after the GWR's original announcement, senior LMS officers, including E S Cox, made a 'secret' visit to Power Jets in Leicester, of which Sir William Stanier was a director, in order to discuss a possible gas turbine locomotive for the LMS. Compared with the diesel-electric locomotive such was considered to have the following advantages:-

The shape of things to come. The two LMS diesel-electrics, Nos.10000 and 10001, power a down Scottish express at Grayrigg in 1949. In 1951 it was estimated that at current prices, despite similar running costs, (engine crew wages plus fuel) of £49, it cost only £84 to work a London-Glasgow express with steam and yet no less than £205 with twin unit diesels. The much higher repair and depreciation costs of the latter held against them. Operated singly they were inadequate, but in tandem they worked well below capacity. It was estimated that a single 2,000HP unit was required. P. Ransome Wallis Collection, NRM (PRW 10697).

The third Bulleid 1-Co-Co-1 diesel-electric was belatedly completed uprated to 2,000HP in 1954, thereby reducing the relative economic advantage of steam traction at a time when coal prices were also rising. The historical significance of BR No.10203, which when new sometimes worked the 'Royal Scot' single handed, scarcely appears to have been appreciated, especially since it was originally authorised before LMS Nos.10000/10001. All three Bulleid diesels, and the LMS 'Twins', were withdrawn from service at the end of 1963, well before the end of BR steam.

1. **Reduced capital and maintenance costs**
2. **Lighter weight for a given power**
3. **Lower fuel costs**

The LMS already had advanced plans for a 1,600HP main line diesel-electric locomotive, and details were forwarded to Power Jets in the hope that an alternative power plant could be accommodated within the same body shell. Unfortunately, the Power Jets enterprise abruptly folded (for political reasons) shortly thereafter. Despite this the LMS initially persevered with discussions until January 1947 with representatives from Brown-Boveri and British Thomson Houston at Rugby, with a view to producing a 2,000HP gas turbine locomotive.

Meanwhile, the LMS also pressed ahead with its various diesel-electric locomotive schemes, of which it liked to think of itself as the British pioneer, having given extensive trial to a variety of 0-6-0 diesel shunters from 1934. In September 1946 it enumerated the perceived advantages of diesel over steam traction as:-

1. **Thermal efficiency was three times higher than that of the normal steam locomotive.**
2. **It provided a new conception of a traction prime mover made up of many light renewable parts which can be serviced or replaced during the turn round times between rostered hours of duty, thus offering very high traffic availability to the vehicle as a whole.**
3. **The advantage of consuming no fuel while standing, and of**

requiring no expensive facilities for provision of coal and water or the removal of ash.

The LMS had initiated studies into a main line diesel-electric locomotive as early as 1942 and had since entered into collaboration with the English Electric Company, which would supply, free of charge, the necessary power plant for two 1,600HP units to be built at Derby. The latter were only formally authorised and made public in March 1947. Despite this, with commendable speed the first, numbered 10000, was completed in December 1947, and so entered service proudly bearing the insignia LMS. No 10001 followed six months later. Individually they were each regarded as equivalent to a Class 4 2-6-4T, but when worked in tandem, the equal of a steam 4-6-2. The last two Stanier Pacifics, Nos. 6256 and 6257, were extensively re-designed with roller-bearings throughout, and hopper ashpan etc., with the intention of achieving 100,000 miles *per annum*, and between heavy repairs for direct operational comparisons with the new diesels. There is no evidence that any such survey was ever actually carried out, but from the copious data available on the surviving engine history cards, the author has attempted to make good this deficiency.

It may well be that the March 1947 announcement by the LMS goaded the rival LNER into initiating a dieselisation programme for the East Coast Main Line, the earliest surviving document concerning which is dated 24 April 1947. This was prefaced as follows:-

"The LNER traffic difficulties of the present day are largely due to the non-availability of steam locomotive power, which in turn is substantially affected by the following factors:-
a)   Inability to obtain delivery of new locomotives either from contractors or railway shops as rapidly as had been hoped.
b)   Inferior quality of coal.
c)   Shortage of coal

Other considerations affect the availability of locomotive power, but the three mentioned above are sufficiently important to warrant examination of the possibility of developing as rapidly as possible traction by other means than coal-burning steam locomotives and thus opening out an additional source of new building and easing the demand for good quality coal of which supplies

TABLE 18	COMPARISON OF LMS 4-6-2S NOS. 6256/7 AND CO-CO DIESEL-ELECTRICS NOS. 10000/1, 1949 - 1957*	
	STEAM 4-6-2 LMS NOS 6256/7	CO-CO DE LMS NOS 10000/1
COST PER UNIT	£21,411	£78,266+
TOTAL MILEAGE	1,296,755	1,223,909
AVERAGE ANNUAL MILEAGE	72,042	67,995
HIGHEST ANNUAL MILEAGE ATTAINED	88,441	130,709
	(6257 IN 1949)	(10001 IN 1957)
TOTAL WEEKDAYS OUT OF USE	2095	2858
AVERAGE WEEKDAYS OUT OF USE PER ANNUM	116	159
AVAILABILITY	63%	49%
AVERAGE MILEAGE PER WEEKDAY IN USE	372	449
TOTAL REPAIR COSTS	£39,823	£111,347
AVERAGE REPAIR COST PER MILE	3.07p	9.10p

*   Taken from Engine History Cards preserved in the National Railway Museum Library & Archive, York

+   The power units were purchased from the English Electric Co. in early 1951 for £81,400 and are included in the above cost.

Under the overall umbrella of dieselisation it is easy to overlook the humble diesel multiple unit, whose initial production actually pre-dated the Modernisation Plan. They not only considerably reduced operating costs on unremunerative routes, but often actually generated considerable extra revenue in rural areas, before the rapid increase in private car ownership. DMUs latterly monopolised several picturesque routes such as Whitby-Scarborough, and Workington-Penrith (shown here) during their final decade of operation prior to closure in the mid-1960s. DMUs were responsible for the premature demise of several hundreds of passenger tank engines. NRM (250/95)

presumably will continue to be short for a considerable period."

In 1945, under Edward Thompson, then CME, the LNER had initiated a five year plan, in which one thousand new steam locomotives were to be built. Many of these would come from private contractors, which at that time were heavily burdened by large orders from overseas. (A later plan to order 20 Peppercorn Class A2 4-6-2s from Beyer, Peacock & Co. had to be abandoned).

It is interesting that the 1947 diesel plan was not initiated by the CME, A.H. Peppercorn, but by C.P. Hopkins, Assistant General Manager, and M.R. Bonavia, Assistant to the Chief General Manager. This was subsequently worked up in some detail, wherein it was proposed to order 25 1,600HP units, to work in pairs. Total operating costs were

estimated as follows for the London - Edinburgh passenger services:-

The diesel repair costs were purely notional and almost certainly too low. It will be seen that the savings would not have been dramatic, but other perceived advantages were:-

a) **Increased availability**
b) **Higher acceleration and better performance on adverse gradients**
c) **Cleanliness**
d) **Publicity and prestige value**

Bids were sought for the supply of the locomotives and fourteen quotations were received, only one from a traditional steam locomotive builder. Prices ranged from £1,035,675 to £1,862,500, and first delivery from 18 months to 36 months. In the event, as a consequence of nationalisation, only a few weeks later the whole project was abandoned and steam remained

supreme on the East Coast Main Line until 1961 rather than 1951.

Nationalisation, paradoxically, undoubtedly *delayed* the demise of steam traction in several areas. Thus, the prestigious 'Golden Arrow' between London Victoria and Dover remained steam-hauled until mid-1961, whereas on 31 October 1946 the Southern Railway had announced plans to eliminate steam traction in the immediate London area and South East by 1955. Third rail electrification was to be extended, involving the construction of 150 Co-Co electric locomotives for freight working, and 200 diesel-electric locomotives were to be built for non-electrified lines. It was proposed correspondingly to reduce the steam locomotive fleet from 1800 to 800. Existing electrification, it was computed, was already saving 400,000 tons of coal per annum, and it was anticipated that under the new proposals a further 300,000 tons would be saved. (Locomotive coal had always cost the SR more dearly than its northern counterparts).

Nevertheless, steam on the Southern had not entirely had its day, for large numbers of three-cylinder 4-6-2s were still being authorised and built, and a revolutionary double-ended tank engine 'The Leader' was ordered in September 1946. In August 1947 the SR announced it had ordered three 1,600HP diesel electric locomotives capable of 100 mph principally for use on the West of England services. These eventually

TABLE 19

LNER ESTIMATES FOR ANNUAL RUNNING COSTS OF STEAM V. DIESEL OPERATION OF THE EAST COAST MAIN LINE, 1947

	STEAM 4-6-2 £	1600HP CO-CO DE x2 £
DEPRECIATION	7,500	33,090
REPAIRS	50,000	35,000
RUNNING REPAIRS	30,000	20,000
CREW COSTS	58,850	58,850
FUEL	127,600	98,560
HANDLING	5,000	2,000
TOTAL	278,950	247,500
COST PER TRAIN MILE	12.7p	11.25p

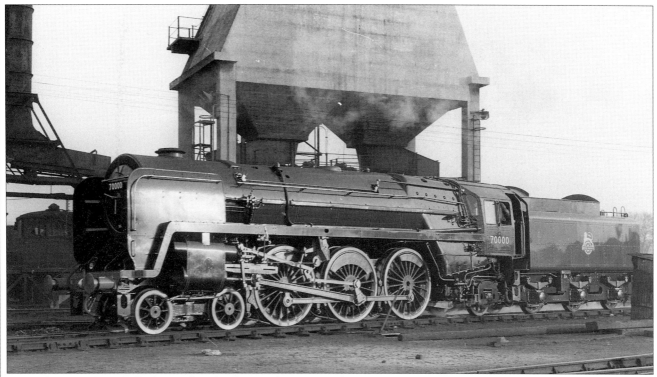

Meanwhile, the British Railways Standard steam locomotive fleet was becoming established. Its doyen was Class 7 4-6-2 No.70000, seen here brand new at Neasden in late January 1951 just prior to being named BRITANNIA. Altogether only 55 of these engines were built specifically for four of the six BR regions between 1951 and 1954, although a further 36 were under active discussion for the 1956 Programme, when they were abruptly abandoned following the major change in British Railways motive power policy. C.C.B. Herbert Collection, NRM.

emerged, the first two uprated to 1,750HP, and the third to 2,000HP, on British Railways between 1950 and 1954.

It is fascinating to note that, during 1946-47, both the LMS and Southern were keenly monitoring progress in the USA with coal-fired gas turbine locomotives, whilst both were also seriously interested in developing diesel *mechanical* locomotives on the complicated Fell system. (In a collaborative venture, Derby Works eventually completed a 2,000HP 2D2 DM in 1951). Thus each of the 'Big Four' at their eleventh hour when

formulating future traction policy were particularly concerned as to fuel cost and availability rather than performance. Fuel cost had always been a major component in total operating costs, but the mid-1940s was a far cry from 1910 when John F McIntosh of the Caledonian Railway remarked 'efficiency and reliability are more to a locomotive superintendent than economy in fuel.'

Prior to 1939, good quality coal supplies at low cost could be assured other than at times of industrial strife in the coalfields, as in 1893, 1912, 1921 and 1926. During World War Two,

however, the actual cost of coal per ton had increased by 157 per cent. Worse, a simultaneous decline in quality meant that more fuel was required, so the effective cost per mile had increased by *181 per cent*. During the first six months of 1946 the cost of coal had risen by a further 25 per cent, prompting the GWR to equip 44 locomotives for oil burning in order to save an estimated 50,000 tons of coal. During the economically depressed 1930s there had been a glut of coal, but now supply could not meet demand in Europe as a whole. In the late summer of 1946, i.e. even before the exceptionally severe winter of 1947 began, the Ministry of Transport requested the four main line railway companies to equip a total of 1,217 specified locomotives for oil burning as quickly as possible. Despite the Arctic conditions which rapidly ensued, exacerbating the already severe situation, only a handful of locomotives were actually converted by each company and the overall impact was minimal. The original intention had been to save two million tons of coal per annum. This quantity, ironically, was precisely equivalent to the increase from the immediate post-war period over immediate pre-war times. The amounts were fourteen million as against twelve million tons, and the difference was due to the intervening decline in coal quality, together with a greater preponderance of slow freight train working.

Within a few days of the Nationalisation of Britain's railways

Although a novelty in Great Britain in 1951, two-cylinder 4-6-2s had been active for over forty years in the United States, where the most outstanding example of the genre was the Pennsylvania Railroad Class K4s, originally introduced in 1914. BRITANNIA amounted to little more than a scaled-down anglicised version, with plate in place of bar frames. PRR No.3740 was pictured in 1941 six years before its demise in the first flush of dieselisation on the Standard Railroad of the World, shortly before BRITANNIA was even conceived. P. Ransome Wallis Collection, NRM (PRW 7393).

The British Railways Class 9F 2-10-0 had originally been envisaged around 1950 as a 2-8-2 version of the Class 7 4-6-2, but instead was revised (in mid-1951) as a 2-10-0. The first significant advance in British steam freight locomotive design for fifty years, 251 were built between 1954 and 1960, mostly at Crewe Works where No.92080 was recorded brand new in primer paint, in 1956. P. Ransome Wallis Collection, NRM (PRW 11413).

on 1 January 1948, the question of how locomotives and rolling stock should from henceforth be painted was debated. It was not until December 1948, however, that Sir Cyril Hurcomb, Chairman of the British Transport Commission, appointed a special non-technical committee to recommend future motive power policy. Nationalisation undoubtedly deferred the replacement of steam traction on Britain's railways, by almost a decade. It would otherwise have commenced earlier, but would assuredly have proceeded at a more measured pace, funds permitting. It took the four-man Committee three years to submit its 181 page report, in October 1951. By this time a new generation of standard British Railways steam locomotives had not only been formulated (in June 1948) but also designed for the most part and pilot batches authorised (in November 1949). The first example, 4-6-2 No 70000 BRITANNIA, was completed at Crewe Works on 31 December 1950.

The previous month, in his Presidential Address to the Institution of Locomotive Engineers, Robert Riddles clearly felt under pressure to justify his continued allegiance to steam. He declared:-

"At present there is undoubtedly a field for steam, for the internal combustion engine and for electric traction. All are in active use, and the three are likely to exist side by side for a very considerable number of years ahead. The case for electrification and the internal combustion locomotive is often and very clearly stated. There is also a case for steam, and it is that at present in a considerable range of circumstances, a pound will buy more tractive effort than in the case of any other forms of traction.

The accompanying table gives a comparison based on present-day prices. The cost for the diesel electric and the gas turbine electric locomotive would undoubtedly be less if larger numbers were ordered.

The money can with steam, moreover, be spent without exceptional investment at any one time. In addition, though thermal efficiency of steam is admittedly low, actual fuel costs per unit of power at the drawbar do not rank very high in the total relative costs, and substantial developments are still being introduced on the mechanical side to reduce maintenance costs and increase availability.

When these facts can no longer be substantiated, then the day of steam is definitely over, and none will deny it ...... I have felt these remarks to be relevant because part of what I have described is the development of a standard range of steam locomotives."

With three leading former LMS locomotive men in charge, R.A. Riddles, R.C. Bond and E.S. Cox, it was not altogether surprising that the new breed represented an extension of LMS practice. The smaller designs amounted to mere refinements in the interests of routine maintenance and increased availability, incorporating roller bearings and self cleaning smokeboxes, in line with Cox's December 1942 recommendations for

TABLE 20

RELATIVE COSTS OF ALTERNATIVE FORMS OF MOTIVE POWER ON BRITISH RAILWAYS, 1951

LOCOMOTIVE TYPE	COST £	STARTING T.E. lb /lb T.E.	COST £/lbT.E.	1 HOUR D/B HP	COST/ DBHP £
BR Std Cl 5 4-6-0 Steam	16,000	26,120	0.61	1200	13.33
1600HP Co-Co Diesel Electric	78,200	41,400	1.89	1200	65.16
2500HP A1A-A1A Gas Turbine	138,700	33,000	4.20	2000	69.35
1500V/DC Co-Co Electric	37,400	45,000	0.83	2120	17.64

post-war steam locomotive development on the LMS. However, there was no resurrection of the proposed stoker-fired express passenger 4-6-4 or its 4-8-4 fast freight counterpart. The keystone of the arch was an entirely new, modest yet well-proportioned two-cylinder mixed traffic 4-6-2, equivalent to an LNER Class V2 2-6-2 or LMS rebuilt 'Royal Scot' 4-6-0.

No fewer than 11 of the 12 Standard classes - 2-6-0, 4-6-0 and 4-6-2 tender, 2-6-2 and 2-6-4 tank, had six coupled wheels, accounting for 748 of the 999 engines built. Only the Class 9F heavy freight 2-10-0 broke new ground, although even this was not particularly remarkable by European standards, except for its quite unexpected high speed (90 mph) potential.

When the so-called Hurcomb Report became available in October 1951 its principal recommendations were:
1.   A pilot main line electrification scheme be planned and costed from north of London King's Cross to at least as far as Grantham, plus selected branches, to be put into effect as quickly as possible.
2.   That, should trials with a 2,000HP single unit diesel-electric locomotive prove satisfactory, then these should be adopted on a fairly large scale for main line passenger workings.
3.   That diesel railcars be extensively employed, on cross country, certain main line and branch line services.
The Committee had little positive to recommend concerning steam traction other than acknowledging that it was likely to be around for some time to come simply on account of its sheer weight of numbers. It concluded that 'there is no evidence that any advance in design can be looked for which will overcome the present inherent limitations of the steam locomotive as an instrument of railway operation.' Writing over a decade later, E.S. Cox remarked that 'there must be few today who would not be prepared to accept this report as a most reasonable and objective presentation.' He seemingly failed to recall the furore it had created *at the time* within the ex-LMS steam triumvirate. On 16 January 1952 R.C. Bond wrote a lengthy memorandum to R.A. Riddles which included the following observations:-
"The Committee seem to have gone out of their way to discredit steam traction and to emphasise the disadvantages, which everyone recognises and admits, without giving a fair statement of the outstanding advantages which have enabled steam traction to retain to itself the major part of

traffic operation in most countries of the world.... The level of performance today is still far below what was regarded as normal in pre-war days, a state of affairs which is not the fault of steam traction.... Let us get back to the standard of performance we enjoyed before the War with the locomotives and equipment that we have ready to our hands."

Three days later E.S. Cox concurred with Bond's 'excellent memorandum' and added:-
"The report is not an objective document and under a guise of fair play it is written from the point of view that at all costs, steam traction must be denied a place in the future."

On 23 January 1952 R.A. Riddles minuted his official response to the Railway Executive in which he made his own personal views clear:-
"Excluding particular cases where there are overwhelming economic advantages, it seems clear that our motive power policy must be founded on coal, which we have, rather than on oil, which we have to import. No better words can be found to express this view than those of Sir Eustace Missenden (Chairman RE) in his paper:-
    'Oil must be imported, no easy task in time of war, and perhaps, paid for in foreign currency. Any large scale changeover to diesel traction would involve an increase in oil consumption sufficiently large to have a direct effect on the whole oil position in this country. Before we could rely on oil as our main source of fuel, we should have to be assured, beyond all doubt, that ample supplies would always be available over a long period, in peace or war, economic prosperity or crisis, and at a cost which would remain favourable in comparison with coal or electric power. The recent experience with the conversion of steam locomotives to oil burning has not inspired our confidence.'
    If this view can be accepted, then the clear alternatives for British Railways are steam traction and electrification. This is broadly the position on the Continent of Europe as distinct from the U.S.A. Electrification will gradually replace steam as justification can be worked out route by route, and as capital can be found. This assumes the co-existence of the two forms of motive power for many years ahead, a point which the report admits. If an orderly and well justified long term programme of electrification is outlined, then

modifications to the relative annual provision for steam and electric rolling stock will follow naturally, but this requires to be done in a manner which will produce the lowest operating costs in steam working during the years in which it still remains."

A further report on Motive Power Policy was submitted to the British Transport Commission in April 1952 which made the following observations as regards steam traction:-
1.   The Commission have been officially warned by the National Coal Board that, whatever the total output of coal over the next few decades, the amount of large coal suitable for locomotives is almost certain to decrease.
2.   The steam locomotive after more than a century of development is reaching the end of a long phase of evolution and it is unlikely than any revolutionary improvements will be made in the future .... The simple reciprocating steam locomotive of today is fundamentally the same as it was a century ago, although a continuous series of important improvements in design has culminated in the latest British Railways standard engines.... We entirely support the policy which has been pursued in developing these standard types, and are of the opinion that within its inherent limitations, this form of motive power will continue to provide efficient service for some time to come."

On 30 May 1952 R.C. Bond made the following comments on the Report to R.A. Riddles:-
"The Report concedes that there is a sufficient variety of traffic to justify the use, in their proper spheres of all the various types of motive power considered. It would be quite wrong, in my opinion, therefore, not to continue to build an appropriate, though decreasing, number of new steam locomotives so as to ensure that, over the years during which steam will still be a major factor in the motive power picture of this Country, full advantage is taken of the reduced maintenance and operating costs made possible by modern design."

During 1952 a practical assessment was made of the overall drawbar thermal efficiency and cost of four forms of motive power on 350-360 ton passenger trains
    Despite the three-fold disparity in thermal efficiency, on this basis steam held its own with diesel, but the coal problem was still acute and would shortly take a different turn. British

TABLE 21
**COMPARISON OF FUEL COSTS AND DRAWBAR THERMAL EFFICIENCY
OF FOUR ALTERNATIVE FORMS OF MOTIVE POWER, 1952**

TYPE	TRAIN SERVICE WEIGHT TONS	DB THERMAL EFFICIENCY %	FUEL COST MILE p	FUEL COST DBHP hr p
Steam 'Castle' 4-6-0	360 Paddington - Cardiff	5.5	5.25	0.50
Diesel-Electric (1750 HP) 1Co-Co1	350 Waterloo - Exeter	18.8	5.33	0.44
Gas Turbine A1A + A1A (No.18000)	360 Paddington - Plymouth	6.6	11.5	0.95
Electric Co-Co (No.20003)	436 Victoria-Newhaven	11.5	9.6	0.60

annual coal production had attained a peak approaching 300 million tons in 1913, but post-1945 it stood at 210-220 million tons. This was in despite of rapid advances in machine cutting, which had doubled from 30 to 60 per cent of total production during the 1930s alone, and by 1950 was approaching 80 per cent. Ironically this ran against railway interests in that hand cut 'large' coal was required for locomotive purposes. The national shortfall in production was made good by imports, once unimaginable, from the USA and Europe which mainly consisted of 'large' coal. In March 1951 it was reported that locomotives in South Yorkshire, at such depots as Mexborough and Doncaster, which were close to a major coalfield, were being fired with American coal! At the beginning of that year, the government had requested that the railways reduce

their weekly coal consumption by 10,000 tons and some passenger services were cancelled. The domestic demand for 'large coal', i.e. for household fires, was actually three times greater than that of the railway. The combined annual requirement of about 50 million tons simply could no longer be met. Furthermore future projections to 1960-65 suggested that by then the *overall* shortfall in coal production could amount to no less than 50 million tons. Another factor then entered the equation.

In December 1952 the city of London was enveloped for 60 hours in impenetrable smog with daytime visibility in places down to less than ten yards, accompanied by exceptionally high concentrations of smoke and sulphur dioxide, which resulted in the deaths of many elderly people. In July 1953 the government

set up a committee under Sir Hugh Beaver to investigate the question of air pollution in Britain. Its findings, published the following year, found that railways were responsible for one seventh of all smoke discharged to the atmosphere. The Committee's decided that the only complete answer was the replacement of coal-fired locomotives by alternative smokeless forms of traction. In particular, it was felt, shunting operations by steam locomotives in industrial areas should be eliminated, by 1960. The Clean Air Bill was published in July 1955 and received the Royal Assent one year later. In practice this had greater impact on the use of industrial steam locomotives (there was a clause which referred to the owners of 'railway locomotive engines') rather than British Railways, which in the mid-1950s administered the second largest steam locomotive fleet on earth, after Soviet Russia. Some of the biggest offenders were locomotive depots, but the Act made allowance for smoke generated during steam raising on shed.

Also in late 1952 Parliament debated the Ridley Report, the *National Policy for the Use of Fuel & Power Resources*. When giving evidence to the Committee, the Federation of British Industries had declared that 'the steam locomotive was in a fuel efficiency sense, one of the least efficient machines to survive in the modern age' and pointed out that British Railways annually consumed approximately 14 million tons of high quality large coal which was in great demand for export and other uses.

This was not strictly true, for the continuing decline in the quality of available fuel was becoming a matter of considerable concern to BR. Wide fireboxes had been specified on the Standard Class 7 4-6-2 in 1948 because 'for locomotives which have to perform main line duties the desired combustion rates can only be obtained by use of the wide firebox' which also made it possible to burn lower grades of coal. Provision was made for the possible later installation of a mechanical stoker, but experience with the SR Merchant Navy class 4-6-2 so equipped experimentally in 1949 showed it to be very wasteful and no answer to poor quality fuel. Nearly twice as much coal had to be fired than by hand to perform the same work, making operation disproportionately costly. The use of cheaper coal in various trials over the years had yielded the same result, greater overall cost, not least due to the greater number of non-productive coal trains

The Pennsylvania Railroad Class I1s 2-10-0 was evolved in 1916 from the L1s 2-8-2, which was the freight equivalent of the K4s 4-6-2 designed in tandem, thereby remarkably anticipating developments on British Railways nearly forty years later. PRR No.4315 was one of a huge order for 475 2-10-0s executed by the Baldwin Locomotive Works for the Pennsylvania Railroad during 1922-23. P. Ransome Wallis Collection, NRM (PRW 7547).

which had to be run to deliver fuel to the depots.

In early 1954 the British Transport Commission entered into collaboration with the British Coal Utilization Research Association at Leatherhead in order to try and solve some of the problems associated with the use of inferior fuel, including clinker formation. For this purpose an original 'Royal Scot' boiler was made available, but despite intensive tests in late 1956 there was no satisfactory outcome. For its part the Locomotive Testing Station at Rugby, opened in October 1948, made little impact on the almost intractable problem of low steam locomotive overall thermal efficiency. During 1955-59 it carried out exhaustive evaluations of the Crosti boiler, Giesl ejector, and

Train (British Transport Commission Member responsible for Engineering Matters):-

"It now seems more likely than at any time in the past, that the necessary funds will be forthcoming to enable a substantial programme of main line electrification to be planned. At the same time, a large number of passenger services at present worked by steam locomotives are proposed, during the next few years, to be covered by multiple unit diesel trains ... while the progressive change from steam traction to multiple unit diesel trains for selected passenger services will take place in self-contained areas over a comparatively short time,

the other hand, taking a shorter period of 20 years, 925 locomotives would require scrapping each year - or dealing with the over-age locomotives first, 1,300 per annum in the first five years and 800 per annum for the next fifteen years. Thus according to these two extremes there will remain the following number of steam locomotives at the years set out below:-

	20 years life	40 years life
1960	12,000	17,500
1965	8,000	14,500
1975	Nil	10,000
1985	6,000	
1995	Nil	

If the eventuality lies between these two limits, it is possible that 5,000 steam locomotives will still remain in 1975. If the stock was not refreshed, the last steam locomotive would go in 1985.

It would appear, therefore, that on any probable rate of steam locomotive breaking up there will still remain at any given time during the next 20 years, sufficient steam locomotives to serve electrification transition periods, and lines not yet electrified, and that no considerable building of diesel locomotives for these particular purposes will require undertaking until the last 10 years before steam elimination.

Whatever the number of steam units at any one time during the period of transition, they will cost money to run and maintain. The ideal would be that as the last 5,000 locomotives was reached, the stock would consist only of types best suited to the traffic to be worked, and of the highest efficiency and lowest repair cost which the current state of the art could achieve. This would require:-

(1) Continued improvement in efficiency and economy of classes likely to survive more than 5 years.
(2) Provision of proper maintenance and servicing facilities where steam traction remains.

A reasonable but decreasing expenditure on modernisation and maintenance facilities for steam should thus form part of the overall plan.

It seems reasonable that new steam construction should be tapered off rather than be brought abruptly to a close. Accepting that possibly express and suburban passenger types will not require any renewals, it may still be economical to build a further number of steam engines, mainly for freight working."

The ultimate in British steam locomotive design, the enigmatic BR Class 8 4-6-2 No.71000 DUKE OF GLOUCESTER, completed at Crewe Works exactly twenty years after COCK 0' THE NORTH, with comparatively little to show for it. Despite the sophistication of poppet valves, both engines proved very heavy on coal and in performance did not match up to other well-proportioned 4-6-2s. Although retired after a working life of only 8½ years, No.71000 was restored to running condition in 1986 and has undergone several design improvements. BR

mechanical stoker, as applied to the excellent BR Class 9F 2-10-0, in the interests of utilising inferior coal. In each instance the enhancement, even under test conditions, was negligible, but by this time the steam locomotive in Britain was living on borrowed time. Sentence had already been passed.

Shortly before a further sharp rise in the cost of coal, in May 1954, the government intimated that it would make some £1,200 million (nearly £17 billion at 1995 prices) available to British Railways in order that it could undertake a major modernisation programme. A sea change in motive power policy, already under debate for several years, was now to the fore at a time when the 1956 Locomotive Building Programme was being decided.

On 6 September 1954 R.C. Bond remarked in a memorandum to J.C.L.

conversion of main lines to electric traction takes a long time.

It is clear that Mr Pope [a fervent diesel railcar protagonist having had experience in Ulster] does not envisage a complete cessation of new steam locomotive construction, and I think it is right that the building of new steam locomotives should be progressively reduced but should not yet be entirely suspended.

Of the existing steam locomotives about a quarter are already above their depreciation life in the respective categories. On the other hand, roughly one half are under 20 years old. If no steam locomotives were built and the present depreciation lives were maintained, the scrapping of 466 locomotives per annum would eliminate this stock in 40 years. On

The British Caprotti poppet valve gear was the one outstanding feature of BR No.71000, conferring very high cylinder efficiency, whatever the engine's other shortcomings. It would probably have received a much wider application had steam development continued offering improved fuel economy *and* reduced routine maintenance, but was otherwise confined to thirty Standard Class 5 4-6-0s, built at Derby Works during 1956-57. Here No.73137, early in its brief career, leaves St Pancras with a Nottingham express. P. Ransome Wallis Collection, NRM.

In January 1955 the British Transport Commission published the *Modernisation and Re-Equipment of British Railways* in which was the stated intention 'to terminate the building of all new steam locomotives within a few years.' It also declared:-
"**The steam locomotive has in the past served the railways well. It has the virtues of low first cost, simplicity, robustness and long life. On the other hand, many factors combine to indicate that the end of the steam era is at hand. These include the growing shortage of large coal suitable for locomotives; the insistent demand for a reduction in air pollution by locomotives and for greater cleanliness in trains and railway stations; and the need for better acceleration.**
It is also a characteristic of steam operation that it involves hard manual labour for such tasks as the firing, cleaning and servicing of locomotives. Not only is much of this work unattractive by present day standards in comparison with that offered by other industries, but it also represents an inherently wasteful use of labour resources."

As early as 1949 the then Chairman of the Railway Executive had observed:-
"**Railway work has, for a variety of reasons, lost much of its relative attractiveness during the last decade, and the maintenance of an adequate establishment of footplate staff and running shed crews has become a serious problem.**"

Two years later the 'Hurcomb Report' elaborated:-
"**It is now extremely difficult, in many parts of the country, to obtain enough young men of the right type to fill the junior positions in the motive power department..... One of the chief deterrence to recruitment to the footplate grades today, with full employment and the current social outlook, is, of course, the irregular hours the men have to work.**"

In their copious memoranda, Messrs. Riddles, Bond and Cox had made no reference whatever to this factor which was actually further exacerbated in the early 1950s by two other phenomena, namely the retirement of many senior footplatemen who had joined the railway service immediately after World War 1, and compulsory national military service. The problem was particularly acute on the essentially 'rural' Eastern and Western regions rather than the heavily industrialised London Midland.

Even the ultimate British Railways Standard steam locomotive designs introduced in 1954, the Class 9F heavy freight 2-10-0 and Class 8 express passenger three-cylinder 4-6-2, in which accessibility was the dominating design feature, still required much traditional hard graft as regards firing and servicing. The 4-6-2, No 71000 DUKE OF GLOUCESTER, had British Caprotti poppet valve gear; on test it boasted the highest cylinder efficiency of any simple expansion locomotive in the world (maximum 15.7 per cent), but ironically its boiler performance was poor. Completed at Crewe almost 20

years to the day after the emergence of COCK O' THE NORTH from Doncaster, the engine represented remarkably little advance in design.

The diesel onrush was still not a foregone conclusion, and in September 1956 a final thirty of the exceptionally versatile 2-10-0s were authorised for the Western Region, bringing the 9F total up to 251. There was no economic diesel alternative on offer and this was done with great reluctance; the last 9F, No. 92220 EVENING STAR, had been authorised on a previous occasion, but did not emerge from Swindon Works until March 1960, almost five years after approval. By this time diesel traction was already making rapid headway on British Railways.

The 1955 Modernisation Plan had originally envisaged the ordering of small pilot batches of main line diesel locomotives from different manufacturers in order to permit the detailed evaluation of their different power units and transmission systems before any further orders were placed *three years later*. In the event, mounting concern as to the rapidly rising BR operating deficit caused large repeat orders to be placed even *before* the first pilot scheme diesel was handed over by the builders, in June 1957.

Although an economic case could not be made for dieselisation on the Southern Region in 1954, in late 1956 the procurement of 4150 main line diesel locomotives (and 1350 electrics) by 1966 was spoken of! Whereas annual capital expenditure on steam traction had peaked at only £6¼ million (actual) in 1948, aided by the massive government funding, this was greatly exceeded in the early diesel era. It rose to no less than £42 million in 1960 alone, when 750 new main line and shunting diesels were delivered. (Actual capital expenditure on steam during between 1948 and 1960 inclusive had totalled £49 million).

In 1955 the Western Region made detailed plans to dieselise completely west of Newton Abbot by 1959, thereby displacing 18 'King' 4-6-0s which it was simultaneously just beginning to modernise. In addition it planned to eliminate steam *completely* by 1968 and to close many branch lines.

In addition to staff recruitment difficulties, the coal problem had become particularly acute on the Western Region. On 1 July 1957 there was a general BR-wide price increase of 6/6d (32.5p) per ton, and serious thought was given to oil-firing on the WR. Its application to the 9F 2-10-0s was even considered, and detailed plans made for trials on a Castle 4-6-0. An 0-6-0PT was actually fitted up, and in 1960 there were proposals to equip thirty Hawksworth 94XX 0-6-0PTs, a class which was then already being retired despite its recent construction.

(One engine lasted only 4½ years). By this time it was envisaged that within three years, steam working would be eliminated in those regions of Britain which were remote from coal supplies - East Anglia, South East England, the West Country, and Northern Scotland, but with a substantial number still remaining in Northern England in 1970. In fact a detailed appraisal of future BR Workshop requirements made in early 1959 anticipated that the steam locomotive might not finally disappear until 1990. The 1955 Plan only looked as far ahead as 1970.

New boilers were still being built and fitted to certain classes in 1962, but the latter half of that year witnessed a massive purge for accountancy reasons in anticipation of the abolition, on 31 December, of the British Transport Commission. No fewer than 2,900 steam locomotives were condemned during 1962, rendering several classes extinct 'at a stroke'. By the end of 1963, the steam stock stood at only 8,000 compared to 18,000 in 1955 and an elimination date of 1972 was announced. In early 1965 elimination by the end of 1967 was predicted with the intention that two regions at a time should complete the process in 1965, 1966 and 1967. On account of their fuel and personnel problems the Eastern and Western Regions were scheduled to be the first

pair, and ironically the Southern one of the last. In the event steam survived on the London Midland Region until 3 August 1968 in North West England.

Delayed by ten years, British Railways mirrored the rapid collective dieselisation of the American railroads a decade before. The indecent haste of it all was criticised at the time, and has been since. Almost to the end Victorian steam locomotives could still be found at work and it could be argued that British steam locomotive design had made no *major* advance in forty years. In 1957 Horwich and Doncaster Works were building Standard Class 4 2-6-0s whose basic characteristics were little different from R.E.L Maunsell's then epoch-making 2-6-0s designed for the Southern Eastern & Chatham Railway in 1914, which combined long travel outside Walschaerts valve hear with a high superheat taper boiler. Even the larger British Railways Standard steam locomotives, the Class 7 4-6-2 and 9F 2-10-0, could be directly related back to Pennsylvania Railroad practice of the same 1914 period. It could be argued that in his controversial 4-6-2s, O.V.S. Bulleid on the Southern Railway, with its pro-electrification policy, genuinely attempted to 'break the mould' by making these more 'user friendly'. However the 'self servicing' chain driven valve gear contained in an

internal oil bath provided erratic steam distribution, which resulted in excessive coal and water consumption, *and* proved prone to frequent expensive mechanical failure. The 'air-smoothed' casing (emphatically *not* streamlining) which was intended to facilitate cleaning, merely impeded routine maintenance. Both features disappeared when 90 of the 140 4-6-2s built between 1941 and 1951, were completely rebuilt between 1956 and 1961. As a consequence fuel consumption was reduced and annual mileage and availability dramatically improved prior to their premature demise in 1964-67, by which time, it has been claimed, the costly reconstruction had already paid for itself.

The steam locomotive could not win in the efficiency stakes either, as E.S. Cox elegantly expressed in 1951:-
"This is the steam locomotive of today and tomorrow, and this is the form which it will fight for survival against the diesel and the electric. As a cheap, rugged tractor, it can still have a part to play, a part which it cannot sustain should it leave its vantage ground and once more descend to the complexities of the compound, the turbine, and the condenser."

The pioneer Bulleid Southern Railway 4-6-2 No.21C1 CHANNEL PACKET as newly completed at Eastleigh Works in March 1941. Despite its designer's genuine intention to reduce traditional drudgery, the concept proved to be badly flawed and the engine would later be extensively rebuilt on more conventional lines, like its 'less enlightened' contemporaries. NRM 395/8/66.

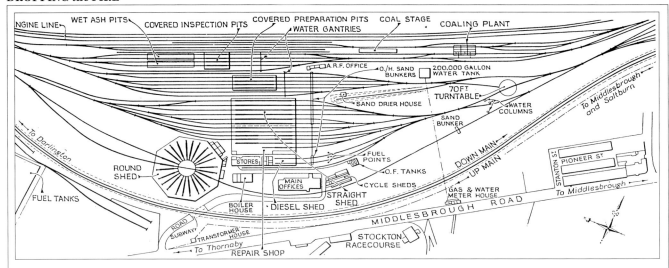

To paraphrase the 1911 observation, 'another, more potent, type of motor did indeed take the place of the steam actuated railway engine.' However, it would be far from 'relegated to the limbo of forgotten inventions.' Thirty years after its final demise large numbers of steam locomotives remain preserved in full working order as a reminder of what could once be found at work every day in every part of the British Isles.

References

(Report) *Visit to America 1945* - Steam Traction, E.S. Cox, January 1946.
Report of the Committee on Types of Motive Power, 1951, 181p.
Report on Motive Power Policy, British Transport Commission, April 1952.
Memoranda on British Railways Motive Power Policy, 1952 - 1954, contained in the R.C. Bond Archive, (National Railway Museum Library & Archive, York).
Modernisation and Re-Equipment of British Railways, British Transport Commission, January 1955.
Locomotive Panorama, Vol.2, E.S. Cox, Ian Allan, 1966, 158p.
British Railways Standard Steam Locomotives, E.S. Cox, Ian Allan, 1966, 158p.
6256 And All That, C.P. Atkins, *Steam Days*, April-June 1987, 12-17.
Britannia, Birth of a Locomotive, C.P. Atkins, Irwell Press, 1991, 92p.
The End of Steam on British Rail, a study in decision making, M.R. Bonavia, *Modern Railways,* (1) September 1975, 359-363, (2) October 1975, 406-410, (3) November 1975, 446-449.

Plan of the Motive Power Depot at Thornaby on Teesside, authorised in 1953 at a cost of £1.5 million and completed five years later as the last new major BR steam depot. It was in fact designed to cater for all three forms of traction, and makes an interesting comparison with the highly sophisticated Norfolk & Western Railway installation at Williamson, West Virginia, illustrated in Chapter 4.

The dismal truth of steam locomotive operation across the world was its highly labour intensive nature; (148,000 souls were directly involved with 19,500 steam locomotives on BR in 1951) there was also the unproductive two-three hours of tedious preparation and disposal at each end of every working day. For coal burning locomotives (the great majority) this involved the highly unpleasant removal of ash from smokebox, firetubes and ashpan, though on post-war designs so-called 'self-cleaning' smokeboxes (which in practice discharged their contents over the countryside through which the engine passed) and hopper ashpans slightly eased the physical burden. Then there were the delights of boiler washout every few days, all carried out under conditions which had scarcely changed since the Victorian period. The necessary provision of purpose-built facilities for diesel traction must have greatly enhanced the psychological reception of the new order. Here is a typical scene in the closing years, at Camden shed. The steam era was, perhaps, not quite as golden as it had been portrayed in retrospect. M.W.Earley collection, NRM (MWE 97/55).

Chapter 7
GERMANY - THE FINAL WHIMPER

Germany ranked a close second to the United States in terms of total steam locomotive production. Likewise this was scarcely reflected in its modest post-war output for the domestic market. Just *before* World War Two, Germany claimed to have the world's largest locomotive export industry. For the home market alone it also built some 2,250 standard steam locomotives for the State Railway (DR), between 1925 and 1939. For 1940-1943, moreover, a major building plan envisaged the construction of no fewer than 5,500 new engines, including 800 of the new Class 23 2-6-2, then under design, as a replacement for the prolific ex-Prussian 'P8' 4-6-0.

In fact most locomotive classes of the former Prussian State Railway (KPEV) were prolific, often numbering several hundreds if not thousands of locomotives. In 1913 the total locomotive stock and route mileage of the KPEV alone approximated to that of Great Britain combined. Not surprisingly, Prussian locomotives, highly standardised, dominated the scene on the formation of the German State Railway in 1920. Nevertheless, a new range of standard locomotive classes was formulated under R.P. Wagner (1882-1953) between the new authority and the leading German locomotive builders. This was inaugurated with the two-cylinder Class 01 4-6-2 in 1925.

In spirit this anticipated the British Railways standard locomotive programme 25 years later, but requirements changed and during the 1930s additional designs appeared. Some, such as high speed 4-6-4s, were in response to the advent of diesel traction. In 1939 Krupp built two hand-fired three-cylinder streamlined 4-8-4s (Class 06) incorporating the same boiler as the Henschel Class 45 three- cylinder heavy goods 2-10-2s introduced in 1937. Even in such a long boiler, as per established DR practice, the firebox was not provided with a combustion chamber.

The 4-8-4s did not survive World War Two, and its outbreak in late 1939 resulted in the cancellation of the 1940-43 building programme. Several thousands of 2-10-0s were constructed instead. These included large numbers of the austerity Class 52 'Kreigslok' variety, but 2-14-0 and (rigid frame) 2-6-8-0 projects did not progress beyond the drawing board. An air raid destroyed two would-be turbine 2-8-4s under construction at Krupp, but an experimental Henschel 2-8-2 having geared high speed 'V' arranged cylinders providing individual axle drive, survived to be shipped to the USA for evaluation.

Such diversions had little place in the austere post-war world. Locomotive construction fell to negligible levels in a Germany that was now divided. Such facilities as remained largely existed in the West, where the railway administration was re-styled the German Federal Railway (DB). The Bundesbahn soon addressed the question of a locomotive policy, and though acknowledging the desirability of extending electrification, the required national power generating capacity to support this did not then exist.

Even for the long established institution and age old culture of the steam locomotive, the German system was extremely bureaucratic, involving government departments, the locomotive industry, and the footplate trades unions, who had a powerful say. Complicating the issue further was the indecisive nature of Wagner's successor from 1942, F. Witte. Priority was given to design a new version of the DR Class 23 2-6-2, of which only two prototypes had been completed in 1941 and which were now located in the East. The first was completed by Henschel in November 1950. Although 105 were built in total up to December 1959, these were produced by four different builders to 12 separate orders, which individually ranged in magnitude from only 4 to 15 engines. Although constructed with characteristic care and finesse, it was no wonder that the German locomotive industry regarded the post-war DB steam orders as little more than irritants, which merely got in the way of substantial export orders,

German Federal Railways (DB) 3-cylinder 4-6-2 No.10.002, the world's last new high speed steam locomotive, delivered by Krupp in late 1957. Always an oil burner, it is pictured undergoing examination at its home depot of Bebra in 1959. P. Ransome Wallis Collection, NRM (PRW 7893).

The two 1941-built Reichsbahn Class 23 2-6-2s provided the basis for the most numerous post war standard steam locomotive classes in both West and East Germany. The first DB example appeared as early as 1950 and there were numerous detail variations amongst the 105 engines built by four different builders, to twelve distinct orders up to 1959. No.23.075 was built by Jung in 1956, and like 55 of the class had roller bearing big ends. DB.

It was, however, deemed desirable to have a steam alternative should diesel traction not prove successful, and two units were ordered from Krupp, which delivered them both during 1957. When new, No.10.001 was a coal burner with supplementary oil-firing, whereas No.10.002 was an oil burner. 10.001 was later rebuilt to conform with the second engine. Although enjoying working lives of only 9-10 years, both, especially when new, achieved very high annual mileages, of the order of 100,000.

The remaining DB standard steam locomotive classes consisted of 2-6-4, 2-8-4 and 0-10-0 tank engines. The 2-8-4T in particular had a direct parallel on the post-war Reichsbahn in the Soviet-dominated East, which also had plans for an 0-10-0T in a standardisation plan which it had drawn up in October 1952 under Hans Schultz (1903-1962). A comparison of the respective post-war German Federal and German State steam locomotive programmes is of some interest.

It should be noted that in 1952 the DR also envisaged a compound 4-6-2. After a slow start DR production eventually greatly exceeded that of the DB, with nearly 200 2-6-2s and 2-10-0s (having a common boiler design) built during 1958-60 alone. In addition, no fewer than 662 engines, of several classes, were completely rebuilt/reboilered between 1957 and 1965, and some 4-6-2s received new boilers as late as 1969. Even after new construction ceased, what amounted to an entirely new design appeared with the complete rebuilding of 35 of the pre-war Class 01 4-6-2s to 01.5 at Meiningen, between 1962 and 1965.

particularly to South Africa. The overall total of DB standard steam locomotives was a paltry 168, which in practice scarcely made any impact on a steam locomotive fleet which at the end of 1950 stood at 12,000, and in mid-1960 at 7,500 engines.

Nevertheless, the early 1950s must have witnessed tremendous activity on many drawing boards, projects which progressed no further included a three-cylinder 2-8-2, and an improved version of the pre-war Class 45 2-10-2, both with mechanical stokers. The question of an express passenger locomotive was particularly vexed. It commenced in 1950 as a large wheeled two-cylinder 2-6-2 with 22 *tonne* axleload, put forward by Witte, but by 1952 a four-cylinder compound 4-6-2 was under active discussion as an alternative to the growing reality of a 2,000HP diesel locomotive. Certain factions were much impressed by the results of compounding on the SNCF, particularly with respect to fuel economy. Witte was not one of these and

finally won the day with a three-cylinder simple 4-6-2 agreed in 1953. Chapelon, who had not enhanced his personal reputation in occupied France by openly engaging in academic discussions on locomotive design with his German counterparts, was asked to scrutinise the drawings, as a consequence of which, uniquely for a German locomotive, a double (but not Kylchap) exhaust was provided. Even so the Class 10 4-6-2 was very nearly not built.

The first DR 2-6-2s, two prototypes, were not completed until 1956, to be followed by 111 more during 1958-59. They were of a more austere yet more purposeful appearance than their DB counterparts, as exemplified by No.23.1042. DR.

TABLE 22

POST-WAR GERMAN STANDARD STEAM LOCOMOTIVES

Wheel Arrangement	RAILWAY			
	German Federal (DB)		German State (DR)	
	Class	Total	Class	Total
2-6-2	23	105 1950-1959	23.10	113 1956-1959
4-6-2	10	2 1957	not built	
2-8-0		-	25/25.10	2 1954-1955
2-10-0		-	50.40	88 1956-1960
2-6-4T	66	2 1956	not built	
2-8-4T (heavy)	65	18 1951-1956	65.10	88 1954-1957
2-8-4T (light)	-		83.10	27 1955-1957
0-10-0T	82	41 1950-1955	not built	
TOTAL		168 1950-1959		318 1954-1960

These included several variations, not least the fact that half were oil burners.

This highlighted the fact that East Germany had fuel problems which were actually more acute than in the West, where German bituminous deposits were located. (In 1938 the 'greater' Reichsbahn had burned 18 million tons). The East had to be content with 'brown' coal which had only about 65 per cent of the calorific value of bituminous coal. The first of the two Class 25 2-8-0s built in 1954-55 had been designed to burn pulverised fuel, and other applications of the necessary equipment were made to a number of existing locomotives.

The situation in West Germany was remarkably similar to that in Britain: both countries were coal producers and exporters, but were obliged to import American coal. As early as 1951 the last two 'Kreigslok' 2-10-0s were turned out with Crosti boilers in the pursuit of fuel economy. A DB Class 50 was equipped with a modified Crosti boiler, and 30 more were similarly rebuilt during 1958-59. As on British Railways, the Crosti 2-10-0s proved highly unpopular with those who had to operate them and were similarly short lived. In 1956 the West German government removed a small subsidy on the price of coal and in December of that year the last 29 Class 23 2-6-2s were ordered. New boilers were built for 4-6-2s and 2-8-2s until 1961. From 1957 the price of fuel oil became increasingly competitive, not least because German export coal could command a higher price than an equivalent quantity of imported oil.

As a result, in the late 1950s several DB 4-6-2s and 2-10-0s were very successfully equipped as oil burners. The 4-6-2s in particular achieved very high monthly mileages (14,000). As on British Railways, however, government funds had at last become available to re-equip the DB, and between 31 December 1956 and 31 December 1960 the number of diesel locomotives on the Bundesbahn dramatically increased, from 235 to 986, and the number of electric locomotives from 529 to 1,015. This gave the German locomotive industry a field day. Unlike BR, however, the steam locomotive in Western Germany underwent a longer and more measured decline, from 7,235 at the end of 1960 to 1,636 at the end of 1970. It finally became extinct in May 1977,

DB Crosti re-boilered 2-10-0 No.50.4021. Having strong parallels with their British counterparts, and produced for similar reasons, the DB Crostis proved equally unpopular and almost as short-lived. DB.

Unlike the DB, the DR built new 2-10-0s in the 1950s. As with the 2-6-2s, two prototypes appeared in 1956, followed by a production run a little later during 1958-60. DR.

when Class 44 three cylinder 2-10-0s finally ceased operation near Hamburg, two years later then earlier envisaged.

In the East, steam working on the standard gauge on the DR ceased eleven years later in 1988, several years after the demise of the 01.50 4-6-2s in the late 1970s. Nevertheless in the 1990s, Meiningen Works retained the capability to cast cylinders and build boilers, and heavily renewed

several 750 mm gauge 2-10-2Ts. During 1984-88 it had built 202 0-6-0 fireless steam locomotives for industry. By the dawn of the 21st century Meiningen could well remain the only plant on earth able to build a new main line steam locomotive, which ironically is something to date it has not so far been called upon to do.

References
Die Dampflokomotive, Transpress, 1964, 912p.
Neubau-Und Rekonstruktions Dampflokomotiven Der DR Nach 1945, W. Meereis, Eisenbahn-Kurier, 1975, 310p.
Katalog der Reichsbahn-Einheitslokomotiven, A.B. Gottwaldt, Franckh'sche Verlagshandlung, 1981, 160p.
Die Neubau-Dampflokomotiven der

Outside the British Isles 2-6-4 tank locomotives were uncommon, but this wheel arrangement was selected for the DB Class 66, of which two prototypes were produced by Henschel in 1956—this is No.66.002. A smaller proposed 2-6-2T was not proceeded with. DB.

Deutschen Bundesbahn, J. Ebel, Kohlhammer, 1984, Vol 1 Classes 23 & 10, 192p, Vol 2 Classes 65, 82, & 66, 184p.

Baureihe 01.50 - Ein Lokportrait, H. Weigard and M. Weisbrod, *Eisenbahn Kurier*, 1995, 106p.

Above. Between 1962 and 1965 the DR completely rebuilt thirty-five pre-war Class 01 4-6-2s with new boilers etc. to Class 01.50. Chronologically speaking this could be regarded as the ultimate European steam locomotive design, and there were numerous detail variations. No.01.505 was an early conversion. DR.

Below. One of the two hundred 0-6-0F fireless steam locomotives built at Meiningen (then in East Germany) during the mid-1980s, pictured at work several years later in Austria. K.R. Chester.

If original plans had matured, in true Russian fashion, by say 1960, the former USSR would have boasted more 4-8-4s of a single design, the P36, than all the North American locomotives of that type (by then all but extinct) put together. Enjoying a new lease of life in the 1990s, after storage for most if not all of the 1970s, and certainly the 1980s, No.P36-0218 poses for the camera at Mineral-y-Vody in May 1993, while working special steam excursions. This design, more than any other, demonstrated the latter-day close affinity of Soviet steam locomotive design with that of the USA, whatever ideological differences might then have existed between the two Super Powers. N. Harris.

Two of the classic Class E 0-10-0s double head a special steam excursion at Goitkh in May 1993. The engine nearest the camera was a late example, built in Hungary by Mavag in 1955. Although originally designed many years before, production of these 0-10-0s actually over-ran that of the much more recent L 2-10-0 and LV 2-10-2. N. Harris.

Chapter 8
RUSSIA AND THE EASTERN BLOC

In terms of total route mileage and locomotive stock, the 5ft gauge railways of the former Soviet Union ranked second only to those of the United States. It has been estimated that the (then dominant) steam stock attained a peak of around 36,000 units in 1956-57 when steam construction abruptly ended on the eve of the Sixth Five Year Plan (1956-60) when a further 6,000 steam locomotives had originally been scheduled to be built. As it was, steam locomotives were built in prodigious numbers during the period 1946-56 in Russia itself, augmented by substantial imports. In addition, over 5,000 narrow gauge 0-8-0 tender locomotives were built for forestry railways, some possibly as late as 1959.

Ten-coupled locomotives dominated the scene in Russia and accounted for the bulk of new construction after 1945. Despite its Tsarist origins, originally introduced in 1912 the classic 'E' 0-10-0 only modestly updated, was 'ordered' in large numbers as reparations from Romania, Czechoslovakia, Hungary and Poland to a total of at least 2,677 units delivered between 1946 and 1957. For a brief period, all except wartime casualties were simultaneously in traffic giving a grand total which has been variously estimated at between 11,000 and

13,000 engines. This was a world record for any steam locomotive design, but it is a remarkable fact that in Russia, with its widely different operating and climatic conditions, from tundra to arid desert, astonishingly few locomotive designs were produced, but were usually built in large numbers. In the early 1950s, in the USSR the steam locomotive had a firm champion in the Minister of Transport, Lazar Kaganovitch, who attached great importance to its basic simplicity, and capacity for hard work. Once a ruthless henchman of Stalin, Kaganovitch survived his master's reign to fall from grace in 1957, an event which presaged the demise of the steam locomotive behind the Iron Curtain.

As elsewhere, steam locomotive development in the USSR was circumscribed by maximum permissible axleload, which was generally fixed at either 18 or 20 *tonnes*. No less than 23 *tonnes* had been permitted in experimental 2-10-4 and 2-10-2 engines imported from Alco and Baldwin in 1931, which injected US technology into Russian practice. However, to produce such locomotives in quantity required a suitable upgrading of track and bridges, which in view of the vast mileages involved would be expensive almost beyond measure. Circumventing the *impasse,* a 4-8-2+2-8-4 Beyer Garratt was

obtained in 1932. It was the largest Garratt ever built, remaining in service until 1957. In 1934 an almost mythical 4-14-4 was built in the USSR itself. This only ever underwent a few trial trips, yet reputedly it was not scrapped until 1960. In the later 1930s the Russians produced large numbers of American-style 2-8-4s for passenger work, and 2-10-2s for freight. Immediately after World War Two, a new 2-10-0 with 18 *tonne* axleload, Class L, was introduced and remained in production until 1955 (the classification derived from the first letter of the designer's name, Lebedyanskii). Greater power was also required and there was something of a repeat of the pre-war scenario with the construction of a prototype 23 *tonne* axleload 2-10-4 (Class OR-23) in 1948. This was followed by an experimental 2-6-6-2 simple expansion Mallet (Class P34) in 1949.

Five prototype 2-10-2 developments (OR-18) of the Class L, later designated Class LV, were built at Voroshilovgrad (Lugansk) in 1952-54 and were later put into serial production there in direct succession to the 2-10-0. Several hundred 2-10-2s were built in 1956 alone, before construction abruptly ceased in December. Prototype 21-*tonne* axleload 2-10-2s (OR-21) were also built in 1954 which were *possibly* the basis of the later Chinese QJ (see Chapter 12).

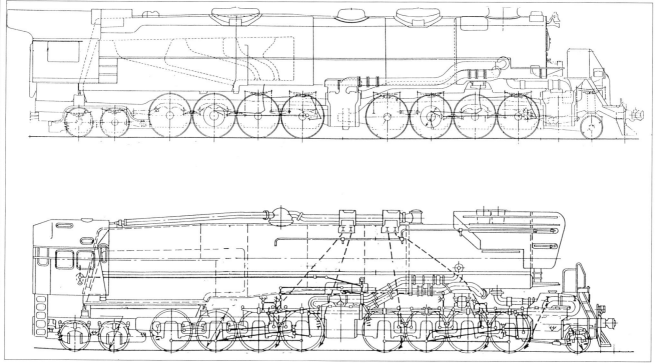

The Russian Class P38 2-8-8-4 of 1954 was the largest and most powerful steam locomotive to be built outside the United States. It was originally to have been larger, to be designed to an axleload of 23 tonnes, but was in fact scaled down to 20 tonnes, to confer with a wider route availability. It weighed only 216.5 tons as against the Baltimore & Ohio EMI's 280.7 tons, whose diagram is reproduced to the same scale for comparison. Nevertheless the Russian engine towered to a maximum height of 17'3" compared to the 15'11" of the American. The four P38s' fate was probably to serve as stationary boilers at industrial plants, (as befell the OR-21s), but a model of one is on display in the railway museum in St. Petersburg.

The outstanding Czech Class 556.0 2-10-0, of which no fewer than 510 were built by Skoda between 1952 and 1958. These were produced in preference to an earlier proposed 3-cylinder 2-10-4 which, it had been decided, would not perform so effectively in relation to its larger size. Skoda.

For passenger work originally 18-*tonne* axleload 4-8-4s and 23-*tonne* axleload 4-6-4 designs were proposed to supersede the Josef Stalin (JS) 4-8-4s, but only the former (Class P36) materialised. A prototype with unsuccessful turbo-fan exhaust was completed at Kolomna in 1950, to be followed by 250 production engines (with conventional exhaust) during 1954-1956. Although appreciably smaller than their US counterparts, with Boxpok coupled wheel centres, mechanical stokers and roller bearings, these were purely American in concept. (A larger 4-8-4 is also reputed to have been considered.)

The same could also be said of the ultimate Russian steam locomotive design, the P38 2-8-8-4 simple expansion Mallet, of which four units were constructed at Kolomna during the winter of 1954-55. These extremely large engines, which had a 20 *tonne* axleload, were reputedly expensive to maintain and were transferred to 'industrial' service in 1959. Their ultimate fate is not known. (What would have constituted Classes P35 and P37 is not clear, although conceivably the latter would have been the 4-6-4).

Early in 1956 it was announced that main line steam locomotive construction in the then Soviet Union would cease almost immediately, with total replacement by 1970. Many years later it would be admitted that this decision was at least partly motivated by the desire to emulate recent developments in the United States, the rival Super Power of that time. There were, however, sound practical reasons. Rail traffic in the USSR was increasing rapidly in the post Great Patriotic War era and steam power could not match the capacity required on long single track main lines. To have provided more powerful steam locomotives would have required hugely expensive track and bridge renewal programmes, as had been recognised in the 1930s. Diesel and electric locomotives, on the other hand, could simply be operated in multiple as required. With the newer forms of traction it was anticipated that track capacity could be increased by 150 to 250 per cent, and that locomotive availabilities of 95 per cent would be achieved. It is rather doubtful if such optimistic aspirations were actually realised.

The vast distances in the huge country exacerbated the problem of high unproductive locomotive mileages accrued through delivering fuel to remote depots. It sometimes took one train of locomotive coal to work two coal trains. At times the railways in the USSR consumed as much as 40 per

The elegant CSD Class 477.0 3-cylinder 4-8-4T, the world's most sophisticated tank engine, of which 22 were built by CKD during 1955-56. The last CSD steam locomotive design was a light 2-cylinder 4-8-4T which had strong affinities with the 556.0 2-10-0 of which only two were built by Skoda in 1956. CSD.

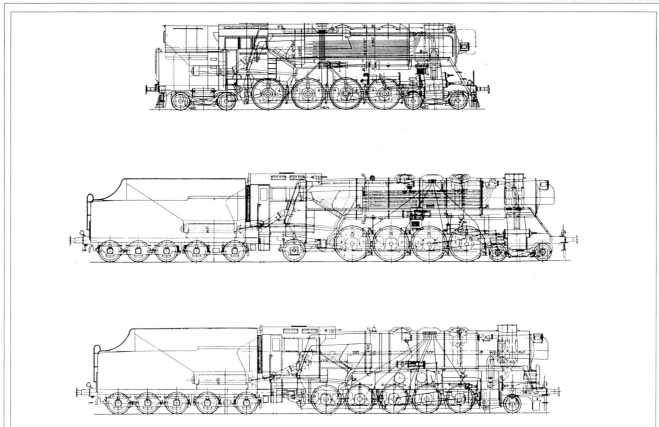

The outstanding Czech steam locomotive trio of the 1950s shown comparatively. The Class 477.0 4-8-4T (top) was undoubtedly the world's most advanced tank engine, while the 498.1 (centre) was the world's fastest 4-8-2. Furthermore the 556.0 2-10-0 (bottom) was the most refined development of that wheel arrangement ever built.

cent of the national coal output, which in 1952 for example, equated to that from British mines. Elsewhere, in arid areas, there were acute water supply problems. There had been experiments with condensing tenders to conserve water supplies, as there had been with combined steam/internal combustion locomotives in the fruitless quest to improve thermal efficiency. As in the United States, in the USSR no ingenuity was spared in genuine attempts to retain the steam locomotive in some form.

As far as main line locomotive construction was concerned, the transition was exceptionally abrupt. However, whereas in most other countries steam locomotives rapidly accumulated in dumps, usually never to operate again, in the USSR such was the continuing upsurge in traffic that contemporary observers initially noted an actual *increase* in steam locomotive mileage, with double-heading frequently resorted to. Although steam traction in the USSR was *largely* eliminated by the target date of 1970,

in practice it still survived in active pockets in remote areas for many years thereafter, even into the 1990s. Some of the last units built, however, had very short *active* lives. For instance, about a hundred 4-8-4s had already been retired by 1967 (having spent much of their earlier years out of use due to component failure, it is understood), yet most were stored intact. It was policy to retain for strategic reasons most post-war steam locomotives until well into the 1980s, at remote dumps far away from likely nuclear missile targets for the military authorities were still unwilling to sanction wholesale scrapping. A few 4-8-4s remained in active use in Siberia until 1974-75, and a small number were returned to service for working special tourist trains in the early 1990s. It was indeed strange to read, in July 1991, of the peaceful demise in Moscow of the once feared Lazar Kaganovitch, a man who had been third in seniority in the Soviet Union after Stalin and Molotov. An arch-survivor, Kaganovitch it was who in 1954 had pledged undying allegiance to the robust and faithful steam locomotive, shortly before his removal from office. A

TABLE 23

MAJOR MAIN LINE STEAM LOCOMOTIVE TYPES
BUILT IN SOVIET RUSSIA 1945 - 1956

Class	Wheel Arr	Axleload *tonnes*	Rated HP*	No.Built	Construction Dates
Su	2-6-2	18.0	1380	400	1947-1951
P36	4-8-4	18.0	2500	251	1950-1956
SON	2-10-0	17.0	-	c.1800	1945-1951
L	2-10-0	18.0	2125	4200	1945-1955
LV(OR-18)	2-10-2	18.0	2420	522	1952-1956
OR-21	2-10-2	21.0	2650	3	1954
23-01	2-10-2	23.0	2800	1	1948
OR-23	2-10-4	23.0	2500	1	1948
P34	2-6-6-2	19.5	2200	1	1949
P38	2-8-8-4	20.0	-	4	1954-1955

* 1 Metric HP = 0.9863 Imperial HP

1 *tonne* = 0.9842 tons of 2240lb

TABLE 24

MODERN CZECH STEAM LOCOMOTIVE CLASSES

Class	Type	No.Built	Years built
486.1	3c 2-8-4	3	1933
486.0	3c 4-8-2	9	1933-1938
498.0	3c 4-8-2	40	1948-1949
498.1	3c 4-8-2	15	1954-1955
475.1	2c 4-8-2	147	1947-1951
+25 for North Korea			
476.0	3cc4-8-2	3	1949
(+12 cancelled and 1 presented to USSR,1951) converted to 2c 1964-5			
534.03	2c 2-10-0	228	1945-1947
556.0	2c 2-10-0	510	1952-1958
464.0	2c 4-8-4T	76	1933-1939
464.1	2c 4-8-4T	2	1940
464.2	2c 4-8-4T	2	1956
475.0	3c 4-8-4T	1	1935
477.0	3c 4-8-4T	60	1950-1955

Note:
2c = 2 cylinder simple
3c = 3 cylinder simple
3cc= 3 cylinder compound

few months after his death the Soviet Union disintegrated, since when harsh economic pressures have compelled several of its former states to re-activate steam locomotives which had long been considered to be museum pieces.

The Russian directive to cease steam locomotive construction almost immediately in 1956 does not appear to have been extended to the various satellite countries in Eastern Europe which were then subject to Soviet domination. For instance, the bulk of post-war construction in the former German Democratic Republic was concentrated in the period 1958-60, but the completion there of DR 2-10-0 No.50.4088 in December 1960 did in fact round off the process for all concerned.

Of all the countries obliged to endure the Soviet yoke during the 1950s, the most enlightened as far as steam locomotive design was concerned was Czechoslovakia, which latterly forged a happy alliance of the best of German and French practices without indulging in the excesses of either. This reflected the influence of André Chapelon as a consultant at this period. Several designs harked back to pre-war antecedents, but were brought thoroughly up to date with extensive resort to welding, especially as regards boiler construction. They also incorporated such refinements as double Kylchap exhaust, roller bearings and mechanical stokers. Three wheel arrangements were particularly popular, 4-8-2 and 2-10-0 tender, and 4-8-4 tank, which were built by either the renowned armaments firm of Skoda, or the longer established (in terms of locomotives) enterprise of CKD.

In 1949 both builders submitted designs for three-cylinder 2-10-4 heavy freight locomotives, developed from the pre-war German Class 45 2-10-2s. Sadly, although five were ordered from Skoda they were cancelled, as were 80 two-cylinder 2-8-2s. Also not proceeded with at this time were a further 12 three-cylinder compound 4-8-2s of Class 476.0, of which three had been built in 1949. This design in particular was indicative of the involvement of André Chapelon, who since 1938 had advocated three cylinder compounds. The Czech design, however, incorporated an ingenious pneumatically operated servo-mechanism for adjusting the respective high and low pressure valve gears to provide optimum cut-offs. The engines are understood to have been rebuilt with two cylinders in 1964.

The high point of Czech design came with the 15 Class 498.1 three-cylinder simple 4-8-2s built by Skoda during 1954-55. In 1964 during the course of special tests, one of these engines achieved a maximum speed of 100.4 mph. The most prolific design, numerically, was the 556.0 two-cylinder 2-10-0 of which no fewer than 510 were built by Skoda between 1952 and 1958. Undoubtedly, they were the most refined examples of their wheel arrangement ever built.

For its part, CKD supplied a series of powerful three-cylinder 4-8-4Ts, which like the 498.1 4-8-2s and 556.0 2-10-0s were equipped with mechanical stokers. This was probably unique in a non-articulated tank engine.

This mighty fleet, tabulated above, remained intact in 1971, but only the following year, on the eve of the world energy crisis, it was resolved to eliminate steam traction on the Czech State Railways (CSD) within five years for reasons which are unclear. In the event the last steam working, powered by 2-10-0 No.556.0506, took place on 1 April 1981.

Less progressive was steam locomotive design in neighbouring Hungary, where 4-8-0s of basically 1924 design continued to be built by the state manufacturer, MAVAG until 1958, and spidery 2-6-2 tanks of even earlier origin until the beginning of 1959. Two 4-6-4 express engines built in 1950 were not multiplied and appear to have suffered an early demise. Normal steam working ended in Hungary in 1986, rather later than the original target of 1975.

In Yugoslavia ten 2-8-0s derived from the Vulcan Foundry 'Liberation' design were built in 1958, followed by 23 0-6-0Ts of the exceptionally austere World War 2 US Army design. In both instances, local construction saw plate frames superseding bar frames, no doubt for ease of manufacture. Steam operations on the JDZ had apparently ceased before the sad disintegration of the country in the early 1990s.

In Poland latter-day construction was dominated by 2-6-2 mixed traffic and 2-10-0 heavy freight locomotives, clearly based on German antecedents, the latter remaining in production until 1958. Plans for an even more powerful 2-10-2 (Class Ty-55) remained on the drawing board. In 1972 Poland also announced its intention to cease steam operation by 1980, but two world energy crises resulted in significant steam working persisting on the PKP until well into the 1990s! At the time of writing Poland remained the only country in Europe which still maintained daily operations involving standard gauge steam locomotives.

In Romania 2-10-0s based on the German Class 52 'Kreigslok' were built until 1960, though they had probably disappeared by the 1980s when the energy crisis hit that country particularly hard despite its oil deposits. This resulted in twelve new 762mm gauge 0-8-0Ts for the forestry railways being built at Reghin between 1982 and 1988, to a long standing design.

This survey leaves only Bulgaria, which could uniquely boast 4-10-0 tender and 2-12-4 tank engines. No developments of any note occurred during the 1950s and the Bulgarian steam locomotive fleet underwent a predictable rapid decline during the ensuing two decades to become the first 'steam free' country in Eastern Europe, in 1980 not withstanding the recent energy crises.

It will be noted that the last main line steam locomotives to be built for service in Poland, Czechoslovakia, Romania and East Germany, as in the United Kingdom and Turkey, within the short period 1958-61, were all 2-10-0s. This was a wheel arrangement which had enjoyed a remarkably short currency in North America, where it had long been regarded as obsolete. In many ways, however, it epitomised the steam locomotive for what it essentially was, a tough no-frills workhorse.

References
Locomotives of the Railways of the Soviet Union, V.I. Rakov, Transheldorisdat, 1955, 456p. Completely revised edition published 1995.

Russian Steam Locomotives, H.M. Le Fleming & J.H. Price, David & Charles, (2nd Edition) 1972, 112p.
Soviet Locomotive Technology During Industrialization, 1928 - 1952, J.N. Westwood, Macmillan, 1983, 240p.
The Steam Locomotives of Eastern Europe, A.E. Durrant, David & Charles, 1966, 160p.
Steam Under The Red Star, R. Ziel & N. Huxtable, Amereon House/Sunrise Special Ltd/Steamscenes, 1995, 256p.
The Steam Locomotives of Czechoslovakia, P. Catchpole, P. Catchpole Ltd, 1996, 197p.

Above. A post-war Polish 2-6-2 which shows a strong affinity with the German DR Class 23, one of several instances world-wide of steam locomotive design transcending international conflict. P. Ransome-Wallis Collection, NRM (PRW 8716).

Below. The only conventional (adhesion) steam locomotives to be built outside China after 1972 have been twelve 762mm gauge wood-burning 0-8-0Ts to a long established design in Romania between 1982 and 1987, for that country's extensive forestry railways. The reasons were the acute shortage of oil and the fact that the engines could be maintained and operated by unskilled labour. This is No.764-412R, then but five years old, at work in typical woodland surroundings in September 1992. K.R. Chester.

The proposed Chapelon 'Super-Power' 3-cylinder compounds did not progress beyond the drawing board, so the 'last word' in France was the unique 232U1 4-cylinder compound 4-6-4. Commenced as a turbine engine almost ten years earlier, this was eventually delivered by Corpet, Louvet et Cie in May 1949, and is pictured here brand new. It was the most powerful six-coupled European locomotive ever built, and unlike most French designs was extremely robust as regards its construction. SNCF.

No.141P305 pictured new at Thionville in 1951, one of the supremely elegant Chapelon SNCF Class 141P 4-cylinder compound mixed-traffic 2-8-2s. By French standards many of these engines, of which no fewer than 200 were ordered in 1946, had unusually short lives, scarcely ten years in fact. Twenty-five were laid aside as early as 1956, rendered redundant by advancing electrification, only four years after the last had been delivered. Paradoxically, other 141Ps accrued unusually high mileages during 1956 as a consequence of the Suez crisis immobilising many oil-burning 141Rs. P. Ransome Wallis Collection, NRM (PRW 3963).

Chapter 9
FRANCE - UNFINISHED BUSINESS

Rebuilt from pre-1914 4-6-2s, the outstanding Paris-Orleans 4-8-0s were designed to the French 'minimalist' tradition as regards their machinery, although the boilers were remarkable performers for their size. Chapelon attracted very considerable international attention when these 4-8-0s were introduced in 1932.

The steam locomotive attained a level of sophistication in France which was without equal elsewhere. The underlying reason was ironically the same as that which led to its eventual demise, which was quite simply the prosaic matter of coal supply.

Coal deposits in France were largely located in the north east of the country, more particularly in Alsace-Lorraine, which was ceded to Imperial Germany in 1871 in the aftermath of the Franco-Prussian War and not returned until after the First World War. Annual French coal output was insufficient to meet national requirements, and large quantities were imported from England and Wales. (Prior to 1914 France was the biggest importer of British coal). During 1913 the French railways burned 7 million tons of coal, of which 5 million tons (70 per cent) was imported, particularly from South Wales. (The largest of the French railways, the Paris-Lyons-Mediterraneé (PLM) even had a fleet of ships dedicated to conveying locomotive coal from Cardiff to Marseilles.) It is interesting to note that prior to 1914 the Belgian railways also depended heavily on British coal, but following the curtailment of supplies as a consequence of the British Miners' Strike in 1912, legislation was enacted which *compelled* railways in Belgium to burn Belgian coal. In contrast to the United Kingdom, where coal was virtually taken for granted, in France there was a strong incentive to conserve supplies, by building more efficient locomotives. Moreover, given the moderate axleload limits which prevailed in France (18 tons was still common in the 1920s) compounding also promised well

balanced locomotives of greater power for a given weight.

Although the first French compound locomotive had been built in 1878, what really attracted world-wide attention was the first Nord express passenger 4-4-2, designed by English-born Alfred de Glehn (1848-1936). This had made its *début* in 1900 and examples were soon built for evaluation in England (GWR), Germany, Egypt, and even the United States (Pennsylvania RR).

Compounding was also extensively applied to goods engines, but the economy it achieved in general was probably not always as great as was fondly imagined by its proponents, especially in early passenger 4-6-2s built from 1907 onwards. Each of the major French railways had extensively built and tested 4-6-2s before 1914, the dominant PLM in particular, where comparisons had been made between various combinations of saturated versus superheated steam, and simple versus compound expansion. By 1917 the PLM had, not entirely surprisingly, found in favour of superheated compounds.

In 1919 French coal producing capacity was greatly increased by the restoration of Alsace-Lorraine. Even so, the necessity to import coal was far from eliminated. French railway consumption peaked in 1930 at 11 million tons, of which 6¼ million tons (56 per cent) was imported. The 1920s witnessed an almost world-wide quest to improve the inherently low overall efficiency of the steam locomotive, often by unorthodox means. In France alone, a rational, systematic, scientific approach was adopted towards the conventional steam locomotive, most notably by André Chapelon (1892-1978). Although Chapelon had received

his training on the PLM, he transferred to the relatively impoverished Paris-Orleans (PO) in 1925 and commenced his classic investigations, which have been extensively documented elsewhere.

By completely re-designing cylinders, valve gear and boiler the maximum horsepower of the original PO 4500 class Pacifics of 1907 was increased by no less than 82 per cent. In 1932 the first of twelve rebuilds of old PO 4-6-2s as 4-8-0s with Nord-style long narrow fireboxes was a veritable *tour de force*, in which the original power output was more than doubled. Hand-fired on test by a super-human fireman, this achieved the phenomenal drawbar thermal efficiency of 11¼ per cent. This was sacrificed somewhat in a subsequent aesthetically improved version which was provided with a mechanical stoker, the Class 240P introduced in 1940. This nevertheless achieved all-time records for power in relation to weight and firegrate area, as will be seen from the table overleaf.

Such compounds could develop as much as 70 per cent more cylinder horse power per square foot of grate area than their British contemporaries. This could be attributed to a 35 per cent greater evaporation rate (1,200lb/ft²) due to sophisticated draughting arrangements, and 25 per cent greater overall cylinder efficiency due to compounding.

In early 1934 Chapelon had published an outline scheme for a *six-cylinder* compound 4-8-4 with two crank axles capable of 6,000HP on an axleload of only 22 *tonnes*, (21.65 tons) and weighing 160 *tonnes* (157.5 tons) without tender. Lacking on line coal supplies and passing though the mountain regions of central France

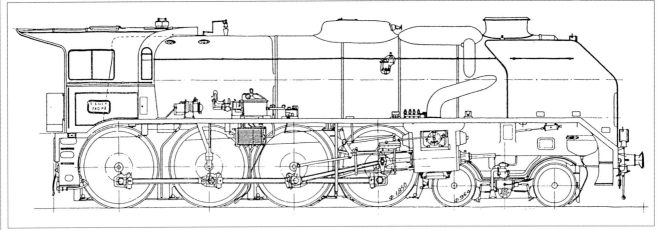

Diagram of the aesthetically improved SNCF 240P 4-8-0, of which twenty-five were 'rebuilt' from old 4-6-2s during 1940-41. These were also provided with mechanical stokers, but like the earlier twelve PO engines, all were retired during 1952-53 after quite short lives.

where cheap hydro-electricity was available, the best long term prospect for the PO was main line electrification. However, its amalgamation at this time with the Midi Railway resulted in Chapelon producing in 1936 a range of six-cylinder compound 6,000HP proposals, including a high speed 4-6-4 with 29 *tonne* (28.5 ton) axleload. To test the six-cylinder principle an old PO 2-10-0 was rebuilt as a 2-12-0, an operation which was not completed until 1940. This was two years after the nationalisation of the French railways, which had taken place on 1 January 1938. Upon its formation the SNCF inherited about 15,500 steam locomotives and began to formulate a locomotive standardisation scheme. Top priority was considered to be a powerful mixed traffic locomotive. Chapelon, who had recently visited the USA, advocated a three-cylinder compound 2-8-4 with cast steel engine bed, but was over-ruled. Instead, a more modest 2-8-2, re-cast from a prolific PLM design, was selected. This was the extremely elegant four-cylinder compound 141P, built between 1942 and 1952, which had the highest recorded cylinder efficiency (17 per cent) of any steam locomotive in the world, achieved by light-weight piston valves rather than by poppet valves.

The first 2-8-2s began to appear during a very difficult period. One was almost immediately destroyed by Allied bombing, and many were stored,

deliberately parted from their tenders, in relatively safe locations. Altogether 358 were authorised, 200 for construction after the war commencing in 1948. Forty, ordered from the leading French builders, Schneider et Cie of Le Creusot, were subsequently re-ordered as 35 modified versions of the PLM 241C four-cylinder compound 4-8-2. It was a measure of the chronic material shortages afflicting French industry immediately after World War Two that although approved in July 1945, the magnificent 241Ps were delivered over a protracted four year period, between May 1948 and July 1952. As a consequence they were not employed on the routes originally envisaged, owing to intervening electrification.

The provision of mechanical stokers on these 4-8-2s, achieved within weight restrictions by substituting a steel for a copper inner firebox, greatly increased their potential, which nevertheless still fell short of what Chapelon had recently shown to be possible. His 4-8-0s were not acceptable in every part of France, however, partly on account of their poppet valves with which some depots were unfamiliar. There have been conflicting reports as to whether or not the 4-8-0s were too powerful for their own good and ultimately knocked themselves to pieces!

Certainly the final French four-cylinder compounds were pushing technology and materials to the limit.

Notwithstanding the provision of outwardly dished driving wheel centres there was a finely balanced compromise between available journal and crank pin dimensions, in association with crank webs of adequate thickness. Crank axle performance was poor, for instance, in the mixed traffic 141P 2-8-2s. When formulating a range of proposed post-war standard locomotives in the dark days of 1942 Chapelon therefore pressed that these should be *three*-cylinder compounds, harking back to an experimental Nord 2-6-0 built in 1887, which could well have been the progenitor also of the numerous W.M. Smith-type Midland/LMS compound 4-4-0s in Britain..

In order to evaluate the principle it was decided to completely rebuild the remarkably unsuccessful Etat three-cylinder simple 4-8-2 of 1933 as a three-cylinder compound 4-8-4. The now legendary 242A1 did not emerge until May 1946. Exhaustive tests followed, which showed it to be an outstanding performer, with a capacity little short of a contemporary American 4-8-4 of nearly twice its size!

The 1942 proposals, 4-6-4 high speed passenger, 4-8-4 heavy passenger, and 2-10-4 heavy freight, were rated at 5,000HP and were scaled down accordingly in weight when compared to the corresponding 1936 PO Midi six-cylinder proposals. By 1946, when these were given some advance publicity, they had been scaled up again to 6,000HP, and included a 2-8-4 mixed traffic engine. The 2-8-4 and 2-10-4 were to have 20 *tonne* and the 4-6-4 and 4-8-4 23 *tonne* axleloads, which would have necessitated considerable track and bridge strengthening. In fact provision was to be made in the 4-6-4,

TABLE 25
IMPROVING MAXIMUM INDICATED HORSEPOWER IN RELATION TO ENGINE WEIGHT AND GRATE AREA, FRENCH EXPRESS PASSENGER LOCOMOTIVES 1907 - 1948

YEAR	RAILWAY	CLASS	WHEEL ARR.	ENGINE WEIGHT	GRATE AREA FT²	MAX JHP	MAX IHP /TON	IHP/FT² GRATE
1907	P-O	4500	4-6-2	89.4	45.9	1873	21.0	40.8
1932	P-O	Rebuilt	4-6-2	100.3	46.2	3400	33.9	73.6
1932	P-O	4700	4-8-0	107.0	40.8	4120	38.5	101.0
1940	SNCF	240P	4-8-0	111.3	40.0	4350	39.1	108.8
1946	SNCF	242A	4-8-4	145.0	53.8	5500	37.9	102.0
1948	SNCF	241P	4-8-2	129.0	53.8	4500	34.9	83.6

This table makes an interesting comparison with Chapter 2, Table 5 which gives corresponding data for American passenger locomotives over a similar period.

which was designed for 125 mph running, to increase this further to 25 *tonnes*. All four classes were to share the same design of boiler, cylinders, and other major components, including a booster on the hind truck. Another interesting feature would have been *triple* Kylchap exhaust, as in the prototype 242A1 4-8-4. Several American features were specified, in line with a more robust approach to construction than had hitherto been the case in France. Early deliveries were to have 10-wheeled tenders with capacity for 15¾ tons of coal and 7,700 gallons of water. Following the installation of larger turntables, 12-wheeled tenders of 9,900 gallon capacity were to be provided.

The 2-10-4 was given priority and was fully designed, with provisional approval for no less than 300. Construction of two began, and cylinders were cast, when the project was abruptly cancelled by government decree. Coal consumption on the SNCF had increased dramatically during the war, as in the UK, due to poor quality and adverse operating conditions. In 1946 only 3½ million tons were imported, but in 1947 coal shortages were Europe-wide. The French government decided that the steel industry took precedence over the railways as regards coal supplies, an argument which cut little ice with Chapelon. He later pointed out that total French coal imports then amounted to 25 million tons, or about one third of total national requirements, half of which was consumed in domestic fires and by industry. The modest 3½ million tons

imported for the railways could be earmarked for express passenger locomotives, while the projected new range of French super power steam locomotives with their mechanical stokers could burn native coal.

Even in 1948 steam was by no means totally out of favour in France, for a range of inter-related 'cheap and cheerful' two-cylinder simple 2-6-0, 2-8-0 and 2-10-0 engines were outlined similar in concept to the recent Vulcan Foundry 'Liberation' 2-8-0s, for potentially rapid construction if required. In 1945 it had been envisaged that between 2,000 and 3,000 new steam locomotives would be required over the next ten years, although much of this quota was effectively taken up by the 1,340 Class 141R 2-8-2s imported from the USA and Canada during 1945-1947 (of which 17 were lost in transit). With their undeniable virtues of rugged simplicity these highly regarded engines, the very antithesis of traditional French practice, increasingly dominated the dwindling SNCF steam locomotive stock in the 1960s. In 1945 it had been calculated that 11,863 locomotives of 177 classes in 1940 would be reduced to 10,239 engines of 134 classes by 1950. With remarkable precision the steam stock was expected to reduce to 8,289 units in 1956, when some Ouest 0-6-0s of 1867 vintage were still expected to remain in use!

The severe wartime damage inflicted on the SNCF gave an added impetus during the ensuing post-war reconstruction to push ahead with major main line electrification projects. As early as November 1945 a ten year

plan to electrify 3,400 miles of track and save 2½ million tons of coal was announced. The electrification of the former Midi main line between Paris and Lyons during 1949-52 permitted the replacement of 750 steam locomotives by only 270 electrics. By 1950 SNCF coal imports had been reduced to only 370,000 tons, compared to 2¾ million tons in 1949, although this increased to 700,000 tons in 1951, when total consumption amounted to 6 million tons. By 1952 the coal burned in French locomotives amounted to only half that in the peak year of 1930.

Although pr-war electrification schemes were usually 1,500V DC, the development of 25 KV AC systems in France significantly reduced the still-high cost of main line electrification. However, for reasons of military strategy, approval to electrify the former Nord route between Paris and Lille was initially withheld. This was home to the de Caso 4-6-4s, three three-cylinder simples (Class 232R) and four four-cylinder compounds (Class 232S). An eighth engine, to have been powered by a Ljungstrom turbine (232T), was only partially fabricated when suspended due to the War. After hostilities ended it was decided to complete it as an improved four-cylinder compound. This, the celebrated 232U1, emerged in May 1949. Unusually for a French compound, it combined robust construction with comparative simplicity as regards its servo-operated steam distribution system. Capable of sustained outputs of 3,500 DBHP, a preliminary order was placed around 1951 for twenty additional

SNCF Class 241P 4-cylinder compound 4-8-2 No.241P35, delivered in June 1952. This was the last new main line compound locomotive in the world. P. Ransome Wallis Collection, NRM (PRW 8831).

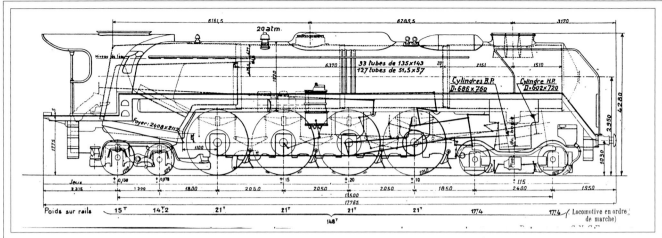

Diagram of the Chapelon 3-cylinder compound 4-8-4 242A1, finally outshopped in May 1946. The triple exhaust was unique, although it had been proposed earlier in Belgium (see Chapter 10) and specified for the proposed range of post-war SNCF 3-cylinder compounds.

engines, which in the event was not proceeded with. The Paris - Lille line was eventually electrified in late 1961, rendering all eight 4-6-4s redundant at a stroke as their 22-23 tonne axleload precluded their transfer elsewhere. Happily 232U1 has been saved for posterity.

On the other hand, the solitary Chapelon 4-8-4 saw little if any use after 1952 and was cut up in early 1961. Chapelon's outstanding 4-8-0s had all been retired during 1952-53. Retirement of the 141P 2-8-2s commenced unusually early, in 1959, only seven years after the last was built, and the class became extinct in 1968. This was partly due to redundancies as a result of increasing electrification, but the 241P 4-8-2s remained intact until 1966 and several covered over one million miles during two decades of life. It was still just possible to travel behind one in an important express after steam working had ended on British Railways.

Over five hundred 141R 2-8-2s still remained active in SNCF stock at the beginning of 1970, but ironically it was World War One vintage 2-8-0s, some of them British built, which performed the last main line steam operations in France, in September 1975, four years later than originally envisaged.

It is a matter for considerable regret that the projected post-war Chapelon three-cylinder compounds were stillborn. Combining the best of the very diverse practices of France and the United States, they would have brought a breath of fresh air into a branch of technology which was rapidly heading for oblivion. Remarkably, as will be related later in this book, the Chapelon 2-10-4, one of the great locomotive 'might have beens' of all time, was seriously re-appraised some thirty years later, in the 1970s, for possible construction both in the USA and China. Equally tantalising is the fact that in 1953, the leading French locomotive builders, Schneider et Cie, commenced design studies into an even more powerful 200 ton 7,500HP 2-10-4 for Mexico. No details have been established, but it would surely have been a compound.

It is a curious fact that no new locomotives of *entirely new* Chapelon design (as opposed to rebuilds) were built for service in France, but *were* built for overseas (for Brazil) in the early 1950s. Even in the late 1940s the Brazilians had requested diesel-electric locomotives, but the French locomotive export consortium Gelsa had persuaded them to accept two-cylinder simple steam locomotives instead. The construction of 24 4-8-4s

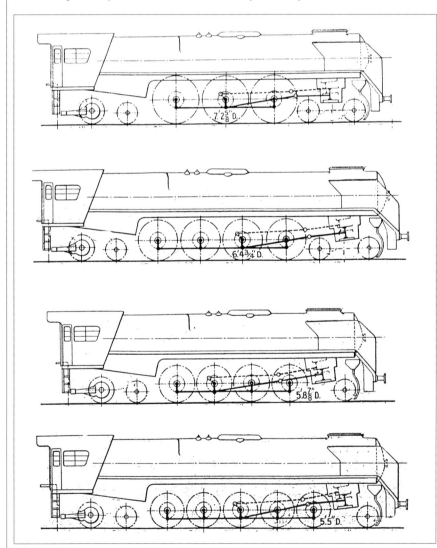

Outline diagrams for the proposed post-war SNCF 3-cylinder compounds. Their back ends especially, firebox and trailing truck with booster, would have been almost identical, although boiler lengths would seemingly have varied. Cylinders and valve gear would have been interchangeable, and the boiler pressure of all four exceptionally high at 328lb. These were to be 4-6-4 high speed passenger, 2-8-4 mixed traffic, 4-8-4 heavy passenger and 2-10-4 heavy freight.

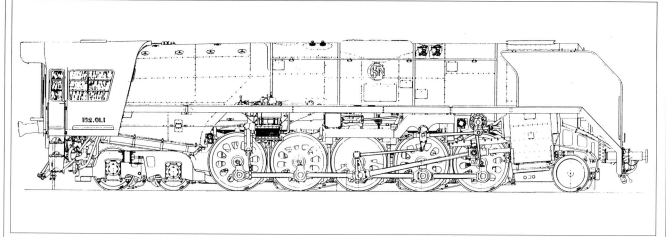

General arrangement drawing of Chapelon proposed 152P 3-cylinder compound 2-10-4, upon which initial construction work actually commenced in 1946. As in 242A1, the inside high pressure cylinder would have been served by two piston valves located beneath it.

and 66 2-8-4s for the metre gauge was divided between four French builders. On completion one of each type was road tested in France on the Reseau Breton before despatch, after which there was almost total silence. Brazil is indeed a very large country but little has been heard regarding the 4-8-4s since their arrival there. One source claims that they were withdrawn around 1956 after only 3-4 years service, although some may have moved to Bolivia. They would have made an interesting comparison with some dimensionally similar and also stoker-fired American 4-8-4s supplied in 1946. The smaller hand-fired 2-8-4s possibly fared a little better, but likewise were reputedly prone to derailment and lubrication problems. Certain railways had not wanted them in the first place, and seven 2-8-4s are said to have been scrapped unused. However, one was photographed in Bolivia, minus smoke deflectors, in 1976. One or two are believed to have ended up in Colombia. Aesthetically, with their Belpaire boilers and 12-wheeled tenders, the 4-8-4s in particular gave the strong impression of a scaled down version of the proposed Chapelon engines which never ran in France itself.

Chapelon's own ultimate objective was *triple*-expansion. A single high pressure (HP) cylinder would take *non*-superheated steam at 570lb pressure and 480°F from a firetube boiler having a water tube firebox. The steam would be respectively superheated and re-superheated between successive expansions in a single intermediate pressure (IP) cylinder and two low pressure (LP) cylinders. All four cylinders would be steam jacketed giving an anticipated overall thermal efficiency of some 50 per cent greater than that of Chapelon's more conventional three- and four-cylinder compounds with 285lb boiler pressure.

With Chapelon as ever, *efficiency* was the goal, maintenance considerations took second place. If triple-expansion was but a pipe dream in 1949 he was *still* working on the idea 20 years later in 1969, by which time, even in France, what comparatively few active steam locomotives still remained, were almost entirely two-cylinder samples!

Chapelon was particularly bitter about the hasty demise of the steam locomotive. In a letter to the author in February 1964, he stated:

'One can only regret that the craze for new motive power which arose after the war was not controlled by a little sense. The balance is now disastrous - as proved by the endlessly increasing defects in operation, the premature destruction of the enormous capital represented by the steam locomotives for the sake of their replacement by so-called 'more economic' power which has been so far from realising its promises.'

References

La Locomotive A Vapeur, A. Chapelon, Librairie J.B. Balliere et Fils; 1st Edition 1938, 914p. 2nd Edition 1952, 648p.
A New 4-6-4 Type Locomotive, French National Railways, *The Railway Gazette*, 14 March 1952, 293 - 296.
Chapelon, Genius of French Steam, H.C.B. Rogers, Ian Allan, 1972, 175p.
Les Locomotives à Vapeur Unifiées de la SNCF: Un Bilan, J.M. Combe, *Rail Magazine*, August 1982, 30 - 43.
L'Oeuvre D'André Chapelon A La SNCF Et Son Influence Mondiale, M. Maillet, Editions du Cabri, 1983, 152p.
Les 'Mountain' Francaises, M. Chavy, A. Gilbert & M. Maillet, Editions du Cabri, 1992, 224p.
The Enigmatic 141P, C. Taylor, & I. Jowett, *SNCF Society Journal*, March 1992, 14-21.

Contrasts. French-built compound 141P and North American simple expansion 141R 2-8-2s stand together at Brest in 1965. The last 'R' outlived the last 'P' by five years, and sadly no 141P now survives. P. Ransome Wallis Collection, NRM (PRW 8830).

Above. Belgian National Railways (SNCB) Type 1 4-cylinder 4-6-2 introduced in 1935. This was the largest and heaviest 4-6-2 design in Europe, with an axleload of 23.6 tons. Its distinctive 'Cock o' the North' styling would have been reproduced in subsequent projected locomotive designs ranging from 2-6-0 to 4-8-4, which in the event were not built. SNCB
Below. Incorporating many modern features the Great Northern Railway of Ireland Class V5 were the most advanced, and last, 4-4-0 locomotives to be built anywhere in the world. However, they were soon displaced by diesel railcars between Belfast and Dublin. Beyer Peacock & Co.

Chapter 10
EUROPEAN MISCELLANY

Several European countries quietly went their own way as regards steam locomotive development. In relation to its relatively small size, Belgium for example, made a remarkable contribution with respect to major design features, - the *Belpaire* firebox, *Walschaerts* valve gear, and *Lemaître* exhaust.

The high point of Belgian steam locomotive design was reached in 1935 on the Belgian National Railways (SNCB) with the introduction of the Type 1 4-6-2, Europe's heaviest Pacific. In initial schemings, the engine had begun life in mid-1932 as a four-cylinder compound, but it was later changed to a four-cylinder simple. This followed a visit to Britain by two Belgian engineers who were impressed by the new Stanier LMS 'Princess' 4-6-2s, of which the first pair had newly entered traffic. Furthermore the front end styling was clearly inspired by the also new LNER 2-8-2 COCK O' THE NORTH. Engine weight was 124 tons and grate area 54ft^2, much higher than the corresponding dimensions for any LMS 4-6-2 or LNER 2-8-2.

These impressive 4-6-2s were largely employed between Brussels and Ostend, until 1962. In capacity they would have been eclipsed, however, by projected 5,000HP three-cylinder 4-8-4 passenger and 2-10-2 heavy freight locomotives outlined in early 1940. Both would have been equipped with *triple* Kylchap exhaust and mechanical stokers and the 4-8-4, with 5ft 11in coupled wheels, was intended for duties in the heavily graded Luxembourg/Ardennes region. The tenders would have been unusually large, running on two six-wheeled trucks and having the capacity for 11,440 gallons of water and 15 tons of coal. Overall length would have been 94ft 9in.

The little known mastermind behind these proposals, Raoul Notesse, who had been closely involved with the Type 1 4-6-2, sadly died in London at the early age of 45 towards the end of World War Two. Even so, neither the 4-8-4 nor 2-10-2 featured in a 1942 locomotive standardisation scheme for implementation on the SNCB after the war had ended. This was to include the Type 1 together with a smaller wheeled version, and a curious inside-cylinder mixed traffic 4-6-0 with wide firebox. Also shown was the 1939 streamlined inside-cylinder 4-4-2, heavy 2-8-0, and light 2-6-0, all with wide fireboxes. In January 1945 it was proposed to order nearly 900 2-6-0s, 4-6-0s, and 2-8-0s straight off the drawing board from the remarkably extensive Belgian locomotive industry, which was still preoccupied with building German Class 52 'Kreigslok' 2-10-0s. In addition, 300 powerful 2-8-0s were being built in Canada, and so it was initially decided to scale down orders to 40 4-6-0s and 60 2-8-0s, from seven builders. In the event, even this was not proceeded with and in fact no new steam locomotive of Belgian design was built after 1939. By 1951 main line electrification was under way, and the first diesels were introduced; by 1958 it was proposed to eliminate steam within ten years. With some ceremony the last steam working on the SNCB took place on 20 December 1966.

Remarkably the first *railway-*built locomotive in the world had been constructed in Dublin as early as 1841, where a century later the peak of Irish steam locomotive design was reached in the magnificent Great Southern Railways '800' class three-cylinder 4-6-0s built at Inchicore Works in 1939. In size these equalled if not exceeded the Great Western 'Kings'. Scarcely had the trio made its *début* than, despite Irish neutrality, World War Two frustrated any real opportunity to exploit the full potential of this outstanding design between Dublin and Cork. During the war and after it, coal supplies were a major problem in the Irish Republic, which was solved by dieselisation in the 1950s. This policy effectively overtook attempts to devise a steam locomotive capable of burning Ireland's prime indigenous fuel, turf. Under O.V.S. Bulleid, CME of the Coras Iompair Eireann since 1949, preliminary experiments had been made around 1952 with an elderly 2-6-0. As a result of data obtained a double-ended 0-6-6-0T, loosely based on Bulleid's earlier 'Leader' class for the Southern Railway, was designed and a prototype completed at Inchicore Works in 1957. Although tested, the engine never entered regular traffic and a once planned fleet of fifty such engines was not proceeded with. Steam operations on the CIE ceased in 1963.

In the north in 1947 the Great Northern Railway of Ireland ordered ten inside-cylinder 0-6-0s and 4-4-0s and five three-cylinder 4-4-0s which were delivered in 1948. The latter (Class VS) were the last 4-4-0s to be built anywhere in the world, but

CP 4-8-0 No. 836, built in 1947 (one of six engines supplied by no fewer than three Spanish builders), the last new steam locomotive to be built for service in Portugal. CP.

proved to be a short-sighted gesture as all too soon on the Belfast - Dublin expresses they were superseded by diesel multiple units, whose economy and success pointed the way for the subsequent extensive adoption of DMUs on British Railways, from 1954 onwards.

The last main line steam locomotives to be built for service in Ireland were eighteen 2-6-4Ts built at Derby Works by the LMS and BR between 1949 and 1950 for the Northern Counties Committee (after 1949 a part of the Ulster Transport Authority). Directly related to the original Fowler LMS 2-6-4Ts of 1927,

examples remained in service until 2 May 1970, nearly two years after the cessation of steam working on British Railways.

Spain had its own special problems in the 1940s and 1950s in the aftermath of its Civil War. The RENFE initiated a locomotive standardisation policy in 1949 and all but ten new steam locomotives built thereafter were eight-coupled tender engines of 2-8-2, 4-8-0, 4-8-2, and 4-8-4 type. The 2-8-2 was designed in Glasgow by the North British Locomotive Company, which adapted it from the Indian XD 2-8-2. The first 25 were delivered in 1953, together with one hundred sets

of parts which were assembled by Spanish builders. These were all coal burners, but later engines manufactured entirely in Spain up to 1960 were oil fired. Indeed, despite initially unpromising experiments with oil burning in 1947, from 1952 a significant number of existing and new RENFE steam locomotives were arranged for oil firing.

The highlights of the fleet were the ten magnificent oil-burning 4-8-4s, delivered in 1955-56 for service between Madrid and Irun, which due to increasing electrification were largely out of a job by the late 1960s. On test, one developed nearly 4,200IHP, a remarkably high figure for a European two-cylinder locomotive. The last new steam locomotives on the RENFE were ten oil - burning 2-8-2+2-8-2 Garratts of 1930 design, which were delivered by Babcock and Wilcox in 1961, nine years after they had been ordered. At the dawn of the 1960s the RENFE steam stock still topped 3,300 and included a highly diverse collection of engines from many different European and American builders, some literally a century old. Inevitably this was soon to change. Between 1964 and 1969 2,400 steam locomotives were condemned, 1,300 during 1966-67 alone, in a drive to eliminate coal burners by mid-1968. By 1971 only 440 remained; all but ten were oil burners and steam working on the RENFE ended in mid - 1975. The last 4-8-4s had lingered until 1973.

Conversely, in Italy on account of increasing electrification, no new steam locomotives had been built for the State Railway (FS) since 1927, yet

SJ 3-cylinder 4-8-0 built by Nohab in 1947. Although the last tender locomotives to be built for service in Sweden, the same builder supplied twenty light oil-fired 2-6-4Ts as late as 1952-53 for branch line service. SJ.

The penultimate in Irish steam locomotive design, the Great Southern Railways '800' class 3-cylinder 4-6-0 of 1939, pictured in CIE condition. M.D. England Collection, NRM.

dwindling numbers could still be found in active use at the dawn of the 1980s. Furthermore, during 1953-54 the unremarkable Italian locomotive industry built the most powerful standard gauge steam locomotives ever for service in Europe for Greece, as a part of a post-war reparations treaty.

It is not clear by whom or where the huge two-cylinder 2-10-2 design was initiated, primarily for *passenger* service between Athens and Salonika. In November 1950 Vulcan Foundry in England did much estimation work on it, and as later built by Ansaldo and Breda (ten each) the engines

incorporated the patent SCOAP coupled wheel centres sponsored by Vulcan. Despite their somewhat American *mièn* the chassis consisted of plate frames 1½in thick. Grate area amounted to 60ft², but whereas the Ansaldo engines were oil burners, those from Breda had mechanical

Iberian excellence, the first Spanish National Railways (RENFE) 4-8-4 stands immaculate at the builders, La Maquinista, soon after completion in late 1955. Nine more engines followed during 1956, but the activities of all were rapidly curtailed by advancing electrification between Madrid and Irun. La Maquinista.

2-10-2s could be found in France, Germany, Spain, Romania and even Turkey by 1945, but all these designs were eclipsed by the huge Italian built engines for Greece. Photographs of these in original condition are rare because of the modifications which had to be made soon after delivery. These were eventually drastic, and the engines were reboilered between 1956 and 1959; No.1017 was recorded after its reconstruction in 1958 by Henschel. Despite the work, some saw little further service. P. Ransome Wallis Collection, NRM (PRW 5771).

stokers. These proved so unreliable that they had to be removed in 1955, which then necessitated the presence of two or even three firemen.

That apart, track inequalities were transmitted through the frames to the boilers, causing the firebox throatplates to crack. Replacement boilers were ordered from Henschel in 1956 and fitted over the next three years. Most were now oil burners but they were never satisfactory and the 2-10-2s were gradually retired between 1964 and 1976. A significant factor in this flawed design was probably its construction date; an acute steel shortage could have caused a resort to inferior materials.

The last new main line steam locomotives to be built for service in Europe were two 2-10-0s completed by

The last Scandinavian steam locomotive was 2-8-2 No.1096, delivered to the Finnish State Railways (VR) in December 1957.

Above. The last new main line steam locomotives for service in Europe were delivered to countries at the continent's eastern and western extremities during 1961, and both were oil-burners. In Spain the RENFE received ten 2-8-2+2-8-2 Garratts from Babcock & Wilcox, which had been ordered nine years earlier; in the event they barely outlasted the decade. P. Ransome Wallis Collection, NRM (PRW 5675). *Below*. Later in that year the Turkish State Railways (TCDD) completed two 2-10-0s of German design in its own workshops, the first of which is pictured here. TCDD.

the Turkish State Railways (TCDD) at its workshop at Sivas and Eskisehir in late 1961. These were also the only locomotives ever built in Turkey. Curiously, like the Spanish Garratts completed earlier in the same year, they were oil-fired for by this date the main justification for prolonged steam locomotive construction was usually the availability of cheap *coal* supplies.

Coal was always an expensive commodity in central and northern Europe. Thus the last main line steam locomotives for service in Switzerland and Italy were built as early as 1917 and 1927 respectively. Electrification was quickly to the fore in both countries, although steam working was to linger on for many years after

World War Two. As a last great flourish, Austria produced a highly distinctive passenger 2-8-4 in 1929, and Norway did the same six years later.

Whereas the Austrian engine was a two-cylinder simple, that in Norway was a four-cylinder compound with the prime intention of producing as powerful a locomotive as possible within an exacting 15½ tons axleload limit. In Denmark four-cylinder compound 4-6-2s of 1914 Swedish design were built as late as 1950, whereas in Sweden itself post-war construction was confined to ten three-cylinder 4-8-0s in 1947 and twenty 2-6-4Ts in 1952-53. Sweden maintained a substantial strategic

reserve of carefully 'mothballed' steam locomotives until the early 1990s, some of which had reputedly been equipped with effectively brand new boilers.

Of all the Scandinavian countries only Finland continued to built new steam locomotives on a significant scale after World War Two and did so until 1957, when the last of its elegant yet unpretentious series of 4-6-2s and 2-8-2s entered service supplied by each of the country's two builders.

References
Vapeur en Belgique. Vol.2, P. Dambly, Blanchart & Ciè, 1994, 352p.
Steam on the RENFE, L.G. Marshall, Macmillan, 1965, 195p.

South African Railways Class 25NC 4-8-4, its remarkable resemblance to the New York Central 4-8-4 readily apparent. SAR.

SAR Class 25C 4-8-4 with condensing tender, at Cape Town, soon after delivery in 1953, when coal in South Africa was the cheapest in the world. SAR.

Chapter 11
AFRICA, AUSTRALASIA AND JAPAN

Several railway administrations in Africa would probably have maintained a pro-steam policy well into the 1960s, if not beyond, had they still been able to obtain new steam locomotives. In the early 1970s a team of consultants advised the Benguela Railway that the ideal motive power for its requirements was steam, if such could still be obtained at a realistic price. By this time only Japanese builders were prepared to take on a major steam order, but *at a price*, quoting something like £250,000 for a 4-8-2+2-8-4 Garratt. Over a decade before, in 1961, the South African Railways had sought quotations for 100 new 4-8-4s, and a large number of light 4-8-2s, but there was no realistic response, even though it was only three years since North British, Beyer, Peacock and Henschel had been building large new Garratts.

The 4-8-4s represented the ultimate in South African steam locomotive development, and constituted a logical conclusion to a long sequence of 4-8-2s, the first of which had appeared as early as 1909. The 4-8-2 had reached its limit in the generally similar 15E, 15F and 23 classes with 62 ft² grates and 18 ton axleload, introduced in the late 1930s. After World War Two a 4-10-4 was briefly considered but a total of 140 4-8-4s was ordered from North British and Henschel in 1951, of which 90 were to have condensing tenders for operation across the arid Karoo desert. Ever since the 1920s, as on certain Australian railways, South African locomotives had incorporated American characteristics, and in the 4-8-4s this process became complete, with a specification for cast steel engine beds for both engines and tenders, and roller bearings throughout. Indeed the result remarkably resembled the New York Central 4-8-4s, even down to the smoke deflector plates.

Delivery was delayed and the condensing engines were not without their teething troubles. Ultimately, 600-700 mile runs between water stops were achieved as per specification. However the engines were expensive to run and were latterly unpopular with their crews. Following replacement by diesels most were rebuilt, from 1975, as non-condensers with conventional draughting arrangements.

The SAR was also the world's largest user of the Beyer Garratt articulated locomotive. After the appearance of the heavy 18½ ton axleload GL class 4-8-2+2-8-4 in 1929-30, development temporarily lapsed in favour of a powerful rigid frame 2-10-4 in 1937, which was not developed further. Between 1938 and 1958 large numbers of light axleload (mainly 15 tons) 4-8-2+2-8-4s with a wide route availability were obtained from British and German builders, and there was no desire nor attempt to produce a modern South African 'Super Garratt' due to electrification of major routes.

During the 1960s SAR steam locomotive withdrawals were only modest, for increasing traffic was covered by extending electrification which had been initiated in the 1920s. Almost in accord with the 'new decade syndrome' experienced elsewhere at other times, in 1970 the SAR seriously began to think in terms of replacing its still extensive steam locomotive fleet. By 1972 a timescale of fifteen years was spoken of, and despite South Africa's then isolated political status and the world energy crisis soon afterwards, large numbers of main line diesel locomotives were ordered, despite a government directive to *private* industry to conserve oil consumption! At the beginning of 1972 almost all the 1,400 4-8-2s built for the SAR between 1909 and 1948 were still in service, and few Garratts had so far been scrapped.

Twenty years earlier only costing one-sixth that of British coal, by now, even in South Africa, available coal was declining in quality. However the main problem was the labour intensive nature of steam locomotive operation and its associated expense and increasing unreliability. However, following a second sharp rise in the world price of oil in 1979, it was calculated that under certain conditions steam locomotive operating costs in South Africa were highly competitive with those of diesel and electric traction. By this time, however, the SAR steam fleet was quickly diminishing, and although scheduled for elimination by the mid-1980s it had still not totally disappeared ten years later. Relatively new Garratts were drastically purged during the 1970s, the last of the once numerous GMAMs going in 1984, on account of their high maintenance costs. The 4-8-4s remained largely intact until well into the 1980s. By 1995, no fewer than 30 were preserved.

Between 1973 and 1980 all but two of the condensing 4-8-4s were rebuilt with conventional draughting. After initial experiments, 85 were reconstructed according to the pattern typified by No.3514, seen here at De Aar on 14 July 1984. E. Talbot.

TABLE 26

SOUTH AFRICAN RAILWAYS MOTIVE POWER TRENDS
1950 - 1990

YEAR	STEAM	DIESEL	ELECTRIC	TOTAL
1950	2540	2	216	2758
1960	2742	76	472	3290
1970	2473	379	1112	3964
1980	1702	1375	1911	4988
1985	775	1635	2198	4724
1990	204	1413	2341	3958

A neighbouring major operator of Beyer Garratt locomotives was the Rhodesia Railways, which ultimately operated engines having the double 2-6-2, 4-6-4, 2-8-2 and 4-8-2 configurations. The latter were the 20 class, dimensionally very similar to the SAR GMA/GMAM class, and likewise were equipped with mechanical stokers. The first had been delivered during 1954. Even as a second series was being built, an order for a further 34, which would have brought the grand total up to 95 was under negotiation. It was abruptly abandoned due to the collapse of the all-important copper industry in 1957. Had this order gone ahead, construction would assuredly have proceeded well into 1959 if not 1960, by which time Beyer, Peacock had no other firm steam orders in prospect.

As it was the first series was soon plagued with boiler problems and litigation ensued between the RR and the builders. There was talk of shipping back a boiler for Beyer, Peacock to examine, or even the latter supplying welded replacements.

Litigation dragged on through the 1960s, which successively witnessed the declaration of UDI by the Smith Government in 1965, followed by the demise of Beyer, Peacock.

The problem could presumably be put down to poor workmanship, as the boilers were virtually identical with those, apparently trouble free, on the South African GMA, and New South Wales AD60. Both the latter designs also incorporated cast steel engine beds, whereas the Rhodesian engines had bar frames, the alignment of which on some engines was also poor. As if all this was not enough, almost as soon as the class had entered service there were major steaming problems, and throughout their lives the engines did not really live up to their imposing appearance.

Electrification was considered in the late 1950s, but the expenditure involved made it non-viable and there was concern what to do with some virtually brand new steam locomotives. So, during the 1970s, dieselisation (with a view to eliminating steam working by 1980)

rapidly increased. Prompted by the acute problem of procuring spare parts for its diesel fleet, when that year dawned for political reasons Garratts of each of the major types were being actively refurbished by RESCO in Bulawayo, in order to give a further 10-15 years of service. A total of 87 Garratts were scheduled for rejuvenation, including 19 4-8-2+2-8-4s. At one stage during the early 1980s there were even serious proposals to have a hundred roller bearing 2-10-2s built, also by RESCO.

A remarkably large number of 4-8-2+2-8-4 Beyer Garratts were built for several railway administrations in Southern Africa during the 1950s, some under sub-contract from Beyer, Peacock & Co. This included a remarkable 2ft 6ins gauge design with only 5 ton axleload for Sierra Leone. At the other end of the scale the largest and most outstanding emanated from the Manchester works for the metre gauge East African Railways, in 1955. This was the 59 class, originally ordered in 1950, which attained a maximum axleload of 21 tons by 'tapering up' of the individual coupled axleloads from 19 tons, and by omitting altogether reciprocating balance (which later had to be incorporated in the interests of smooth running at speed). After 1945 the EAR had increasingly resorted to oil firing as a consequence of the unreliability of South African coal supplies during World War Two, but provision was made to revert to coal burning should circumstances change.

Introduced at the height of the 'Mau Mau' troubles in Kenya, the 59 class was employed on the heavily graded single track Nairobi - Mombasa main line. Such was the rapidly expanding traffic that scarcely had it appeared than the railway began to

The world's most numerous Garratt class was the SAR Class GMA/GMAM 4-8-2+2-8-4, of which 120 were supplied by Henschel, Beyer, Peacock, and North British between 1952 and 1958. Many ran coupled to a supplementary water tank as shown here. SAR.

Egyptian State Railways oil-fired 4-6-2 built in France during 1954-55 to imperial dimensions. SACM.

plan in its own drawing office a considerably larger Garratt, with 27 ton axleload an estimated 372 tons total and 123ft long.

At least three alternative schemes were produced during 1956-57, one a 4-8-2+2-8-4. The other two were to be 4-8-4+4-8-4, and one of these would have an SAR-style condensing tender. Doubtless Beyer, Peacock would have welcomed such an order at this difficult time, but matters never progressed that far. The inevitable need to upgrade track and infrastructure to take such large engines, which would almost have rivalled the big American Mallets, was circumvented instead by resorting to diesel-electric traction in multiple. As it was, after 1960 the 59 class became the most powerful steam locomotives in active use in the world, following the recent demise of the last Mallets in the USA. Later in the decade their performance was further enhanced by the provision of Giesl ejectors, which were widely applied by the EAR at that time. Whatever, by the early 1970s steam traction was scheduled for elimination by about 1975; in the event

it held on until mid-1980. The steam locomotive vanished relatively early in Northern Africa. In Algeria it had disappeared possibly as early as 1950. Egypt on the other hand placed substantial orders for new units after World War Two, including even streamlined Sentinel steam railcars. Its final contract was placed in France in 1952, for 20 4-6-2s which were delivered in 1954-55 for high speed service between Cairo and Alexandria. Before 1914 the Egyptian State Railways had imported best Welsh steam coal, but latterly it employed a by-product of oil refining termed *mazout*. The new 4-6-2s (which had originally been envisaged as three-cylinder 4-6-4s) were possibly unique in having long narrow fireboxes set behind the trailing coupled axle, which also contained long combustion chambers in order to reduce tube length. Shortly after the 4-6-2s entered service the Suez Crisis occurred, and soon after that the ESR, which had obtained diesel-electric locomotives from Britain as early as 1949, rapidly dieselised. Main line steam working officially ceased in early 1963. Unlike

Africa, Australia did possess an indigenous locomotive industry, whilst several of its major railways enjoyed locomotive building capabilities. This had even extended to producing large 4-8-4s, not to mention some disastrous narrow gauge 4-8-2+2-8-4 Garratts during World War Two. Nevertheless, owing to serious arrears and internal shortages soon after the end of the War, each placed large orders for new steam locomotives in Great Britain. This was understandable enough at the time in view of the desire to replace ageing war-weary locomotives, but it quickly came to be much regretted in at least two instances.

In July 1949 the New South Wales Government Railway ordered twenty five 4-8-4+4-8-4 standard gauge Garratt locomotives of new design from Beyer, Peacock & Co. In August 1950 the order was increased to fifty and the first two engines were unloaded in Sydney in June 1952. The makers commissioned a documentary colour film recording their design, construction and entry into service in anticipation of their approaching centenary in 1954, but by the time the

New South Wales Government Railways Class AD60 4-8-4+4-8-4 Beyer Garratt No.6002 (built in 1952), pictured in service in 1970. Befittingly, No.6042 of this class, the highest numbered steam locomotive on Australia's largest railway system, worked the country's last scheduled steam working in early 1973. However it was not the same engine of that number which had entered service in 1956, but a replacement assembled as recently as 1969 from the plethora of spare parts remaining from the part-cancelled order. Regrettably a unique opportunity to photograph officially the two 6042s together was missed owing to a misunderstanding at the time. P. Ransome Wallis Collection, NRM (PRW 10153).

film made its *début*, things had turned distinctly sour. Although in many ways the most advanced Beyer Garratts yet built, incorporating cast steel engine beds (imported from the USA) for the first time, and mechanical stokers, the design met concerted opposition from the footplate trade unions (for one reason or another) for several years. The initial criticism concerned the hot and smoky conditions in the cab when working through tunnels, which resulted in at least one engine receiving an experimental snorkel device. The remedy proved to be simply to work bunker first.

Significantly, the first diesel-electric locomotives had begun to appear on the NSWGR the year before the first Garratt, and were very well received. Despite the existence of the New South Wales coalfield the 'coal factor' was not as strong as might be thought. There had been disruptions to coal supplies through industrial action during the 1940s, as in the USA and 20 Baldwin 2-8-2s (eventually delivered to the NSWGR, much delayed, in 1952) came as oil-burners. Attempts were made to cut back on the Garratt order in early 1954 to the obvious chagrin of the builders. In the event, in addition to the thirty seven already in service, a further five were despatched and assembled in Australia, the last entering traffic in January 1957. Three more arrived as complete sets of parts, and two as incomplete sets, The last three being cancelled altogether. Incorporating a variety of modifications, which were

applied to some engines and not to others, the engines then gave sterling service until retired between 1969 and 1973. No.6042 performed the last rites on 24 February 1973, which was also the final scheduled main line steam working in Australia as a whole, although this engine was actually a 1969 assemblage of spare parts!.

A more woeful tale concerned the Class R 4-6-4s of the 5ft 3in gauge Victorian State Railways, the full story of which was only revealed by two meticulous researchers, R.M. Carlisle and R.L. Abbott, in 1985 in their book *Hudson Power*. The engines were originally to have been built by the railway itself in its own Newport Shops, but owing to a variety of problems an order was placed for fifty with the North British Locomotive Company in Glasgow in September 1949. Delivery was to have been made at the rate of ten per month, commencing in December 1950. Almost immediately, in January 1950, the order was increased to seventy. The first engine was completed in March 1951 and unloaded in Melbourne at the end of May; in no time acrimonious correspondence passed between contractor and customer. The 4-6-4s were despatched fully erected as deck cargo, and because they incorporated roller bearings, detailed instructions were issued by the Australian CME concerning stowage to prevent damage in transit. These, it seems, were wholly disregarded both by NBL and the shipping authorities, and the bearings indeed suffered damage through

movement and ingress of sea water. To add insult to injury, on arrival when the engines were being prepared for service, evidence of poor workmanship came to light. In several cases this considerably delayed entry into traffic, by which time diesels were arriving in force. Many 4-6-4s were stored after 1956, when two were actually retired after only four years, never to run again. Such was the magnitude of the situation that it was officially 'covered up', for even after 1960 only 21 out of the original 70 saw any further use. Overall, the design enjoyed a revenue earning operational span of 17½ years, with engines averaging only 175,000 miles each - a mere 14,300 miles per annum.

Although discreetly concealed for so many years, the Victoria 4-6-4 saga reflected badly on the largest British locomotive builder. The underlying reasons could probably be traced back to the late 1930s. NBL's workforce declined from an all time peak of 8,262 in 1919, to merely 389 in 1932 when no locomotives were built. When trade modestly picked up a few years later, difficulty was experienced in recruiting skilled staff. If this was a problem in 1938, it must have been more so in 1951, a time of full employment with Clydeside enjoying what would prove to be its last major shipbuilding boom. Other builders were not immune, but one locomotive order which did uphold the long tradition of British excellence was that placed by the 3ft 6in gauge Western Australian Government

Victorian Railways 4-6-4 No.707 was the last of the 70 R class engines to enter traffic, in early 1954, by which time it was already three years old. It ran experimentally at first, burning pulverised brown coal on the STUG system, when a sudden collapse in the price of oil rendered this both uneconomic and unnecessary. There are several 4-6-4s now preserved, one of which may be re-gauged from 5ft 3in to 4ft 8½in gauge, a possibility provided for when originally designed. No.707 was recorded at Melbourne in 1970. P. Ransome Wallis Collection, NRM (PRW 10161).

New Zealand Government Railways 4-8-2 No.1274, the last new steam locomotive to be built in New Zealand (December 1956). NZGR.

With 5ft 9in diameter 'Boxpok' type coupled wheels, these engines could attain 82mph, and represented the high point of Japanese steam locomotive development. Replete with mechanical stokers these had a look of being 'pocket NYC Hudsons', and the similarity was no coincidence. The reconstruction was masterminded by Colonel Howard Hill (1895-1983) who is better remembered for his World War Two US Army 2-8-2s and 0-6-0Ts. As part of the US Military Administration in post-war Japan, Hill's brief was to survey the railway system and restore it to full efficiency as quickly as possible.

Railways for 24 2-8-2 freight locomotives. This was the only facet of a grand plan which envisaged 4-6-2/4-6-4 passenger, 2-8-2/2-8-4 freight, and large Beyer Garratt locomotives actually to materialise, and even here some seven years elapsed between initial conception (in 1949) and the final engine entering traffic in November 1956. Both Vulcan Foundry and Beyer, Peacock & Co. actively responded to enquiries from the WAGR in March 1950. An order was placed for some 2-8-2s with Beyer Peacock, who were currently happily overwhelmed with steam orders, including sixty 4-8-2s for the WAGR. When the order was increased to 24 engines in late 1951, the builder felt unable to accommodate it and sub-let the engines to Robert Stephenson & Hawthorn in Darlington. These exceptionally handsome engines, whose boilers were comparable in size with those of a BR Class 9F 2-10-0, were designed to burn the local Collie coal, which they also hauled in large quantities.

In early 1971 the WAGR announced it intended to retain a strategic reserve of steam locomotives. Yet in mid-June twenty 2-8-2s were withdrawn at a stroke and broken up. A Class V 2-8-2 operated the last steam working on the railway on Christmas Eve 1971, although the four remaining engines were not formally condemned until August 1972.

The disparate Australian state railways were remarkably consistent with each other with regard to the run down of steam power, a phenomenon to which even the distant New Zealand Government Railways conformed. The NZGR took delivery of its final steam locomotive in late 1956, yet eliminated steam working only fifteen years later in 1971.

Steam locomotive construction for domestic service ceased remarkably early on the 3ft 6in gauge in Japan, in 1948 with five 2-10-4 banking tanks. Having a unique wheel arrangement for a tank engine, these were very quickly displaced by electrification. Redeployed, they were finally retired in 1962, partly on account of the low grade materials employed in their construction.

The long established Imperial Japanese Government Railways were reconstituted as the Japanese National Railways during 1948/49. The JNR opted not to continue with major steam locomotive development. Japanese coal was of poor quality, having low calorific value, c.8000 BThU/lb, and was very dusty. On account of the 3ft 6in gauge, many older Japanese locomotive designs had inadequate grate areas and so the coal was burned very inefficiently with a high proportion ejected straight up the chimney. Electrification, already well established, was seen as the future policy, not least on account of the availability of hydro-electricity, although on occasions this could prove vulnerable to drought conditions. The changeover effectively began in 1952 and took 25 years to achieve.

There was also a surplus of 2-8-2 goods engines built at the end of the War, some of which were rebuilt as either 2-8-4s or 4-6-4s. This helped get around the chronic materials shortage which existed in Japan immediately after World War Two. A total of 49 'heavy' 4-6-4s of Class C62 were produced during 1948-49 by utilising the still new boilers of recently built Class D52 'heavy' 2-8-2s.

This same Administration at the time of the Korean War issued a *verbal* order to leading Japanese locomotive manufacturers for standard gauge 2-8-2s. By the time that these had been completed they were no longer required and so they were offered for sale. No interest in the engines was expressed, however, and they were cut up unused, even though they were almost identical with JF 2-8-2s currently being built in China! Despite such *contretemps*, the Japanese locomotive industry remained in the steam market for longer than most, until well into the 1960s in fact, when it supplied new engines to Patagonia and Indonesia.

References

Steam Locomotives of the South African Railways, Vol 2, 1910 - 1955, D.F. Holland, David & Charles, 1972, 144p.
Steam Locomotives of the East African Railways, R. Ramaer, David & Charles, 1974, 96p.
The 60 Class, K.T. Groves, H.J. Wright, & M. Morahan, New South Wales Transport Museum, 1994, 226p.
Hudson Power, R. Carlisle & W. Abbott, Australian Railway Historical Society (Victoria Division), 1985, 156p.
A History of WAGR Steam Locomotives, A. Gunzburg, Australian Railway Historical Society (Western Australia Division) 1984, 156p.
The Roots of Steam, Steam Locomotives in Japan 1872 - 1972, Vol 4, S. Usui, Koyusha, 1978, 200p.
The Red Devil and Other Tales from the Age of Steam, Chapter 1, D. Wardale, pub. author, 1998, 522p.
Steam Revitalised (Rhodesia), E.D. Hamer, *The Railway Magazine*, February 1980, 64-65.

Nearly forty years old, the prototype Class WP 4-6-2 No.7200 (BLW, 1947), heads a Daund-Manmad train at Shrigonda Road, on 17 February 1986. The progenitor of some 5,500 broad and metre gauge 4-6-2s and 2-8-2s built over a period of twenty-five years, this engine is now preserved. L.G. Marshall.

Class YP 4-6-2 No.2870 (Telco, 1970), was not only the world's last 'Pacific' to be built, but also the world's last new steam passenger locomotive. Highly decorated and, unofficially named 'Evening Star', the engine stands at Lallaguda depot, South Central Railway, on 26 February 1988. L.G. Marshall.

Chapter 12

FAR EAST FINALE - INDIA AND CHINA

By the early 1960s the steam locomotive was extinct in North America and in headlong retreat in Europe, whilst no new orders whatever were outstanding in either Africa or Australia. In contrast, new construction continued to proceed apace in India for the simple practical reasons that traffic levels continued to increase. Steam locomotives could be built cheaply and indigenously to meet this, and fuel supplies did not have to be imported for them.

Prior to 1924 Indian locomotive practice mirrored British, most engines being supplied by British builders with only a relatively small number erected locally, for both the broad (5ft 6in) and metre gauges. Following incursions by the American locomotive industry in 1900 attempts were made to standardise Indian locomotives for ease of manufacture and from 1903 a range of supposedly standard 4-4-0, 4-4-2, 0-6-0, 4-6-0 and 2-8-0 designs were evolved which in actual practice varied widely. At this time it was normal practice for Indian railways to import Welsh steam coal.

In order to utilise lower quality indigenous Indian coal, in 1924 prototype broad gauge 4-6-2 and 2-8-2 locomotives were supplied by Kitson & Co. in England and the Baldwin Locomotive Works in the USA, and a new range of standard locomotive designs with wide fireboxes, the X series, was subsequently evolved. These were as follows:-

TABLE 27

STANDARD INDIAN 5FT 6IN GAUGE 'X' SERIES STANDARD LOCOMOTIVES

Class		Axle load tons	Grate Area ft²
XA 4-6-2	Passenger	13.0	32.0
XB 4-6-2	"	17.0	45.0
XC 4-6-2	"	19.75	51.0
XD 2-8-2	Freight	17.0	45.0
XE 2-8-2	"	22.5	60.0

Although the two 2-8-2 designs proved highly satisfactory and were still being ordered in the 1940s, the 4-6-2s were not so outstanding. They displayed poor riding qualities at speed which resulted in a sequence of major derailments with high loss of life, and displayed an alarming susceptibility to plate frame fractures. During World War Two a large number of 2-8-2 locomotives with bar frames were supplied from North America, which provided the general inspiration for a new post-war range of Indian Standard locomotives.

The keystone was to be the Class WP 4-6-2, for the broad gauge to which the Vulcan Foundry in England devoted much energy calculating and estimating in late 1946, as it regarded the Indian market as its special preserve. However, a pilot order for sixteen engines was passed to Baldwin in January 1947, probably because Vulcan was fully booked with orders and BLW could deliver the same year. North British of Glasgow received an order for no fewer than 125 WPs in April 1947, which was later transferred to North America and replaced by an order for 100 WG 2-8-2 freight equivalents. NBL completed

Rather curious was the construction of 94 light Class WL 4-6-2s at Chittaranjan between 1966 and 1968, replicas of a pilot batch supplied by Vulcan Foundry in 1955. This is a somewhat embellished late example, No.15087, at Bathinda, on 26 November 1979. L.G. Marshall.

the first of these in 1950 and the WGs proceeded eventually to become numerically the largest single class of steam locomotive in the British Commonwealth, with examples built by no fewer than eight countries in three continents.

Although pre-war 4-6-2s had been built to 21½ ton, and 2-8-2s to 22½ ton axleloads, the new post-war WP and WG designs were tailored to an 18½ ton axleload in order to work relatively light 300 ton passenger and 1,500 ton freight trains respectively. The *rationale* behind working light trains lay in the need to employ low grade Indian coal with high ash content, having a calorific value of 11,000 BThU per lb. This required large firegrates (46ft^2) at the upper limit of manual firing capacity. The various advantages of working light as opposed to heavy trains was enumerated in 1948 thus:-

1.   *Ability to burn lower-grade coal and continue hand-firing.*
2.   *Economies in wear and tear of the track through lighter axle-loading.*
3.   *Avoidance of capital expenditure and the provision of long sidings and second lines.*
4.   *Reduction of delay at starting and stopping stations in making up trains.*
5.   *Reduction in wagon delay in awaiting full train-loads.*
6.   *Increased daily mileage of locomotives and wagons from the above causes, and also through increased ability of locomotives to make up lost time.*
7.   *Consequent quicker movement of freight.*

The disadvantages of the light train were considered to be:-

1.   *Loss of line capacity on heavy-traffic sections unless double-tracking were carried out.*
2.   *The increased number of locomotives and brake-vans required (although of smaller individual size and cost).*
3.   *Capital expenditure in increasing the reception capacity of certain yards.*
4.   *Some additional staff.*

Scaled down versions of the broad gauge 4-6-2 and 2-8-2 for the metre gauge, the YP and YG, were also evolved, to an axleload of 10 tons. Collectively these four designs represented the bulk of new steam locomotive construction for India for 25 years from 1947. In addition, in 1948, a 4-8-2+2-8-4 Beyer Garratt and 2-10-6 heavy shunting tank engine had been envisaged for both gauges which in the event never materialised. Tenders were called for twenty broad gauge Garratts in the 1954-55 programme but Beyer Peacock's quoted price was more than twice that of two German or Japanese-built 2-8-2s. Notwithstanding the very high cost of fifty Baldwin-built WGs at the same period (doubtless funded by Marshall Plan aid), Beyer's price was not accepted.

Major post-war steam locomotive proposals and actual construction for the Indian Government Railways are summarised opposite. Some later 2-8-2s were provided with roller bearings, and there were experimental applications of mechanical stokers and Giesl ejectors to selected WPs and WGs. Drawings were completed for a welded version of the WP/WG boiler but this was never put into production. Supplementary oil firing was tried on both classes, but haulage power then outstripped adhesive capacity.

One design not envisaged in 1948 was the Class WT heavy suburban 2-8-4T, which was entirely Indian designed and built. Introduced in 1959 it almost certainly constituted the last entirely new design of main steam locomotive to appear anywhere in the world. Although no fewer than 146 of these engines were originally ordered, only thirty were actually built owing to increasing electrification, and similar numbers of WG 2-8-2s and WL light 4-6-2s were substituted.

The moderate axleloads of the WP 4-6-2s and WG 2-8-2s ultimately proved to be an inhibiting factor in the face of ever increasing passenger and freight traffic. Around 1960 the Indian Central Design Office outlined a 4-8-4 passenger engine with 12-wheel tender. No details of this have ever been published but it would possibly have been comparable to the Russian P36. About the same time a scheme was worked out which envisaged two WG 2-8-2s working back to back, sharing a large 10,000 gallon tender between them.

Had either of these two intriguing schemes ever materialised they would have been built in India, which after 1959 became entirely self sufficient as regards steam locomotive construction. Although a few hundred locomotives had indeed been built, or at least assembled in India over the years, the possibility of establishing a national locomotive plant in the country had been investigated in some detail on the eve of World War Two. After Indian independence in 1947 the Chittaranjan Locomotive Works was set up in East Bengal with considerable technical assistance from

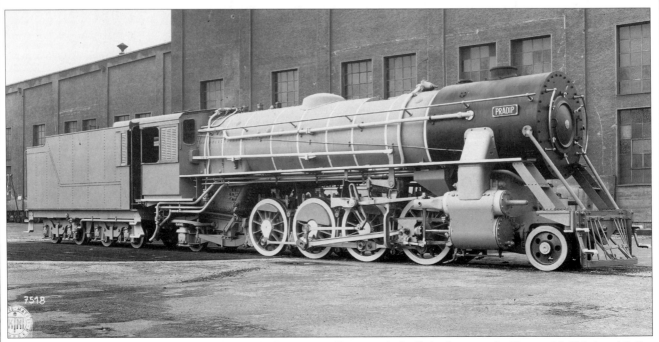

The metre-gauge version of the WG, the Class YG. This is an early example, built in Germany by Krauss-Maffei. As with the broad gauge WG, the last Indian metre gauge steam locomotive was also a 2-8-2. Krauss-Maffei.

TABLE 28

INDIAN STANDARD STEAM LOCOMOTIVES 1947 - 1972

Class	Wheel Arrangement	Axleload tons	Grate area ft^2	No built	Years Built
WL	4-6-2	16.9	38.0	104	1955-1968
WP	4-6-2	18.5	46.0	755	1947-1967
WG	2-8-2	18.5	46.0	2450	1950-1970
WT	2-8-4T	18.0	38.0	30	1959-1967
WS	2-10-6T	17.0	30.0	not built	
WHG	4-8-2 + 2-8-4	17.0	70.0	"	
YL	2-6-2	8.0	17.75	264	1952-1957
YP	4-6-2	10.5	28.0	876	1949-1970
YG	2-8-2	10.5	28.0	1096	1949-1972
YS	2-10-6T	10.5	14.9	not built	
YHG	4-8-2 + 2-8-4	10.0	48.75	"	

TOTAL 5575   1947-1972

the British locomotive industry, although this was officially contrary to the latter's long term interests.

The first locomotive, WG 2-8-2 No.8401, was ceremonially unveiled at Chittaranjan on 1 November 1950. Over the next few years the imported content, initially high, and the cost were progressively reduced, and output peaked during the period 1959-63 at around 170 units per annum. Between 1952 and 1970 the Tata Locomotive & Engineering Company (Telco) supplied a total of 1,155 metre gauge YP 4-6-2s and YG 2-8-2s from its plant at Indian steam

locomotive stock (all gauges) peaked during 1964 at 10,800. This was actually no more than the rapidly declining total about two years earlier on British Railways, and the Indian railways were experiencing a similar problem: coal, its steadily increasing price and declining quality. In 1957 it had been calculated that the annual fuel bill could double by 1966, and so a target of only 50% reliance on steam traction by 1975 was set. Of the balance, the preferred option was electrification where this could economically be justified, for there was a reluctance to import oil. Later, in the

early 1960s, Indian appraisals of the BR 'crash' dieselisation programme and its results did not arouse enthusiasm in India for extensive dieselisation there.

In late 1965, on the eve of the Third Five Year Plan (1966-71) it was announced that steam locomotive production would cease thereafter. In June 1970 the last broad gauge steam locomotive, Class WG 2-8-2 No.10560, named *Antim Sitara* (Morning Star) left Chittaranjan. The works had recently received an order for 100 metre gauge YG 2-8-2s. This was quickly cut to 70, and subsequently to 60 and the last, No.3573, was outshopped in February 1972.

Even before the world energy crisis broke late the following year, the Indian government was becoming concerned as to the procurement of diesel fuel supplies and barely one year after the emergence of the final 2-8-2, serious consideration was given to the resumption of steam locomotive construction, on a limited scale. Ironically, the Chittaranjan boiler shop had been dismantled almost immediately in 1972 and it was envisaged that boilers would be obtained from private industry and a government-owned shipyard. At that time, it was thought that some steam locomotives might thereby remain in use for the next 40-50 years. Despite

The classic Chinese QJ 2-10-2, of which about 4,700 were built over a period of thirty years. No.2822 pictured here in ex-works condition at Changchun in November 1989 was a relatively early example with 8-wheeled tender. Some later series had 12-wheeled tenders. A few were built to 5ft gauge for service in Inner Mongolia, but otherwise variations were remarkably few for such a large class. E. Talbot.

the ensuing quadrupling of oil prices this plan was not put into effect. The Southern Railway eliminated steam working on the broad gauge as early as the end of 1982.

As of mid-1981, the post-war IGR standard steam locomotive classes stood virtually intact except for a handful of accident casualties. The situation soon changed for the worse and by early 1986 the target steam elimination date of 2013 had been brought forward to 2000. Only two years later that date was brought forward still further, to 1995. Underlying this policy decision was the rising cost of coal, its inefficient use on the menial duties which by then were the lot of steam traction, and the huge level of pilfering of coal from depot stocks, and even from the locomotives themselves.

Heavy repairs to broad gauge steam locomotives ceased in August 1992 and normal steam operation on the broad and metre gauge in India came to an end during 1995. The last scheduled broad gauge steam working took place on 25 November, a passenger train between Firozpur and Jalandhar. The locomotive was not a 1970 Chittaranjan-built WG 2-8-2, but a forty year old British-built Class WL light 4-6-2, No.15005, which has since been retained for preservation. Steam

working lingered on the metre gauge for a little longer, but the metre gauge itself was steadily being converted to 5ft 6ins gauge in order to accommodate continually increasing traffic.

Following the end of steam locomotive construction in India in the early 1970s it was popularly supposed that this once widespread activity had now ceased the world over. But it was not so. Since the Communist take-over in 1949 China had been a forbidden land, although there had been the

TABLE 29

INDIAN GOVERNMENT RAILWAYS MOTIVE POWER TRENDS

1948 - 1996 (Broad, Metre & Narrow Gauge)

YEAR	STEAM	DIESEL	ELECTRIC	TOTAL
1948	7988	18	72	8078
1955	8554	72	75	8701
1960	10154	181	91	10426
1965	10711	621	289	11621
1969	9700	1091	552	11343
1976	8496	1803	797	11096
1984	6212	2805	1194	10211
1987	4950	3182	1366	9498
1990	2915	3759	1743	8417
1993	1725	4069	2012	7806
1996	207	4308	2387	6902

occasional report in the 1960s indicating that steam locomotives *were* still being built there. After 1971 China began modestly to open up to tourists and in July 1976 three brand new 2-8-2s were photographed at Tangshan, only two weeks before a catastrophic earthquake devastated that region.

About three years later it became apparent that large stoker-

fired 2-10-2s were still in serial production. Quite exceptionally, this design had been described in *The Railway Gazette* during February 1957. Purely American in concept, it is now known that during the 1956-1960 period prototype 2-10-0 (Class HQ) and 2-10-2 (Class HP) engines were built in China, developed from recent Russian designs (Class L and LV). Only three of the 2-10-0s, which were virtual copies adapted to 4ft 8½in from 5ft gauge, were built and they were not repeated. The 2-10-2, however, was by no means identical and it seems probably that the boiler was more closely related to that of the Russian P36 4-8-4 and the design might have been derived from the subsequent Russian OR-21. The Chinese 2-10-2s had a nominal axleload of 20 *tonnes* as against only 18 *tonnes* on their Russian counterparts. The hydraulic device on the latter, whereby adhesive weight could be increased whilst in motion by transference from the leading and hind carrying axles, was perpetuated in the Chinese design. As 42 pilot 2-10-2s were produced in six different works in China, it is possible that these were supplied by the Russians in 'kit' form just as steam construction was winding down in the USSR. (The full details of Sino-Soviet

In contrast to the rather appealing Class SY light 2-8-2s for industrial service, the larger JS 2-8-2s, some of which were also built for industrial users, were rather clumsy-looking even though their basic design dated back to 1918. Disfigured by its prominent smoke lifting equipment, No.6103 approaches Dayancha on 20 December 1989. E. Talbot.

steam locomotives co-operation during the 1950s remain unknown) The only major improvement was the reduction in tube length from 21ft 4in to 17ft 7in and a substantial increase in firebox volume and heating surface by the incorporation of a combustion chamber to suit local coal, as the original design steamed badly..

A few locomotives had been built at Tangshan (then Tongshan) as early as 1898, and possibly some 4-6-2s and 2-8-2s by the Dalian shops of the Japanese-controlled South Manchurian Railway during the 1930s and 1940s. However *regular* steam locomotive production did not begin in China until 1952. One source maintains that a total of 1,400 locomotives, mainly 2-8-2s, were built in China at the Dalian and Sifang Works up to 1959, when the new plant at Datong (formerly Tatung) commenced production. With a workforce of 8,000 this huge enterprise produced no fewer than 5,571 steam locomotives during the course of exactly 29 years. This represented an overall average of one locomotive every two days, but there were peaks around 1975 and 1985 when *one per day* was attained. Remarkably, only two major steam locomotive classes were ever built at Datong, the QJ 2-10-2 (85 per cent of the total output) and JS 2-8-2. Although regular 2-10-2 production had not begun until 1964, the 500th was built in 1968, the 1,000th in 1970, the 2,000th in 1974, the 3,000th in 1979 and the 4,000th in 1982. (The QJ designation was first applied in 1974).

In splendid isolation, at the dawn of the 1980s *one thousand* 2-10-2s and a few hundred 2-8-2s were still to be built in China, and although prototype diesel and electric locomotive construction had begun in 1958, government policy still favoured steam on two main counts:-

1. Its low capital cost, a new QJ 2-10-2 cost only about £80,000 compared to £450,000 for an equivalent new diesel at a time when traffic was still rapidly increasing. Longer life, few spare parts and lower skilled staff required.
2. China had abundant cheap coal supplies of good quality and only limited indigenous oil fields. Chinese coal production escalated from 300 million *tonnes* in 1970 to 1000 million *tonnes* in 1990. (Described as 'black rice', Chinese coal is not ideally suited to locomotive use. Its annual consumption peaked at 10 million *tonnes* during the late 1970s).

The government did, however, recognise the inherently low thermal efficiency of the steam locomotive, which was nevertheless remarkably

high at 8.8 per cent on the QJ, and gave directives that attempts should be made to increase this to no less than 20 per cent. This was an impossibly high figure, and possibly a purely arbitrary one, although it roughly equated with the corresponding figure readily attainable with diesel traction.

In the pursuit of more power from less fuel, three experimental 2-10-2s, each incorporating differing Porta gas producer firebox systems (see Chapter 14) emerged from Datong during 1986-87. No official photographs or technical details were ever released by the Chinese authorities concerning any of these.

These experiments were directly inspired by David Wardale's recent reconstruction of 4-8-4 No.3450 in South Africa (again, see Chapter 14) as a result of which he was officially invited to China in order to improve the QJ 2-10-2. On arrival in 1985 he discovered there was much scope for improvement, not least the woefully inadequate cylinder insulation, on locomotives which were called upon to operate in winter temperatures of *minus* fifty degrees Centigrade! The standard of workmanship at Datong also often left much to be desired. Under contract, Wardale proceeded completely to redesign the QJ down to the smallest detail, with the objective of raising overall efficiency from around 8% to 12% and power output by means of a gas producer system as in SAR No.3450.

As a preliminary the three 2-10-2s were built, one of which, was already in hand when Wardale arrived. QJ$_2$0001 was provided with a gas producer tender, which on the three test runs made by the locomotive (piloted by another), the engine crew were in mortal danger of carbon monoxide poisoning.

Wardale was initially permitted to modify No.7036, one of three newly built QJs which had been rejected as sub-standard by their would be operator. A triple exhaust was installed in the smokebox and a cyclone gas producer system in the firebox. It underwent a series of static and road tests prior to reconversion to standard form in 1988, for sale to an industrial user (as was the fate of QJ$_2$0001 in 1992).

Another QJ, specially numbered 8001, was modified during construction, having a more conventional firebox and incorporating a Chinese version of the Giesl exhaust. On test this engine (which never subsequently entered revenue earning service) began to show quite promising results. However by this time, 1988, steam locomotive construction was clearly tapering off at Datong, and Wardale realised there was no possibility of his modified QJ ever materialising. For some time he had been increasingly frustrated by local

inertia and bureaucracy, and was convinced that there was no official desire for his experiments to succeed. In reality, steam had probably only been tolerated by default in China for the past decade.

Ten years earlier, shortly after the outside world became aware of the apparent pro-steam policy in China, the Minister of Railways announced in 1978 that during the forthcoming Sixth Five Year Plan (1981-85) the proportion of steam working would be greatly reduced from the current 87 per cent to only 40 per cent. The Chinese main line steam locomotive stock stood at a peak of 7,800 units between 1975 and 1980. The steady decline thereafter was temporarily reversed by an upturn in construction at Datong around 1984-85. In early 1986 it was decided to end steam locomotive construction, but such was the continuing increase in traffic that it could not be matched by diesel and electric output alone. However by this time a target elimination date of 2001 was becoming spoken of, i.e. the end of the century. It has been reported that many of the last 2-10-2s built were scrapped when the first heavy repairs fell due. Some may even have been scrapped unused due to over-production by government decree, rather than built to railway requirements.

The later 2-10-2s and 2-8-2s were in fact produced against the railway's own wishes, for the Ministry of Energy wanted indigenous coal supplies utilised rather than imported oil. However, increasing traffic levels outstripped the 2-10-2s' haulage capacity (as had happened earlier with WG 2-8-2s in India) and it was not unusual for QJs to work in pairs or even threes. Although equipped with mechanical stokers, these were only resorted to at times of high demand; two firemen were carried and they were financially rewarded for achieving good fuel economy. After 1985, this good fuel husbandry began to decline, as steam locomotives became increasingly disliked in certain areas. This may not have been wholly unconnected with a pay bonus scheme instituted in 1986 related to productivity achieved in terms of ton-miles, or more accurately *tonne*-km. Between 1980 and 1990 the proportion of gross *tonne* kilometres worked by steam locomotives in China fell from 79.9 to 29.1 per cent. (However, as freight traffic increased overall during that period by no less than 85 per cent, the *actual* fall was only 33 per cent.) By 1985 it was down to only 11 per cent. Remarkably, in the mid-1970s, serious consideration was given in China to building the still-born French Chapelon post-war three-cylinder compound 152P 2-10-4. The latter's estimated weight was only 161 *tonnes* as against 134 for a QJ, although rated

Two Class SY 2-8-2s of early 1980s vintage at an industrial graphite plant at Jilin in November 1989. A. Wild.

horsepower was *twice* as great, at 6,000HP. The grate area of the 2-10-4 was actually *less* at 64.6ft² as against 73.2ft². This would surely have gone some way to both meeting the traffic department's requirements and returning a higher overall efficiency, in line with the later government edict, possibly as high as 12 per cent at the drawbar. The suggestion was made in 1974 by Kenneth Cantlie, who had very strong associations with China, and whose friend, George Carpenter,

through his own close collaboration with Chapelon, possessed a full set of working drawings for the 2-10-4.

The only major reason why this fascinating idea was not taken up was that locomotive production at Datong would have had to cease for a whole year, while the plant re-equipped from 1920s American practice to 1940s French!

Little priority was correspondingly accorded to passenger locomotives, for whereas some 2,400

'main line' 2-8-2s and 4,700 2-10-2s were built in China between 1952 and 1988, only 400 4-6-2s were built, between 1956 and 1966. In 1957 it was announced that an improved version of the Vulcan Foundry 4-8-4s supplied from Britain in 1935-36 was scheduled. This never appeared, nor did the 2-10-4 heavy freight engine originally designed in parallel with the latter, although this would have been eclipsed in any case by the QJ 2-10-2, let alone by the Chapelon 152P.

Two early QJ 2-10-2s, Nos. 1872 and 1278, at work in sub-zero conditions at Tianzhu, on 3 January 1990. The Chinese QJ 2-10-2, the world's last main line steam locomotive design to remain in regular production, like the last Indian 4-6-2s and 2-8-2s, mechanically speaking was not so very far removed from the pioneer Pennsylvania Railroad 4-6-2 No.7067, of 1907. E. Talbot.

Both JS 2-8-2s and QJ 2-10-2s were emerging from Datong in the closing months of 1988, and the very last engine was QJ No.7207 in late December, by which time the associated equipment, some of its Russian, had already been removed and sold. However, Tangshan Works, which had recovered remarkably quickly from the devastating July 1976 earthquake (outshopping its first new engine thereafter as early as January 1978) was still turning out Class SY light 2-8-2s for industry, albeit at a reduced rate. Prior to the earthquake, output had averaged 150 per annum, subsequently following recovery, this did not exceed 90 per year. In early 1990 it was announced that production would cease later that year, but five years later, new 2-8-2s were still being built. Furthermore, at least one other plant, Changchun, *and* possibly Junin, were simultaneously outshopping 2-8-2s, from parts supplied by Tangshan. In 1994 Changchun produced a bizarre oil burning 2-8-2, No.3016. Its draughting, by means of electric fans, provided a novel and surely final chapter in the long history of unorthodox steam locomotives.

By 1997 serial production appeared to have ceased. Whereas the SY 2-8-2 *in essence* dated back to 1934, the larger JS design harked back to 1918 on the South Manchurian Railway. One of the final 1988 JS engines from Datong, and three SY engines from Tangshan, were built to the special order of American railroad preservation enterprises. Three were shipped simultaneously to the USA in late 1989. The third SY sadly was lost at sea in the Bay of Bengal in June 1991, an event which has surely not happened since 16 141Rs for France sank in a gale in mid Atlantic in April 1947. There was talk of China also building 2-8-2s for Cuba and Brazil, but nothing came of this. The unashamed display of a 2-10-2 at a Rail Fair in Japan in 1983 did not result in any orders.

At the time of writing, the target date for elimination of main line steam traction in China is 2001. Despite the construction of new 2-8-2s and 2-10-2s as recently as 1988, the rapid decline in steam power during the 1980s alone and the continuing downward trend means such a goal does not seem unrealistic. It has been suggested in some quarters that the rapid downgrading of the steam locomotive in China is simply on account of it being incompatible with

the image of a rapidly emerging superpower. However, it should be remembered that it was the railways and not the government which first expressed dissatisfaction in the mid-1980s before the emergence of the modern China began. Furthermore, even the extremes of the Chinese climate must play its part, ranging as it does through plus to minus 50 degrees Centigrade. It made steam locomotive operation a sometimes unattractive proposition to those directly involved!

Finally, the preference of Chinese industry for steam and the production of light 2-8-2s for it in 1995 would suggest that it could be many years yet before steam locomotives vanish completely in China. The emerging Super Power will very probably be the last place on earth where they will be found actively at work on *ordinary* duties.

References

Standard Locomotives in India, *The Railway Gazette*, 2 December 1949, 636-637.

Steam in India, H.C. Hughes, *The Railway Magazine*, May 1964, 441-446, June 1964, 517-522.

Locomotive Building in India, F. Lehmann & H.C. Hughes, *Motive Power International* No.8, 1-29, c.1972.

Indian Locomotives Part 4, 1941 - 1990, H.C. Hughes, The Continental Railway Circle, 1996, 112p.

Freight Locomotives for China, K. Cantlie, *The Railway Gazette*, 22 February 1957, 218.

China's Class 'QJ' 2-10-2, K.R. Chester, *Locomotives International* No.9, May 1991, 11-18.

Chapter 7, *The Red Devil and Other Tales from the Age of Steam*, D. Wardale, pub. author, 1998, 522p.

Issues of *The Continental Railway Journal* and *Locomotive Club of Great Britain Bulletin* from 1975.

TABLE 30

CHINESE STEAM LOCOMOTIVE PRODUCTION*

WHEEL ARR.	CLASS	QUANTITY	YEARS BUILT
2-6-2	YJ	202	1956 - 1966
4-6-2	SL	151	1956 - 1961
	RM	258	1958 - 1966
2-8-2	JF	455	1952 - 1960
	JS	1916	1957 - 1988
	SY	c.1800	1960 - 1995
2-10-0	HQ	3	1958 - 1959
2-10-2	QJ	4708(+3)	1956 - 1988

* some minor classes have been omitted

TABLE 31

CHINA - MOTIVE POWER TRENDS 1952 - 1990

	LOCOMOTIVE STOCK			% WORKING			
YEAR	STEAM	DIESEL	ELEC	TOTAL	STEAM	DIESEL	ELEC
1952	4180	0	0	4180	100.0	0.0	0.0
1957	4251	0	0	4251	100.0	0.0	0.0
1962	6202	17	29	6248	99.9	0.0	0.1
1965	6142	66	30	6283	99.7	0.1	0.2
1970	6878	566	60	7504	97.1	2.3	0.6
1975	7824	1352	191	9367	88.7	9.7	1.6
1980	7801	2190	287	10278	79.9	18.0	2.1
1985	7674	3511	587	11772	60.9	32.9	7.1
1990	6279	5680	1633	13592	29.1	53.2	17.7
1996	3781	8944	2678	15403	-	-	-

TABLE 32

STEAM LOCOMOTIVE PRODUCTION IN INDIA AND CHINA,* 1960 - 1995

YEAR	INDIA	CHINA	YEAR	INDIA	CHINA
1960	196	N/A	1978	0	267
1961	209	N/A	1979	0	N/A
1962	235	N/A	1980	0	342
1963	227	N/A	1981	0	N/A
1964	225	N/A	1982	0	N/A
1965	202	98	1983	0	260
1966	205	N/A	1984	0	N/A
1967	158	N/A	1985	0	361
1968	148	N/A	1986	0	N/A
1969	89	N/A	1987	0	270
1970	50	375	1988	0	228
1971	10	N/A	1989	0	53
1972	5	N/A	1990	0	24
1973	0	N/A	1991	0	12
1974	0	N/A	1992	0	35
1975	0	366	1993	0	32
1976	0	N/A	1994	0	15
1977	0	N/A	1995	0	8

* standard gauge only

The 1,340 Class 141R 2-8-2s built in the United States and Canada for France during 1945-47 constituted the last large steam order to be undertaken by the North American locomotive industry. Ten years on No.141R1138, an oil burner with cast steel engine bed and Boxpok coupled wheel centres, stands at Marseilles in 1957. P. Ransome Wallis Collection, NRM (PRW 6242).

During a similar period the Canadian industry produced 300 2-8-0s for Belgium. These were still numerous when the author travelled through the country in 1965, but all had gone just over a year later. SNCB

Chapter 13

THE END OF AN INDUSTRY

The once extensive commercial steam locomotive construction industry essentially disappeared within the space of just ten years. The decline began with the 100 per cent commitment of the American Locomotive Company to diesel locomotive production in mid-1948, and ended with the completion of what proved to be their last steam locomotive orders by the North British Locomotive Company and Beyer, Peacock & Co. in Britain, and Henschel & Sohn in Germany, during 1958. All four enterprises could trace their origins back a century and more. Thereafter, new commercial steam locomotive orders were very few and far between indeed.

Excluding seven British Railways workshops and the national plants of the USSR, India and China, as of 1954 there were at least forty private enterprises in twenty countries still actively engaged in steam locomotive construction. By 1964 the total had fallen to barely half a dozen located in four countries, England, Germany, India and Japan. Thirty years later still, Switzerland would have a unique distinction in this regard.

Despite the collapse of the domestic market in the United States, Baldwins continued to take on the occasional steam order until well into the 1950s, culminating in 50 2-8-2s for India in 1955. The following year the Canadian Locomotive Company completed a batch of related 4-6-2s for the same customer.

The German locomotive industry was particularly active in the early 1950s, meeting large orders from South Africa especially. This even included Garratts built under licence from Beyer, Peacock & Co., which owing to pressure of work was obliged to sub-contract a number of orders at this time. This would not last, and Beyer Peacock, once the immediate post-war flush had passed, would be very grateful to receive any at all.

The British locomotive industry was indeed overloaded with orders (some delayed from 1939) for several years after 1945, and to expedite delivery many orders were transferred between builders. A particularly outstanding example concerned the order originally placed by the Iranian State Railways in 1940 with Beyer, Peacock & Co., for 24 oil-fired 2-10-2s. Owing to the War this was not pursued, but after 1945 the number was increased to 64 units and transferred to the Vulcan Foundry. Vulcan completed the engines during 1952-53, by which time the United Kingdom was in serious conflict with Iran and shipment of the final 24 engines was postponed until the crisis had been resolved. The 2-10-2s appear to have enjoyed very brief working lives indeed, for most were out of service by 1962.

Vulcan later completed what proved to be its last steam locomotive as early as 1956, by which time the other British builders were finding that they had very few steam orders on hand. The recently announced British Railways Modernisation and Re-Equipment Plan attracted some blame, for influencing traditional Commonwealth customers into moving away from steam. A little earlier there had been dismay that the Indian Railways had placed extensive steam locomotive orders with European builders. Attempts to get British Railways to order steam locomotives from private industry also failed, although contracts were nearly placed with North British and Vulcan for 9F 2-10-0s, and with Robert Stephenson & Hawthorns for Class 5 4-6-0s in 1953.

The passing of the Clean Air Act in 1956 seriously reduced the demand for industrial steam locomotives, thereby hitting the smaller builders.

South America was a major market for the British locomotive industry. The most prominent single customer was probably the Buenos Aires Great Southern Railway, which in 1948 became a part of the Argentine State Railway. Arguably the ultimate in South American steam locomotive design was the improved Argentine 3-cylinder Caprotti 4-6-2. A large order for ninety was placed with the Vulcan Foundry, later cut back to only sixty engines (in favour of diesels) which were delivered between 1950 and 1953. Many of these evidently saw little service on those lines previously unfamiliar with poppet valve gear. Here a pristine example, brand-new from the builders, awaits despatch overseas at Gladstone Dock, Liverpool in September 1950. T.J. Edgington.

TABLE 33

ANNUAL STEAM LOCOMOTIVE PRODUCTION
BY THE PRIVATE BRITISH LOCOMOTIVE INDUSTRY 1947 - 1972

YEAR	TOTAL	YEAR	TOTAL	YEAR	TOTAL
1947	472	1954	377	1961	3
1948	484	1955	287	1962	5
1949	555	1956	101	1963	0
1950	524	1957	67	1964	2
1951	484	1958	43	1965-70	0
1952	389	1959	3	1971	1
1953	354	1960	2	1972	0

(Statistics from the Locomotive & Allied Manufacturers' Association, now Railway Industry Association)

TABLE 34

ANNUAL SPARE BOILER PRODUCTION
BY THE PRIVATE BRITISH LOCOMOTIVE INDUSTRY 1949 - 1972

YEAR	TOTAL	YEAR	TOTAL	YEAR	TOTAL
1949	216	1957	125	1965	6
1950	215	1958	74	1966	5
1951	218	1959	44	1967	4(+8*)
1952	217	1960	16	1968	3
1953	178	1961	8	1969	3
1954	215	1962	14	1970	0
1955	183	1963	6	1971	1
1956	150	1964	4	1972	1

Statistics for 1949 - 1962 from LAMA, production from 1963 was confined to the Hunslet Engine Co.

*   8 boilers for new 2-6-2 + 2-6-2s built in South Africa

The sharp decline in steam orders after 1955 is clearly apparent from the statistics given left.

Excluding one fireless engine, only two steam locomotives were built commercially by British industry in 1959, by the small Hunslet Engine Company of Leeds. This enterprise envisaged, however, that a substantial market would continue for major spare parts, particularly boilers, for British-built main line locomotives overseas, and to this end Hunslet acquired the necessary flanging blocks from other builders. These even included the blocks for large Garratt boilers, which still lay unused in the Leeds works yard in the late 1970s. In fact, the anticipated spare boiler market did not materialise, except for ten completed during 1965-67 for 4-6-2s and 4-8-2s in the Sudan. The remainder were small items for colliery locomotives, and narrow gauge railways in Wales and the Isle of Man. A British pioneer in the field, back in 1932, Hunslet successfully made the transition to diesel locomotive production, and was to remain in business until the mid-1990s. Less happy was the fate of the larger British manufacturers, such as North British and Beyer, Peacock & Co. which ceased to trade in 1962 and 1966 respectively. Rather more successful as regards the manufacture of main line diesel locomotives for both the domestic and overseas markets was the English Electric Co.

This unremarkable engine, a modified Hunslet 'Austerity' 0-6-0ST for the National Coal Board, was the last standard gauge steam locomotive to be built in the United Kingdom, in March 1964. (HE 3890/1964). It is pictured at Cadeby Colliery in South Yorkshire 18 months later, in October 1965. It only enjoyed a short working life, but is now preserved at the Buckinghamshire Railway Centre near Aylesbury. Brian Webb Collection, Industrial Railway Society.

British industrial steam locomotives were almost invariably 0-4-0 or 0-6-0 tanks (only three industrial 0-8-0Ts were ever built). Abroad, 'industrials' could be much more exotic, as in Spain where this imposing 4-8-4T was built in 1958 for the then recently constructed Andorra-Escatron Railway, by Spain's longest established locomotive builder, La Maquinista, as its final steam locomotive. La Maquinista.

Although in the past not always able to meet domestic demand, the French locomotive industry enjoyed a brief final flowering in the early 1950s, building metre gauge 2-8-4s and 4-8-4s for Brazil, and standard gauge 4-6-2s for Egypt, the fate of which is still shrouded in mystery. The last French-built steam locomotive, an industrial 0-8-0T, was completed by SACM in June 1956, eight years before the last British 0-6-0ST by Hunslet and German 0-4-0T (by Jung) in March and December 1964. It is an interesting fact that the last steam locomotives to be built in the United States, France, Britain and Germany for domestic service, were all shunting engines. Fireless 0-6-0s continued to be built in Germany for another 20-odd years.

Elsewhere, builders in Austria, Poland and even Yugoslavia all built steam locomotives for India as late as 1959, and one Polish plant continued to supply 0-8-0Ts to China until 1963.

By this time steam locomotive exports from anywhere had become extremely rare, but in that year Mitsubishi in Japan shipped ten narrow gauge 2-10-2s to Patagonia. During 1964-67 German and Japanese builders supplied seventeen 3ft 6in gauge 0-10-0 rack and adhesion tank engines of modified 1916 design to Indonesia, seemingly by way of reparations twenty years after World War Two had ended.

In 1971 Hunslet supplied a diminutive 0-4-2ST of 1905 design, also to Indonesia, and for many years this

appeared to be positively the last commercially-built steam locomotive to come out of Europe. Then the Swiss Locomotive & Machine Works (SLM) announced in 1989 that it was building three 0-4-2 rack locomotives for service in Switzerland and Austria. Designed for one-man operation and oil-fired, these were completed in 1992 and orders were subsequently placed for five additional locomotives. SLM had not built a steam locomotive since 1952, which proved that a lack of staff acquainted with the procedures of a former age did not preclude the resumption of steam locomotive construction. SLM have recently also outlined plans for a 75 ton oil-fired narrow gauge (750mm-3ft 6in) 2-10-2T which it would be prepared to build, should any takers emerge.

It is indeed curious that the first builder anywhere to construct the last main line steam locomotive for service in its own country (as early as 1917) should, *eighty* years later, be the world's *only* builder prepared to accept an order for new steam locomotives. Indeed since the late 1980s SLM's stance has been proactive in this field. Around 1995 SLM entered into discussions concerning the possible supply of new steam locomotives, to basically very old designs, for two Indian mountain railways with great tourist potential. These related to the British-designed (1888) 0-4-0STs for the 2ft gauge Darjeeling-Himalaya (adhesion) line, and Swiss (1914) 0-8-2Ts for the metre gauge Nilgiri rack railway.

Negotiations were apparently still continuing in 1998, when SLM was completely rebuilding a German class 52 2-10-0. Like the recent 0-4-2RTs and Indian proposals it will be oil-fired, thereby eliminating much traditional drudgery and even permitting remote lighting up by telephone! The provisional livery for the 2-10-0 is blue, and the project is aimed at the tourist luxury train business. It now appears increasingly unlikely that any new steam locomotives will be built *commercially* in future, for the *real* world.

References

Last Japanese Export Order For Steam Locomotives, (750mm gauge 2-10-2s), *The Railway Gazette*, 20 March 1964, 226.
Steam Locomotives For Sumatra, *The Railway Gazette*, 5 February, 1965, 107-108.
Boiler Renewals For The Sudan *The Railway Gazette*, 3 February 1967, 105-106.
Narrow-Gauge Garratt Locomotives For SAR, *The Railway Gazette*, 19 July 1968, 551-552.
End of An Era, Hunslet's Steam Locomotive Production 1949-1971, D. Townsley, *Railway World*, May 1987, 277-281, June 1987, 413-416.

Seemingly by way of war reparations, seventeen 4-cylinder 3ft 6in gauge rack and adhesion 0-10-0Ts were built in Germany and Japan between 1964 and 1967 for the Padang Railway in Sumatra. Here is a German-built 1964 example outside the Esslingen plant, with boiler supplied by Jung. The basic design dated back to 1916, but these engines ranked amongst the very few steam locomotives to be built new with Giesl ejectors. These engines ceased operation in late 1984 alongside some of the original 1920-built series. M.F. Esslingen.

Both Nigel Gresley on the LNER and William Stanier on the LMS sought to improve the efficiency of their conventional 4-6-2s by unorthodox means. Brand new at Edinburgh Haymarket in 1929, this is the LNER experimental 4-cylinder compound 4-6-2-2 No.10000, with 450lb Yarrow water-tube boiler. It was converted to a conventional 3-cylinder simple locomotive in 1937. No.10000 was never formally authorised and its costs have never been revealed, nor have any reliable coal consumption figures ever surfaced. P. Ransome Wallis Collection, NRM (PRW 990).

The LMS turbine 4-6-2 No.6202, 'the Turbomotive', newly fitted with improved high superheat boiler in 1936 (the year after it was built) waits its next turn of duty at Camden shed. No.6202 cost about twice as much as a standard LMS reciprocating 4-6-2 compared to which it showed a fuel economy of only 4% under test conditions. The engine saw some fifteen years of service in 'turbine' form prior to conversion in 1951/52 to a conventional reciprocating locomotive. P. Ransome Wallis Collection, NRM (PRW 1797)

Chapter 14

RISING TO THE CHALLENGE

After the end of World War One the steam locomotive could no longer rest on its laurels. Fuel economy, a factor hitherto disregarded in many quarters, was now to the fore, and operators were less sanguine about the very low thermal efficiency of the steam locomotive. Alternative forms of traction were stirring; railway electrification was already well established by 1914, and the first true diesel locomotives were built in Germany and the United States during the 1920s.

The various attempts worldwide to improve the steam locomotive after 1918 were legion. Some involved sophisticated conventional technology, such as compounding in association with high boiler pressures and steam temperatures, as in France. This realised peak efficiency in the Chapelon PO 4-8-0 rebuilds of 1932-34, which achieved a drawbar thermal efficiency of 11¼ per cent or nearly double the typical 6 per cent of the period.

At the same time, in the United States an experimental four-cylinder *triple* expansion compound 4-8-0 on the Delaware & Hudson Railroad (with hand-fired 500lb water tube boiler and poppet valves) achieved 12 per cent in

1933. So elaborate was this locomotive, which followed earlier two-cylinder compound high pressure 2-8-0s, that it never entered revenue earning service and was scrapped after accruing only 9,000 miles during trials.

Inherent complexity also bedevilled such British experiments as the LNER four-cylinder compound 4-6-4 No.10000 with 450lb marine type boiler, and LMS three-cylinder semi-compound 4-6-0 with ultra high pressure Schmidt Henschel boiler, No.6399 FURY, both built in 1929. The LNER so-called 'Hush Hush' did enter, albeit sporadic, revenue earning service, but not so its fearsome LMS counterpart which suffered an explosion with fatal results on its first trial run on the main line.

More promising was the LMS turbine-propelled 4-6-2 No.6202 built in 1935, which followed previous turbine locomotives with conventional boilers (4-6-2s in Germany, and 2-8-0s in Sweden). It appears to have inspired the Pennsylvania Railroad 6-8-6 (originally ordered as a 4-8-4) completed in 1944. The builders, the Baldwin Locomotive Works, in an internal document claimed the following advantages for a geared (steam) turbine locomotive:

1. More power possible
2. Approximately 20 per cent improvement in efficiency
3. Elimination of reciprocating parts, hammerblow and unbalanced forces
4. Reduction of 20 per cent in stops for fuel and water
5. Smaller driving wheels
6. Lower centre of gravity
7. Improved high speed performance
8. Possible reduction in maintenance costs

It was pointed out that the geared turbine locomotive was not a cheap product due to the high level of workmanship and high grade steels required to build the turbine itself. Although cost per horsepower would be higher than that of a conventional reciprocating locomotive it would still be lower in this respect than for a comparably rated diesel-electric locomotive.

This engine operated for about four years until 1948. Ironically its turbine equipment gave little if any trouble, but problems were experienced with the conventional locomotive boiler. This suffered heavy staybolt fracture due to the excessive

Pennsylvania Railroad geared turbine 6,900HP 6-8-6 locomotive completed by the Baldwin Locomotive Works in 1944 and inspired by the LMS turbine 4-6-2. Taken out of use in 1949, it was scrapped three years later. BLW.

The Chesapeake & Ohio Railway 6,000HP steam-electric express passenger locomotive, one of three delivered by the Baldwin Locomotive Works/Westinghouse Electric during 1947-48, and out of use by 1950. BLW.

demands for steam when moving away from a stop with a heavy load. Although a replacement boiler was designed, it was not built and the engine was eventually scrapped in early 1952.

Scarcely had the turbine 6-8-6 entered service than in March 1945 the Pennsylvania Railroad announced a design for a more advanced 'Triplex' geared steam turbine locomotive rated at 9,000HP, intended for both passenger and freight service. This would have consisted of a 32½ (short) ton coal bunker at the leading end, followed by the cab and back to front conventional locomotive boiler. This was to be mounted on a cast steel underframe carried on two 'eight-coupled' power bogies, each powered by a 4,500HP turbine. Trailing behind would be a 21,000 US gallon water tender. The wheel arrangement was to be 4-8-4-8-0.

This (in the event, abortive) scheme was designed in association with Baldwins and Westinghouse, and at the same time the Chesapeake & Ohio Railway placed an order for three rather similar engines, but with electric rather than direct mechanical transmission. This made for increased weight, from an estimated 282 tons to 367½ tons (without tender) and the wheel arrangement was therefore increased to 4-8-4-8-4. Although it was accepted that the turbine electric drive would be much heavier, the advantage was perceived as a greatly reduced steam demand at starting. In effect it was hoped to secure the claimed advantages of diesel-electric traction whilst still remaining true to the coal industry. The C&O engines were ordered in 1945 to work a planned luxury 10-hour Washington DC - Cincinnati daylight service at speeds of up to 100mph. They constituted

some of the longest (140ft) and heaviest (533 tons) locomotives ever built, rated at 6,000HP.

By the time all three locomotives had been delivered during 1947-48 the passenger market for which they had been devised had collapsed. The final pair were in service for scarcely more than one year. Tests quickly showed that barely half of the rated 6,000HP at the turbine shaft emerged at the drawbar. A major problem was draughting and to remedy this, twin Giesl exhausts were proposed, as the inventor was currently at hand in the USA. However, the C&O was already beginning to move away from the 'coal standard' and this extremely ambitious, and costly, venture was quietly abandoned. The three 'steam-electrics' were scrapped in 1951.

Seemingly undeterred, the Norfolk & Western Railway ordered a 4,500HP 4-8-4-8-0 steam turbine-electric locomotive from Baldwins in mid-1948, with electrical equipment, as before, supplied by neighbouring Westinghouse. As first envisaged, this locomotive (numbered 2300) was similar to the Chesapeake & Ohio 4-8-4-8-4s. By the time it was delivered, in May 1954, its wheel arrangement had become 6-6-6-6, it incorporated a 600lb pressure water tube boiler, and it was 21ft longer still than the C&O engines. An overall efficiency of 13 per cent as against 8 per cent by a 2-8-8-2 was anticipated.

Long-awaited by the N&W management, which hoped the new engine pointed the way ahead, No.2300 was soon pitted against the latest Y6b 2-8-8-2s, developing a maximum of 3,950DBHP at 17 mph, compared to 5,600DBHP at 25 mph on the part of the Mallet. Nevertheless the steam-electric could handle a higher unassisted tonnage on a given gradient than a Y6b, *and* it returned a distinct

Southern Railway 'Leader' 0-6-6-0 double-ended tank engine No.36001 in steam at Brighton on a test train circa 1949. Of the five ordered, only this engine was completed and steamed before the project was cancelled in 1950, after over £3 million (at 1995 price levels) had been spent. NRM (BTN 628).

British Railways Crosti-boilered 2-10-0 No. 92021 new at Nottingham in August 1955. J.P. Wilson.

fuel economy. In November 1954 the N&W President announced that the new locomotive 'had made a splendid showing in preliminary tests. Particularly gratifying is the high thermal efficiency and low fuel cost per unit of traffic.'

Two months later the N&W Test Engineer proclaimed '(There is) a bright future for the coal burning steam locomotive. In over 19,000 miles no major difficulties have been experienced, 13 per cent more tonnage and 30 per cent fuel saving with only a small sacrifice in overall speed.'

Then there was total silence. There are unconfirmed reports that the N&W had been seriously interested in ordering a fleet of such engines, but the builders raised the price. Another version is that the N&W would have ordered more if it could have found other railroads also prepared to purchase some in order to reduce the unit costs of a minimum batch of 40 locomotives. During its brief life No.2300 was mainly employed in banking duties at Blue Ridge, before it was condemned on the last day of 1957, by which time diesels were arriving on the railroad in force. Curiously, in announcing its demise, the N&W did not seem to dismiss entirely the possibility of further such locomotives. It revealed that maintenance costs had been prohibitive (there had been frequent failures of the complex automatic control systems) but the experience gained indicated that 'a more economic and dependable steam-turbine locomotive could be designed and built.' However in mid-1958 a total diesel policy was announced. Two designs of 'automatic' steam locomotive had

earlier been built in the United States, for shunting purposes. Diesel locomotives had first made an impact in the realm of yard shunting, having the high economic advantage of requiring one man operation. During 1935-37 the Baldwin Locomotive Works built three attractive 48½ ton 0-4-0 saddle tank locomotives, two for its own use and one for the Atlantic Coast Line, which were oil fired and so likewise required only one man to operate. The safety valves were electrically linked to the oil burners and blower so that steam pressure could automatically be maintained at 180lb without the valves blowing off. Sufficient oil fuel was carried for 24 hours operation, and sufficient water for 8 hours. The provision of roller bearing axleboxes also reduced routine maintenance to a minimum. Remarkably, all three of these engines, which were not further multiplied despite the claims made for them, still exist in preservation.

This basic idea was carried one stage further in 1947-48 by the Norfolk & Western Railway, when it rebuilt two 4-8-0 tender engines of *circa* 1910 vintage with mechanical stokers. These were automatically controlled, in order to maintain boiler pressure, in conjunction with a steam turbine induced-exhaust (to reduce noise). Although technically speaking they were successful, both engines were scrapped in 1951, when the utterly conventional Class S1 0-8-0s were becoming available.

In Britain the passing of the Clean Air Act in 1956 seriously reduced the demand for steam shunting locomotives. The only significant orders placed thereafter were from the

National Coal Board, whose Northumberland Division actually ordered a few *oil-burning* outside-cylinder 0-6-0STs from Robert Stephenson & Hawthorns! However, the NCB received two *inside*-cylinder 0-6-0STs as late as March 1964 from the Hunslet Engine Co. of Leeds. These were equipped with the patent Kylpor (*Kyl*chap/*Por*ta) exhaust system recently developed by the builders to reduce smoke emission, and underfeed stokers to permit one man operation. A number of older tank engines were similarly equipped for the NCB up to 1971, but by then diesels had a virtual monopoly across British industry. By the end of the 1970s the industrial steam locomotive was all but extinct in Britain, although one of the last active examples, ironically enough, was employed by the nuclear industry! It was unusual for steam locomotives to be built to counter diesel locomotives, but such a thing happened on the Southern Railway in England, shortly after World War Two. The Southern was committed to third rail electrification but several routes would not be dealt with for the foreseeable future, if ever. Although an extensive fleet of diesels was also planned, the unorthodox SR Chief Mechanical Engineer, Oliver Bulleid, conceived a double-ended steam locomotive mounted on two three-cylinder power bogies, giving rapid acceleration and cutting out the need for turning. High cylinder efficiency was sought through the use of sleeve valves, and the firebox was to be lined with firebrick. This was in order to avoid staybolt problems, but came at the expense of losing valuable evaporative heating surface. Five such engines were authorised in August

Dr. Adolph Giesl-Gieslingen and BR 2-10-0 No. 92250, equipped with the Giesl Ejector, at Rugby Locomotive Test Plant in 1959. J.G. Click Collection, NRM.

1946, and the first was completed at Brighton in June 1949. Numerous problems were encountered on trials, not least the intolerably hot conditions inflicted upon the fireman in his compartment amidships. The project was formally abandoned in November 1950 after an outlay of £179,000; the four remaining engines were never completed.

The marked coal supply problems of the post World War Two era were also responsible for the extended trial of two variants of the basic Stephensonian locomotive concept, the Italian Crosti boiler and the Austrian Giesl ejector. These emanated from two countries where major steam locomotive development had ceased around 1930, but where there were strong economic pressures to improve the stock alongside main line electrification.

The Franco-Crosti system sought to utilise the residual heat in the gases reaching the smokebox by diverting them back through a pre-heater to which cold feed water was admitted prior to injection into the boiler proper. This necessitated the exhaust, or exhausts, to be mounted half way along the side of the boiler, which with the Italian 2-6-0, 2-6-2, and 2-8-0 locomotives so fitted between about 1930 and 1960 produced distinctly bizarre results. After World War Two the German Federal Railways and British Railways made applications of these boilers to 2-10-0 heavy freight locomotives between

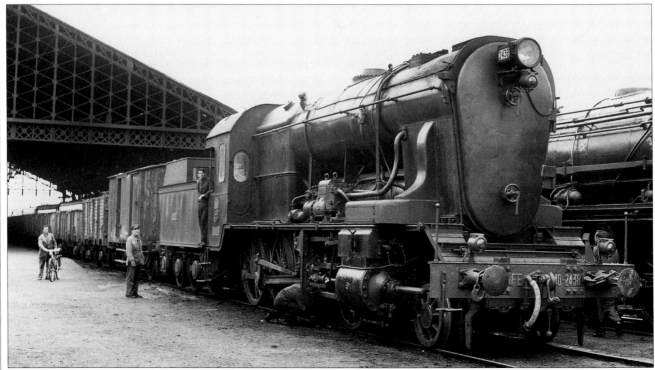

RENFE ex-Norte 2-8-0 No.140.2438 fitted with the Chapelon-Crosti boiler in 1959. P. Ransome Wallis Collection, NRM (PRW 5493).

Brand-new Mitsubishi 760mm gauge 2-10-2 being loaded on board ship for Patagonia in 1963. Compared to the original 1956 batch, this engine incorporated highly effective L.D. Porta modifications. Mitsubishi.

1950 and 1959, encouraged by Italian claims of fuel savings of as high as 20 per cent. Neither administration achieved such a reduction, for the simple reason that the locomotive designs to which they *were* applied were much more modern and therefore more efficient than those in Italy - there was much less scope for improvement. Furthermore, in both countries the engines in question were unpopular with their crews because of the dirty conditions on the footplate. On BR there were severe draughting problems and the engines only ran from 1955 until 1959 as originally designed, before conversion to orthodox working. It was also a question of the choice of work. Had the BR Crostis been employed on the briskly timed Annesley-Woodford 'runners', for instance, then somewhat better results might have been obtained than on the Toton - Brent coal trains, with their frequent signal checks and high standby losses.

The late 1950s witnessed widespread applications of the Giesl Oblong Ejector developed by Dr Adolph Giesl-Gieslingen (d.1992), which consisted of an in line row of small nozzles discharging through a flattened chimney. This produced a given smokebox vacuum for a much reduced back pressure when compared to conventional exhaust systems. By the time it appeared on the scene around 1956, following initial experiments in Austria and the United States, many railway administrations had lost interest in any further forms of steam locomotive development. However, several saw the device as a

cheap means of enhancing locomotive efficiency for a few more years, and as a way of coping with inferior grades of coal. It was this incentive which underlay the installation of a Giesl ejector on British Railways Class 9F 2-10-0 No.92250 in 1959, but the results were disappointing. Similarly, the German Federal Railways were unimpressed, yet the German State Railways made extensive applications. The South African Railways made one little-known application, to a Class 25 4-8-4 and left it at that, whereas the East African Railways produced very dramatic results by equipping many of its oil burning Beyer Garratts. The much-reduced back pressure greatly enhanced their performance up the very severe gradients between Nairobi and Mombasa. In China some 4-6-2s and 2-10-2s were also provided with Giesl-type exhausts, referred to as 'flat chimneys' which had been manufactured locally.

In Spain there was a unique combination of the Giesl exhaust with a Crosti boiler. In 1959 an ex-Norte 2-8-0 was rebuilt with a new variant of the Crosti boiler. In this the hot gases made a return pass through the preheater beneath the boiler to the smokebox which contained a Giesl ejector, a project in which André Chapelon was involved.

This obscure experiment seemingly marked the end of world-wide attempts to improve the steam locomotive, which had become increasingly unacceptable on account of its smoke emission and very low overall thermal efficiency. Drawbar thermal efficiency amounts to

something less than the product of boiler efficiency and cylinder efficiency. In a conventional locomotive boiler thermal (absorption) efficiency declines as output increases but final superheated steam temperature also increases. This enhances cylinder efficiency, which is further improved by minimal back pressure. In Argentina, in the 1950s, Dante Porta sought to tackle these inter-related problems and by relatively simple means achieved improvements in efficiency far in advance of those attained by more complex methods in the past. Drawbar thermal efficiencies of the order of 11 per cent were now possible with *simple* expansion.

Many years later, on 7 March 1969 he addressed the Institution of Locomotive Engineers in Manchester. In 1949 Porta had rebuilt at his own expense an Argentine metre gauge 4-6-2 as a four-cylinder compound 4-8-0 Chapelon-style, and with re-superheat and 135 degree crank setting, which resulted in equally dramatic increases in power output in relation to weight. Particularly impressive were more recent developments on the remote 750mm gauge 160 mile Rio Turbio branch of the Argentine Coal Authority (YCF) in Patagonia. This was operated by diminutive 2-10-2s built in Japan in 1956 and 1963 which despite having a grate area of only 23ft^2 were nevertheless equipped with mechanical stokers. In the second series, boiler pressure was increased from 199lb to 228lb, and a revised tube and flue arrangement yielded a final steam temperature of 780°F. Maximum sustained DBHP was thereby boosted from 700 to 1,200, and although normal train weights were 1,700 tons, no less than 3,000 tons were handled on test despite an adhesive weight of only 38 tons. The dramatic enhancement in performance had also been due to the introduction of secondary air and superheated steam into the firebox in a controlled manner which greatly improved combustion efficiency at high power outputs. This became known as the gas producer system. It obviated the hitherto conventional decline in efficiency as the firing rate increased and high final steam temperatures were realised, which had not always been compatible with high boiler efficiency in the past, Furthermore, dark smoke emission was eliminated as a consequence of the Lempor (Lemaître/Porta) exhaust system. 160 mile through runs were possible despite the Rio Turbio coal having an ash content as high as 15-20 per cent, there being no clinker formation.

With regard to rising coal production and existing line capacity, 4000HP compound 2-10-10-2 and then 2-12-12-0 Mallets with 13½ ton axleload, capable of working 8000 ton trains were very seriously proposed in the later 1970s, of which six were envisaged. Porta also designed a less powerful three-cylinder compound 2-12-0 which he considered more

realistic but in the event none of these schemes materialised. Twenty years later the remaining ageing 2-10-2s finally ceased 'main line' operation in November 1996, succumbing to second hand diesels from Eastern Europe, despite proposals for new steam locomotives from SLM.

In the late 1960s Porta had proposed a new design of two-cylinder compound 2-8-0 for general service on a variety of rail gauges in Argentina. This too never saw the light of day, despite a confident prognostication by Porta in the immediate aftermath of the 1973 Energy Crises that the steam locomotive would experience a 'Second Coming' world-wide by the end of the twentieth century at the expense of the recently all-conquering diesel.

Porta's paper prompted the by-then elderly but still active André Chapelon to write to *The Railway Gazette* (5 September 1969). He pointed out how close the New York Central steam *versus* diesel tests had been, and that whereas the 'Niagaras' had developed only 49DBHP/ft² of grate area, his own contemporary 242A1 4-8-4 had produced 74DBHP/ft². Had the technical features he employed been incorporated in the NYC design, then the latter should have been able to sustain 7,500 DBHP, thereby requiring as an equivalent five 2,000HP diesel-electric units, a much more expensive alternative.

He went on to say that, similarly modified, the largest American Mallets could have been upgraded to produce 11,000DBHP, and by adoption of triple expansion with re-superheat, and a 570lb high pressure boiler with water tube firebox, 15,000DBHP would have been possible with a single locomotive.

Chapelon also pointed out popular misconceptions regarding the cost of energy as brought to the locomotive. He suggested, for instance, that it was cheaper to convey coal from the mine to the locomotive depot by train rather than generate electricity at the pithead and lose a considerably greater equivalent amount of energy through transmission on high voltage overhead power lines.

Just four years later, in the closing months of 1973, the world became very energy conscious indeed, when for political reasons the price of oil increased three-fold. In the United States the Duluth, Missabe & Iron Range Railway seriously considered re-activating its three preserved 2-8-8-4s, and there was a sudden re-awakening of interest in coal-fired locomotives. This concern was sustained by a further near-tripling in the price of oil in 1979. During the 1970s Chapelon was actively involved in proposals to rebuild an American Mallet articulated as a *five* cylinder compound. One scheme was to rebuild a preserved

South African Railways Class 26 4-8-4 No.3450 as modified by David Wardale and named L.D. PORTA, at Beaconsfield Shed, Kimberley, in May 1985. E. Talbot.

The last commercially built American 4-8-4, Chesapeake & Ohio Railway No.614 (Lima, 1948) already relegated to freight working by about 1952, shortly before its premature retirement. The C&O President declared that 'the greatest single advance in railroad efficiency in recent years has been the introduction of the diesel-electric locomotive', though 614 was briefly returned to active service during the coal boom of 1955-56. After that it went into store for twenty-five years.

Union Pacific 4-8-8-4 with an additional inside cylinder to give two high pressure and three low pressure cylinders which, it was estimated, could develop 15-16,000IHP/13-14,000DBHP. Alternatively there were plans for the penultimate Norfolk & Western Y6b 2-8-8-2 (No.2199) which still languished in a Roanoke scrapyard. This would have received an additional high pressure cylinder making it capable of 11-12,000IHP. Regrettably nothing came of these proposals, but the action now switched to South Africa where a substantial if declining fleet of modern steam locomotives was still at work.

Following preliminary experiments in 1979 with a Class 19D 4-8-2 incorporating a gas producer system, in order to counter the worsening quality of available coal, David Wardale sought to modify more radically an SAR Class 25 NC 4-8-4. Somewhat grudging permission was granted and No.3450 was rebuilt with a larger superheater, double Lempor (*Le maitre*/*Porta*) exhaust, improved cylinders and valve gear, and gas producer system in the firebox. The engine was outshopped from Salt River Works in 1981 and named *L.D. Porta*. Its scarlet livery earned it the popular title 'The Red Devil', but officially it was re-designated Class 26.

Comparative tests with an unmodified 4-8-4 returned fuel economies of 28 per cent, water consumption reduced by 30 per cent, and maximum power increased by 43 per cent. At high power outputs, specific fuel consumption was reduced

by 60 per cent. During trials in 1983 a maximum cylinder horsepower of 4,492 was measured at 47 mph, from which it was computed that 5,000HP could have been attained at 62mph. In terms of power per ton weight and per square foot of firegrate these figures were comparable with that achieved by Chapelon compounds.

The SAR 4-8-4s resembled to a remarkable degree a scaled-down sub-standard gauge version of the New York Central 'Niagaras'. One can only speculate on what might have been achieved by applying similar modifications to one of these, without the need for incorporating the complexities of three-cylinder compounding à la Chapelon.

Shortly before SAR No.3450 appeared in its new guise, the second newest surviving 4-8-4 in the United States returned to work after an absence of 25 years. This was Chesapeake & Ohio Railway 4-8-4 No.614, built by Lima in 1948, its tender newly rebuilt to double coal capacity to a record 50 short tons.

In January 1985 this engine was fitted up with instrumentation and worked 6,000 ton coal trains between Huntington and Hinton, WVA, to provide basic data for an advanced steam locomotive project. This was the ACE 3000, promoted by American Coal Enterprises, which was the most publicised of a number of coal-fired locomotive proposals (which also included the Chapelon 2-10-4) spawned in the wake of the second oil crisis in the late 1970s, when there was concern as to the dependence of US

transportation systems on Middle East oil.

Rated at 3,000 drawbar horsepower, it was carefully designed to incorporate several constructional and operational features of the diesel-electric locomotive in order to reduce the very considerable psychological barriers presented by the prospect of a return to the steam locomotives in North America. These would include one man operation, bi-directional running, and the capability of being worked in multiple, if necessary, with diesel-electric locomotives. The engine itself would consist of a condensing rigid-frame four-cylinder compound 4-4-4-2 with tender. Although the 300lb pressure boiler was to be of a conventional fire tube type, it would incorporate a chain grate, which had been a successful feature of the N&W's *Jawn Henry*, a veteran of which project sat on the ACE design committee, which also included Dante Porta. Modern electronics were also to be employed for combustion management.

With an estimated efficiency of 18 per cent the engine would have been capable of running 1,000 miles between water stops, and 500 miles between refuelling. It was seriously investigated for possible fleet operation by the Burlington Northern Corporation for service on its recently opened (1979) line to the Powder River Basin in Wyoming which had been built to tap vast quantities of high grade low sulphur coal deposits. However, by 1986 oil prices had substantially fallen and stabilised and

the incentive to progress the project, despite the on-line coal supplies, had disappeared. Serious hopes of also interesting the Chinese also floundered, no doubt because in China at this time policy was beginning to move away from steam traction. A leading participant in the ACE 3000 project, has conceded that the latter could not, ten years later, compete on economic grounds with the latest advances in diesel-electric traction. In 1996 General Electric unveiled their 192 ton 6,000HP *single-unit* Co-Co having AC traction motors. c1948 to have obtained the same horsepower required cumbersome *triple*-units weighing about 500 tons in aggregate.

Nevertheless, in early 1995 proposals to build advanced Garratt locomotives in Australia were announced. Two types were projected, both having five-cylinder triple-expansion power units. One was to a 4-10-4+4-10-4 condensing engine fuelled by natural gas, whereas the other was to be a 2-14-2+2-14-2 with 900lb pressure water tube boiler fuelled by a colloidal suspension of coal in alcohol. Rated horsepower would be 13,400 and overall efficiency 20 per cent. These projects soon foundered.

To the writer's mind, however, the ultimate steam locomotive would not be so extreme, but consist of Chapelon's proposed three-cylinder compound 2-10-4 refined with British Caprotti poppet valve gear, and Lima-type 'double Belpaire' firebox incorporating a Porta-style gas producer system. Further features, not in the original French drawings, would be a cast-steel engine bed, all-welded boiler and roller bearings (also applied to crank pins). Such a design might

Chesapeake & Ohio 4-8-4 No.614 was restored to working order in 1980. Five years later it underwent road testing, as seen here at Milton, West Virginia, ostensibly to provide data for the abortive ACE 3000 advanced steam locomotive project. During the tests, it was temporarily renumbered 614T, after which it effectively disappeared from view until 1996, when it once again came out to power special excursions. V. Hand, per W.L. Withuhn.

Chinese Railways Class QJ 2-10-2 No.2826 and Class JS 2-8-2 No.5713 working hard with a freight between Mudaoshi and Daguanling on 12 March 1989 in a scene reminiscent of the United States four to five decades earlier. Remarkably, both types were still in production less than a year before this photograph was taken, although by this time early elimination of steam working in China was already officially decreed. E. Talbot.

In the first country in the world to begin to forsake the main line steam locomotive, almost 80 years earlier, a brand new 1996-built Swiss 0-4-2RT awaits despatch from the makers to neighbouring Austria. Based on a 1935 design, the redesigning of these new rack engines with oil firing immediately eliminated several traditional problems. These were noxious exhaust emissions, and the need for tedious fire cleaning, while this also permitted rapid steam raising and one man operation. The extensive employment of welding throughout eliminated rivets and significantly reduced weight, which in turn resulted in an increased payload. The engines were all built for tourist lines on which the continued use of steam locomotive power would provide an added attraction. SLM.

conservatively be capable of developing say 8,000IHP and return a drawbar thermal efficiency of 15 per cent, more than double the latter-day norm. If necessary, the projected SNCF 4-6-4, 2-8-4 and 4-8-4 engines outlined in tandem could be developed in due course, similarly updated.

As the Millennium approaches this is all surely but a pipe dream. Curiously, in 1998, in real terms the world price of oil is no higher than it had been 25 years earlier, in 1973. However, its alarming behaviour between times at least ensured a lingering commercial interest in steam locomotive technology, which might otherwise have been extinguished many years before.

References

Automatic Oil-Fired Steam Switching Locomotive, *Baldwin Locomotives*, October 1935 - January 1936, 11-13.

N & W Automatic Switcher, *Railway Mechanical Engineer*, August 1947, 402-407.

Turbine Electric Locomotives for the Chesapeake & Ohio Railway, *The Railway Gazette*, 5 March 1948, 277-280.

'Jawn Henry', *Railway Locomotives and Cars*, August 1954, 41-43.

N & W Tests Turbine Locomotive, *Railway Locomotives and Cars*. January 1955, 56-60.

The Suppression of Smoke (Hunslet 0-6-0ST), *The Railway Magazine*, August 1963, 580-581.

Steam Locomotive Development in Argentina, L.D. Porta, Paper No.721, *Journal of the Institution of Locomotive Engineers*, Vol.59 No.2, 1969-70, 205-256.

Lokomotivbau und Dampftechnik, W.Stoffels, Birkhauser Verlag, 1975, 308p.

The World's Most Advanced Steam Locomotive, (YCF 2-10-2) M.Swift & R. Wilkinson, *The Narrow Gauge* No.82, Winter 1979, 7-21.

Steam is more economical than diesel traction, R. Freeman, *Railway World*, September 1985, 472-475.

Steam Locomotive Development in South Africa, D. Wardale, *Continental Railway Journal*, No.62, Winter 1985/86, 39-43.

Modern Steam Locomotives - Traction for the Future? M. Thorpe and D. Wardale, *Developing Railways*, 1985, 32-35.

Chapter 3, *The Red Devil and Other Tales from the Age of Steam*, D. Wardale, pub. author, 1998, 522p.

Did We Scrap Steam Too Soon? W.L. Withuhn, *Trains*, June 1974, 36-48.

Time to Reinvent the Steam Locomotive?, W.L. Gwyer, *Trains*, June 1982, 66.

Chapter 6, *The Red Devil and Other Tales from the Age of Steam*, D. Wardale, pub. author, 1998, 522p.

The only steam locomotive in regular serial production in the 1990s was the Chinese standard gauge Class SY 2-8-2, first introduced in 1960—something approaching 2,000 have now been built, principally at Tangshan, including three for export to the USA. Some were still being built in 1995 since when one or two more have been assembled to order. Variations have been remarkably few, and No.1678, a 1988-built engine, was recorded at a steel works in January 1994. E. Talbot.

CONCLUSION

The fortunes of the steam locomotive were inextricably linked to coal. Coal as a prime energy source reached its zenith in 1913, after which alternatives, particularly oil but also electricity generated by burning coal, increasingly displaced it. Except by industrial action, usually of short duration, coal supplies were not seriously threatened for a further 25 years, at the end of which the steam locomotive had apparently reached its technological limit in North America and Western Europe. In these regions from 1945 the steam locomotive lived on borrowed time, surviving for a further 15 and 30 years respectively. Its fall from favour was not so much a matter of prejudice, but primarily due to a genuine concern as to the long term procurement of locomotive fuel, for different reasons in different countries. Abandonment was facilitated by the rapid rise and development of a viable alternative, the diesel-electric locomotive, which enjoyed the added virtue of much higher overall thermal efficiency and the availability (prior to 1973 at least) of cheap oil.

The one remaining unassailable virtue of the steam locomotive, its simplicity and low capital cost, was recognised even after 1960 in both India and China, where traffic levels were still rapidly increasing. However, in both countries, the few designs of 1940s/1950s vintage which remained in production were built to a modest axleload, in order to permit widespread use. This inevitably placed a limit upon their haulage capacity, at least as single units, and they were eventually overtaken by traffic requirements, as had earlier been the case in the then Soviet Union. Diesel-electric and electric units could alternatively be operated in multiple without resort to heavier rail and expensive bridge renewals. However, the proposed Lima 4-8-6 and Chapelon 2-10-4 showed what advances could have been achieved within already established axle load limits in the United States and Europe, with further enhancement possible via post-1940s 'Porta technology' which made high efficiency compatible with simplicity.

The steam locomotive was clearly an expensive luxury in Scandinavia and Central Europe, but in most major countries, including the United States, its rapid or even total elimination was not envisaged when replacement began. Worldwide experience showed, however, that once steam was pushed into second place, its continued operation became disproportionately uneconomic, thereby accelerating its elimination. In most regions the process effectively took 15-25 years, which was also the typical life of a locomotive boiler. The dismantling of the manufacturing capability to produce this fundamental component almost invariably triggered the countdown towards eventual oblivion, which also resulted in the eventual demolition of the time-honoured infrastructure—water towers, coaling plants, roundhouses and the rest.

The demise of the steam locomotive worldwide can be summarised thus: North America 1945 - 1960, Western Europe 1955-75, Eastern Europe and the former Soviet Union 1960-85, Southern Africa 1970-95, India 1980-95, and China 1985-2000. Remarkably though, in 1995 a handful of new steam locomotives were still being built in Switzerland and China.

Just fifty years on from the symbolic 'beginning of the end' at Schenectady in June 1948, it would seem that 1998 is the first ever year since the reign of King George III in which no steam locomotives whatever have been built anywhere in the world.

Several projected steam locomotive designs produced in India failed to materialise, but an exception was the little publicised Class WT heavy suburban 2-8-4T. This was probably designed in the early 1950s and incorporated Class WP cylinders and valve gear, and a narrow firebox Belpaire boiler closely based on that of the two Class WMS 4-6-0s built for the Bengal-Nagpur Railway in 1938 by Robert Stephenson & Hawthorns. 1959-built No.14002 is seen at Bandel shed on 2 January 1979. L. G. Marshall.

One of eight 2ft gauge 2-6-2+2-6-2 Garratt locomotives built mainly in South Africa for the SAR, by Hunslet-Taylor Ltd in Johannesburg, with boilers from the Hunslet Engine Co. in England, during 1967-68. A. Jorgensen.

Appendix

FINAL MAIN LINE RAILWAY STEAM LOCOMOTIVES TO BE BUILT IN MAJOR COUNTRIES 1917 - 1988

COUNTRY	RLY	LOCOMOTIVE	NO.	DATE
Switzerland	SBB	2-10-0	2978	1917
Italy	FS	2-8-2	746.110	1927
Belgium	SNCB	4-4-2	1206	July 1939
Norway	NSB	2-8-4	473	Aug 1941
Japan	JNR	2-10-4T	E105	1948
Canada	CPR	2-10-4	5935	Mar 1949
Denmark	DSB	4-6-2	999	1950
France	SNCF	2-10-2T	151TQ22	Sept 1952
USA	N&WR	0-8-0	244	Dec 1953
Sweden	SJ	2-6-4T	1929	1953
Russia	SDZ	2-10-2	LV. 0522	Dec 1956
New Zealand	NZR	4-8-2	1274	Dec 1956
Finland	VR	2-8-2	1096	Dec 1957
Australia	QGR	4-6-2	1089	Mar 1958
Czechoslovakia	CSD	2-10-0	556. 0510	May 1958
Poland	PKP	2-10-0	Ty 51-232	1958
Hungary	MAV	2-6-2T	375. 1032	Feb 1959
Germany (West)	DB	2-6-2	23.105	Dec 1959
United Kingdom	BR	2-10-0	92220	Mar 1960
Germany (East)	DR	2-10-0	50. 4088	Dec 1960
Roumania	CFR	2-10-0	150.282	1960
Yugoslavia	JDZ	0-6-0T	62.129	1960
Spain	RENFE	2-8-2 + 2-8-2	282 - 0430	Apr 1961
Turkey	TCDD	2-10-0	T56.202	Oct 1961
South Africa	SAR	2-6-2 + 2-6-2	NG156	1968
India	IGR	2-8-2	3573	Feb 1972
China	CR	2-10-2	7207	Dec 1988

PERCENTAGE OF STEAM WORKING ON SELECTED MAJOR WORLD RAILWAYS 1955 - 1970
(Normally calculated on a train mileage basis)

COUNTRY	RLY	1955	1958	1961	1964	1967	1970
United Kingdom	BR	87.4	77.0	54.4	24.2	3.4	0.0
France	SNCF	50.2	42.1	29.6	20.6	8.8	2.8
Germany (W)	DB	76.1	66.2	53.9	37.3	22.5	8.4
Germany (E)	DR	-	-	88.9	79.2	64.7	37.0
Spain	RENFE	78.7	71.3	62.3	51.9	25.5	5.6
Poland	PKP	-	87.2	85.3	76.9	-	49.3
USSR	SDZ	86.0	74.5	-	21.1	7.6	3.5
India	IGR	95.2	93.5	90.9	84.5	70.9	62.4
Japan	JNR	62.0	50.5	37.6	-	19.8	10.0
South Africa	SAR	81.0	78.8	64.7	56.8	47.1	38.3
East Africa	EAR	100.0	-	-	-	79.1	60.2
Rhodesia	RR	-	90.0	-	68.4	-	52.7
Australia							
New South Wales	NSWGR	69.5	58.8	-	20.5	11.0	3.0
Western Australia	WAGR	76.0	54.5	-	-	33.0	17.3
Victoria	VR	-	14.6	13.0	11.0	-	-

These statistics are taken from various editions of Jane's World Railways.

DOMESTIC MAIN LINE STEAM LOCOMOTIVE CONSTRUCTION IN VARIOUS COUNTRIES, 1945 - 1961
(excludes exports, imports, industrial and narrow gauge locomotives)

YEAR	USSR	FINLAND	CZECHO-SLOVAKIA	POLAND	HUNGARY	ROUMANIA
1945	8	9	40	45	0	0
1946	243	2	107	87	0	0
1947	674	5	97	122	3	25
1948	1032	10	143	149	11	0
1949	1187	2	24	114	16	0
1950	985	3	78	18	18	0
1951	665	3	28	56	16	30
1952	254	3	58	27	3	0
1953	668	7	102	4	5	0
1954	758	6	3	40	0	0
1955	654	15	152	65	20	51
1956	490	5	38	81	64	65
1957	0	6	66	39	} 57	57
1958		0	40	6		33
1959			0	0		17
1960					0	19
1961						0

DOMESTIC MAIN LINE STEAM LOCOMOTIVE CONSTRUCTION IN VARIOUS COUNTRIES, 1945 - 1961,
(excludes exports, imports, industrial and narrow gauge locomotives)

YEAR	USA	CANADA	UK	FRANCE	SPAIN	WEST GERMANY
1945	115	50	295	N/A	18	N/A
1946	86	36	608	N/A	48	N/A
1947	69	8	384	N/A	20	N/A
1948	86	52	395	80	21	10
1949	69	6	357	114	2	11
1950	12	0	385	48	44	34
1951	18		297	} 66	38	48
1952	19		211		57	8
1953	15		251	0	36	2
1954	0		208		65	27
1955			174		35	26
1956			138		41	9
1957			141		23	12
1958			62		26	6
1959			15		12	13
1960			3		8	0
1961			0		10	

APPENDIX 4 US CLASS 1 RAILROAD COAL CONSUMPTION AND FUEL COSTS 1923 - 1960

YEAR	RAILROAD CONSUMP. M US TONS	TOTAL OUTPUT M US TONS	% RAIL-ROAD Consump	AV COST $/TON	Railroad COAL COST $ M	Railroad TOTAL FUEL COST $ M	% COAL OF TOTAL FUEL COST
1923	158	565	28.0	2.68	537	618	86.9
1924	126	484	26.1	2.20	388	472	82.2
1925	131	520	25.3	2.04	358	459	78.0
1926	140	573	24.3	2.06	376	473	79.4
1927	131	518	25.2	1.99	355	439	80.9
1928	120	501	23.9	1.86	312	385	81.0
1929	124	535	23.2	1.78	296	364	81.3
1930	109	468	23.2	1.70	249	307	81.1
1931	91	382	23.9	1.54	204	245	83.3
1932	75	310	24.1	1.31	147	178	82.6
1933	75	334	22.6	1.34	151	181	83.4
1934	79	359	22.1	1.75	178	217	82.0
1935	81	372	21.8	1.77	185	233	79.4
1936	92	439	20.9	1.76	213	272	78.3
1937	92	446	20.6	1.94	220	294	74.8
1938	75	349	21.4	1.95	183	244	75.0
1939	82	395	20.7	1.84	198	257	77.0
1940	89	461	19.2	1.91	209	274	76.3
1941	104	514	20.2	2.19	263	350	75.1
1942	121	583	20.8	2.36	315	426	73.9
1943	130	590	22.0	2.69	379	527	71.9
1944	136	620	21.9	2.92	434	586	74.1
1945	123	578	21.3	3.06	400	555	72.1
1946	108	534	20.3	3.44	391	553	70.7
1947	110	631	17.4	4.16	463	692	66.9
1948	99	600	16.5	4.99	492	833	59.0
1949	65	438	14.8	4.88	324	564	57.4
1950	64	516	12.4	4.84	323	609	53.0
1951	54	534	10.2	4.92	277	621	44.6
1952	38	467	8.1	4.90	196	539	36.4
1953	28	457	6.1	4.92	149	510	29.2
1954	16	392	4.1	4.52	81	433	18.7
1955	15	465	3.3	4.50	77	454	17.0
1956	12	501	2.5	4.82	69	477	14.4
1957	8	493	1.7	5.08	52	460	11.3
1958	4	410	0.9	4.86	25	376	6.6
1959	3	412	0.7	4.77	19	392	4.8
1960	2	416	0.5	4.69	14	365	3.8

APPENDIX 5

MOTIVE POWER TRENDS ON BRITISH RAILWAYS
1948 - 1968

YEAR	STEAM LOCOMOTIVES				DIESEL LOCOS		DMU	ELECT. LOCO
	STOCK 1 JAN	NEW	2ND HAND	WITH DRAWN	STOCK	NEW	NEW	STOCK
1948	20023	395	563	767	53	14		16
1949	20211	357	39	817	67	34		17
1950	19790	385		577	100	24		17
1951	19598	297		792	125	20		10
1952	19103	211		453	145	62		33
1953	18859	251		426	207	49		58
1954	18584	208		372	256	60	25	65
1955	18420	174		639	316	113	56	71
1956	17955	138		571	452	107	275	71
1957	17527	141	3	712	607	145	528	71
1958	16959	62		913	802	400	**1070**	71
1959	16108	15		1666	1201	601	832	72
1960	14457	3		1184	1799	**751**	575	85
1961	13276	0		1585	2550	631	183	135
1962	11691	0		**2924**	3179	506		158
1963	8767	0		1720	3683	482		178
1964	7050	0		2075	4060	408		194
1965	4973	0		1987	4462	354		198
1966	2987	0		1298	4811	168		277
1967	1689	0		1329	**4962**	59		340
1968	362	0		359*	4742	48		362

*   From September 1968 the only steam locomotives remaining in BR stock were 3 narrow gauge Vale of Rheidol Railway 2-6-2Ts

APPENDIX 6

BRITISH RAILWAYS STEAM LOCOMOTIVE
MAJOR OPERATING COSTS
1948 - 1962

YEAR	FUEL £m	WAGES £m	REPAIRS £m	TOTAL £m	LOADED TRAIN MILES (Million)	COST/ loaded TRAIN MILE p
1948	36.4	42.0	25.5	103.9	296	35.1
1949	36.3	41.8	24.8	102.9	307	33.5
1950	35.9	41.1	23.5	100.5	311	32.3
1951	37.7	44.7	25.1	107.5	304	35.4
1952	41.4	47.1	27.7	116.2	304	38.2
1953	43.8	48.4	31.3	123.5	305	40.5
1954	46.2	50.5	31.7	128.4	303	42.4
1955	48.0	51.8	32.7	132.5	286	46.3
1956	55.4	**56.9**	33.4	**145.7**	293	49.7
1957	**63.8**	41.5	**37.0**	142.3	289	49.2
1958	62.8	39.6	35.5	137.9	268	51.5
1959	56.6	36.1	31.6	124.3	240	51.8
1960	53.9	37.3	31.4	122.6	199	61.6
1961	50.3	33.0	31.2	114.5	166	69.0
1962	44.3	29.3	27.5	101.1	135	74.9

Statistics are taken from the British Transport Commission Annual Report & Accounts, 1948-1962.
Comparable figures were not published by the British Railways Board from 1963.

Note the almost 50 per cent increase in operating cost between 1959 and 1962.

APPENDIX 7

BRITISH RAILWAYS COAL CONSUMPTION AND FUEL COSTS
1948 - 1962

YEAR	COAL CONSUMP M TONS	UK COAL OUTPUT M TONS	% RAILWAY CONSUMP	UK COAL IMPORTS M TONS	BR COAL BILL £M	AVERAGE COST/ TON £
1948	13.89	214.9	6.5	0.1	36.4	2.62
1949	13.94	221.7	6.3	0.0	36.3	2.60
1950	13.75	223.1	6.2	0.0	35.9	2.61
1951	13.55	229.2	5.9	1.2	37.7	2.78
1952	13.33	232.0	5.7	0.3	41.4	3.10
1953	13.08	230.7	5.7	0.6	43.8	3.35
1954	12.92	230.8	5.6	3.0	46.2	3.58
1955	12.09	228.8	5.3	12.0	48.0	3.97
1956	12.13	229.2	5.3	5.4	55.4	4.61
1957	11.57	230.8	5.0	2.9	63.8	5.51
1958	10.75	222.8	4.8	0.8	62.8	5.84
1959	9.64	212.8	4.5	0.1	56.6	5.87
1960	9.02	199.8	4.5	0.0	53.9	5.98
1961	7.80	196.7	4.0	0.0	50.3	6.45
1962	6.27	203.8	3.1	0.0	44.3	7.06

APPENDIX 8

BRITISH RAILWAYS ENERGY COSTS 1948 - 1968

YEAR	ENERGY COSTS £ MILLION					LOADED TRAIN MILES MILLION			
	COAL	OIL	ELECTRICITY	TOTAL	% COAL	STEAM	TOTAL	% STEAM	Energy COST per LTM p
1948	36.4	-	3.4	39.8	91	296	338	88	11.8
1949	36.3	-	3.6	39.9	91	307	353	87	11.3
1950	35.9	-	3.8	39.7	90	311	358	87	11.1
1951	38.0	-	3.9	41.9	91	304	352	86	11.9
1952	41.4	-	4.4	45.8	90	304	357	85	12.8
1953	43.8	-	4.7	48.5	90	305	353	86	13.7
1954	46.2	-	5.4	51.6	90	303	352	86	14.7
1955	48.0	-	5.7	53.7	89	286	337	85	15.9
1956	55.4	-	6.2	61.6	90	293	349	84	17.7
1957	**63.8**	0.8	6.9	**71.5**	89	289	357	81	20.0
1958	62.8	1.4	7.9	71.2	88	268	351	76	**20.3**
1959	56.5	2.4	7.2	66.1	85	240	347	69	19.0
1960	53.9	3.3	7.7	64.9	83	199	335	59	19.4
1961	50.3	4.7	8.7	63.7	79	166	332	50	19.2
1962	44.3	5.6	9.4	59.3	75	135	328	41	18.1
1963	31.8	9.3	8.5	49.6	64	103	325	32	15.3
1964	26.2	9.7	10.2	46.1	57	76	313	24	12.5
1965	15.3	9.5	11.4	36.2	42	44	290	15	12.5
1966	9.7	9.4	12.3	31.5	31	24	276	9	11.4
1967	4.4	10.4	13.0	27.8	16	9	264	3	10.5
1968	0.9	12.8	13.0	27.6	3	1	258	0	10.7

Statistics are taken from the British Transport Commission Annual Report & Accounts, 1948-1962, and British Railways Board Annual Report & Accounts, 1963-1968.